D1643360

IRELAND

l'Organisation Mondiale
pour l'Education Préscolaire

*Proceedings of the Conference
held in
Dublin Institute of Technology
on
Saturday, 24th April, 2004
entitled*

Children of the Global Village

Edited by
Mary Horgan & Francis Douglas

Contents

SECTION THREE
DISADVANTAGE AND SPECIAL NEEDS

SECTION FOUR
ASPECTS OF QUALITY

SECTION FIVE
SPIRITUALITY

NEW BOOKS

Welcoming Address
Children of the Global Village?

Dear chairperson, friends, colleagues and distinguished guests.
I am very honoured to open this year's OMEP Ireland Conference and would like to thank OMEP for this wonderful opportunity to share some of my thoughts with you.

As you know I am the Director of the Centre for Early Childhood Development and Education and the relationship between the CECDE and OMEP has been very close and fruitful since the establishment of the CECDE in October 2002. These conferences of OMEP Ireland are very important in providing an arena and possibly the most important forum for research in the field of early childhood care and education in Ireland. The CECDE is of course a member both of OMEP International and its Irish branch, and very active members indeed. The CECDE and OMEP have assisted each other in many ways for example by promoting events in our respective publications and so on. Staff of the Centre delivered two presentations at last year's conference in Cork and this year we are represented with three papers including the present one which you are now – I am afraid – forced to endure.

When I was preparing this opening paper, I had a choice to discuss the development of a quality framework for early childhood care and education in Ireland, which is after all the core objective of the CECDE, or to take my cue from the title of this year's conference "Children of the Global Village". I am glad to say that I decided to do the latter although it turned out to be the more challenging theme to cover. I note with interest that the title of OMEP's World Conference later this year in Sydney, "One World: Many Childhoods", is also raising this important issue of tension between the global and the local and what this means for children everywhere.

The term "global village" in the title of our conference was of course coined by the legendary sociologist and theorist of media and communication, Marshall McLuhan. However, his metaphor of the "global village" for a world connected by modern electric and electronic media has frequently been misunderstood. McLuhan saw the "village" as riven by war and conflict, not peace and harmony. He was no follower of Rousseau. He thought electric media – as opposed to print media – reduced the ability to think abstractly and would return us to a tribal world of identities in conflict. It is useful to remember this understanding of McLuhan's global village when we unpack and test contemporary delusions in relation to "globalisation".

In the following 30 minutes or so I will look at some issues, which arise from the current globalisation debate as it impacts on early childhood settings. However, let me remind you: I am not primarily a researcher or academic. The following is not a review of the literature but if you like musings of someone who is very engaged with the matter not only as a policymaker but also as a parent and citizen. I will present research but only in a very eclectic and random way to explain the sources of my thoughts and lend them some weight. I would like to concentrate on three questions which I believe are of major consequence and have implications for the way we want to develop early childhood care and education in Ireland. These are: (1) Is childhood sufficiently uniform across the globe with universal needs and rights demanding a global response? (2) Why is the answer to the first question important for our response to the needs of young children in Ireland? (3) How is the Centre for Early Childhood Development and Education approaching the development of a National Quality Framework for young children here in Ireland?This is an image taken from an advertising campaign by a multinational manufacturer and retailer of clothing, particularly children's clothing. We all know the name of the company – it is a global brand.

The picture – and the campaign in general – plays in to our desire to see childhood as an age of innocence when later adult divisions and conflicts have little or no impact. The sub-text to the picture is the populist phrase "children are the same all over the world" and implies that childhood is an era of harmony and equality.

However, the reality often disturbingly varies from our desires and prejudices: In October 1998, an Italian newspaper alleged the exploitation of child labour in a Turkish plant working for the Benetton group. Italian trade unions, together with their Turkish counterparts, intervened and concluded an agreement, which forbids the use of child labour in the Turkish textile plants working for the Benetton group. The company explained the events as unusual and unfortunate.

This little story illustrates the tension between the view that childhood is a universal age of man and exists aloof of time and place and the opposite view that childhood is socially constructed and deeply affected by local culture and social conditions. Or in other words, do "All children smile in the same language" (US bumpersticker)? Or do "children speak hundred languages" (Reggio Emilio motto)?

As so often the case, both perspectives are reasonable and based on evidence but I fear that we will not see the whole picture if our view is limited to one or the other perspectives.

I will look first at aspects of childhood which may reasonably be regarded as "universal" or common to all children. Multi-lateral agreements between states are based on the reasonable assumption of a number of common aspects, needs and rights of children no matter where on earth they live. The classic example for this is the UN Convention on the Rights of the Child, ratified by all countries – except Somalia and the United States.

Another example for aspects of childhood, which may have universal application, is the consensus on ranges, sequence and direction of processes and events in early childhood such as motor, cognitive or social development. "Normality" here is often defined by proximity to the apex of the bell curve. Certain physical requirements are also the same for all children, for example the need for food, sleep or shelter.

Based on these similarities across countries and cultures some organisations especially in the USA have attempted to design universal standards for early childhood care and education. One such example is the "Global Guidelines for Early Childhood Education and Care in the 21st Century" by the Association for Childhood Education International[1]. These guidelines come complete with a detailed assessment tool in the format of a checklist.

However, whenever we look at childhood across different countries and communities we quickly arrive at a point where the diversity and differing contexts of childhood become apparent.

A large number of cross-cultural studies particularly in the field of anthropology examining child rearing practices, child development and behaviour have shown "how certain Western cultural practices and beliefs regarding infancy make sense in the American and European contexts but are not universal or natural. 'Natural' childbirth, mother-infant bonding, father's rough-and-tumble play, and getting the infant to sleep through the night are important practices in a contemporary American cultural context, but are infrequent or insignificant features of infant care in other parts of the world."[2]

The following short narrative is based on the findings of just one well-known study observing childrearing practices of two neighbouring people:

> In a densely forested section of central Africa, a woman goes about her daily chores in a camp of Aka foragers. No matter the task, she keeps her 3-month-old baby strapped to her chest. The baby rarely loses contact with her, even at night. Breast-feeding occurs frequently, often on demand. If the youngster begins to cry, the woman may gently rock her or even pass her to a female friend for some supplemental breast-feeding. A short walk away, another mother of a 3-month-old works in a farming community of the Ngandu people. She usually leaves her baby on a soft mat and picks up the child from time to time. Breast-feeding occurs when the mother takes a break from planting, weeding, and preparing food. Her baby's cries often go unanswered.[3]

It is clear that the childhood experiences of members of these two communities are very different, that children are developing at different pace and in a different sequence from each other.

One may query the studies of these small, often remote communities and their relevance at a global scale. However, similar evidence can be found across most countries, regions and cultures. I would even suggest that we would find a number of very differing child-rearing practices within many residential streets in any city of Ireland!

International comparative studies of early childhood care and education have consistently shown substantial differences in policy and practice across different countries and communities. In 2001, the OECD published a summary report, "Starting Strong", of their thematic review of early childhood education and care policy in twelve countries. The report provides an overview of policy and practice in these countries which surprises by its diversity given the fact that the participating countries are all modern industrialised societies. The report clearly links the shape of early childhood care and education in a specific country to its cultural and social context: "The reasons for investing in ECEC policy and provision are embedded in cultural and social beliefs about young children, the role of families and government and the purposes of ECEC within and across countries"[4]

Another interesting and quite recent comparative study is the International Review of Curriculum and Assessment (INCA), carried out by the National Foundation for Educational Research in England and Wales, on behalf of the Qualifications and Curriculum Authority in England. Tony Bertram and Chris Pascal authored a summary review of a number of participating countries. The review focussed on early years education and suggests that "Childhood is a social construction deeply embedded within societal norms and values. Different societies and sub-groups within societies, especially in multicultural societies, view what is an 'appropriate' curriculum for young children differently."[5]

The authors of the report continue to emphasise the diversity of findings across the participating countries of the survey and locate the reasons for this diversity: "Policy and practice in ECEC is deeply located in national understandings of the place of family and childhood in society. Such social constructions underpin the choices that are made and these cultural norms differ, even within the relatively economically-homogenous group of nations of this study."

The IEA Preprimary Project 1986 – 2002 is another example of an international comparative study and illustrates particularly well the difficulties comparing early childhood settings and experiences across countries.

Why are the answers to the previous discussion important? Does it really matter whether childhood is defined as a timeless and universal phenomenon or as socially constructed and reconstructed, changing over time and across cultures? I believe it matters a lot for three main reasons: First of all, there is strong evidence that continuum of care from family to early years setting is crucial for child outcomes. Indeed, the presence or otherwise of this continuum can be identified as an important indicator of quality. Secondly, the implementation of any policy, curriculum or practice in early childhood education requires acceptance and "buy-in" among parents, practitioners and the interested public to be ultimately successful. Finally, the design of policy and practice frameworks for early childhood care and education has to match the stage of development any particular country or community is in. In other words, it has to "pick people up where they are".

Commenting on the issue of continuity, Lisa da Silva and Sarah Wise from the Australian Institute of Family Studies in their recent paper on continuity between parental child rearing beliefs and practices across different child care settings, summarise the research evidence as such:

> Although complete continuity between parents and care providers is near impossible, due to the different roles and experiences of parents and care providers, research investigating continuity across care settings is important. Levels of continuity or discontinuity across care settings influence the experience of the child in care, and are increasingly being recognised as an important dimension of good quality childcare. Continuity is also thought to be optimal for children's development.[6]

The following anecdote recounted by Lisa Delpit illustrates the important aspect of "buy in" or acceptance by the community of learners and teachers:

> The teacher wanted to bring the children's culture into the class. She asked D. (Alaska Native bilingual aide in an Anglo teacher's classroom.) to write the directions for making an animal trap on the blackboard so the children could make traps in class during the activity period. D. told me she had a hard time writing up the directions, but struggled through it. The kids, however, were the ones who really had a hard time. They found the directions impossible to follow. Finally, in utter frustration, D. went home and got a trap. She took it apart and let the children watch as she put it

back together. Everyone made his or her own trap in no time.[7]

And Louis Laosa points out, "Groups differ in their views of what constitutes desirable behaviour on the part of their children; they differ, moreover, in the conceptions of the attributes that define 'optimal development'"[8].

I have been in correspondence with a colleague from British Columbia in Canada who has been working with the British Columbia Aboriginal Child Care Society on the development of a statement that defines quality from the perspective of Aboriginal peoples in British Columbia. Her name is Victoria Mulligan and she describes herself – quite tongue in cheek! – as an advocate of "locally appropriate practice". I find myself agreeing with her and furthermore believe that the "whole child perspective" or holistic view of children as documented in our National Children's Strategy[9] as well as an ecological understanding of childhood encompasses both our knowledge of how children develop and the culture and values of their communities.

Sometimes administrators ask me why we couldn't just "import" a successful framework of early childhood care and education from another country, for example New Zealand or Sweden? Wouldn't this save us much time and expense on our own journey? Why not take a convenient short cut? The answer to this question is evident from the above: It just wouldn't work for three reasons: (1) It would not match the cultural and value pattern of contemporary Irish communities. (2) It would not find the necessary acceptance among stakeholders. (3) It would ignore the particular stage of development of the Irish early childhood care and education sector. But there is another important reason why we have to take the longer and less travelled road: The process and the debate towards a framework is in itself a great opportunity for development and cannot be skipped.

How, then, is the Centre for Early Childhood Development and Education approaching the development of a National Quality Framework? To take account of the various contributing strands the Framework will be developed and supported by three main areas of work:

▸ Reviews of National and International research, policy and practice in relation to quality in early childhood care and education

- Consultation with stakeholders in early childhood care and education in Ireland
- A conceptual framework of early childhood care and education in Ireland

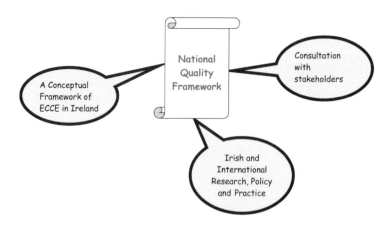

The process so far leaves me very confident that the National Quality Framework will be soundly based on current research evidence and at the same time reflect the socio-cultural reality of contemporary Ireland. I believe that our framework – with your help – will emerge through a fruitful process of debate and that it will enjoy broad participation and acceptance.

I will refrain from going into further detail at this stage, as I don't want to overstay my welcome and test your kind patience for too long. In any case, two of my colleagues, Maresa Duignan and Jacqueline Fallon will present papers on some of the aspects and details of our

work later today. We are very much looking forward to a lively debate on your views on all of these issues.

I started of with a picture of idealised childhood from a commercial advertising campaign and would like to leave you with a couple of different pictures clearly based in their cultural and social context.

Heino Schonfeld
Director of the C.E.C.D.E., Dublin

1   Association for Childhood Education International: "Global Guidelines for Early Childhood Education and Care in the 21st Century", 2002
2   Hewlett, Barry S.: "Diverse Contexts of Human Infancy"
3   Bower, Bruce: "Raising Trust (relation of child-rearing technique to social development of children)"
4   OECD: "Starting Strong", 2001
5   Bertram, Tony and Pascal, Chris: "Early Years Education – An International Perspective", 2002
6   da Silva, Lisa and Wise, Sarah: "Continuity of childrearing models across childcare settings", 2003
7   Delpit, Lisa: "Other people's children: Cultural conflict in the classroom." 1995
8   Loasa, Louis. M.: "Parent education, cultural pluralism, and public policy: The uncertain connection." In R. Haskins & D. Adams (Eds.), Parent education and public policy, 1983
9   Department of Health and Children: "National Children's Strategy", 2000

Introduction

We were greatly honoured when Heino Schonfeld, the Director of the Centre for Early Childhood Development and Education, agreed to open the OMEP Conference held in the Dublin Institute of Technology on Saturday 24th April, 2004. In his address, which forms the first part of these 'Proceedings', he draws attention to the theme of the 2004 Conference "Children of the Global Village" asking three thought provoking questions which he then proceeds to answer. "(1) Is childhood sufficiently uniform across the globe with universal needs and rights demanding a global response? (2) Why is the answer to the first question important for our response to the needs of young children in Ireland? And (3) How is the Centre for Early Childhood Development and Education (CECDE) approaching the development of a National Quality Framework for young children here in Ireland?"

In many ways the answers to Heino's first two questions are encapsulated in the United Nation's Convention on the Rights of the Child (1989). Ireland signed this Convention on the 30th September, 1990 and subsequently ratified it, without reservation, on the 21st September, 1992. With its 54 Articles, this Convention is a veritable "Bill of Rights" for all the children of the World. As such it provides benchmarks against which quality provision can be judged. What follows in the sixteen articles in these 'Proceedings' are insights into and analysis of Early Childhood Education and Care which assist in the assessment of Irish provision. The first paper by Dr. Noirín Hayes sets the scene.

Section One – Aspects of Quality

Dr. Noirín Hayes states in her paper that it is "A series of musings on the direction in which Irish Policy making is going in Ireland with respect to young children and early education." Noirín stresses the importance of distinguishing between a Welfare and a Wellbeing Approach. She says:

> The increasing use of the term wellbeing in policy documents could be seen as reflecting a positive shift in thinking. A wellbeing approach to children and childhood would break through 'the web of paternalistic protectionist constructions that emphasise children as powerless dependents separated off from adult society

and effectively excluded from participation in shaping their own destiny'. (Woodhead, 1977)

Noirín says that the Irish Department of Education and Science mostly adopts the welfare approach. This can be seen in their view that early education is driven by two main policy agendas (1) Educational Disadvantage and (2) Labour Force Equality. She mentions in her paper a recent example from Canada of the development of a Wellbeing Approach – The Early Childhood Development Agreement (Canada, 2000, 2001).

Maresa Duignan provides an interesting insight into the CECDE's consultation process on quality in ECEC. She says that the core function of the CECDE is to produce a National Framework for Quality for ECCE in Ireland. This she says involves three key strands. Firstly, the provision of a Conceptual Framework. Secondly, a review of National Policy, Practice and Research and thirdly, a nation-wide consultation with the 'Stakeholders'. In her paper, Maresa briefly outlines the rationale, methodology, findings and implications of the national consultation process with these 'Stakeholders' in ECCE. She gives, in considerable detail, the stakeholders' views concerning: The Definition of Quality; The Assessment of Quality; The Support of Quality; And The Implications for the Development of the National Framework for Qualifications. She concludes by saying "The wealth of data generated during the consultative seminars outlined in this report provides valuable insights (concerning quality early years provision) from a diverse array of stakeholders".

Mary O'Kane considers the impact of the Child Care (Pre-School Services) Regulations (1996) on the Quality of Early Childhood Services in Ireland. She does this by revisiting the IEA Pre-Primary Project which took place between 1994 and 1995 as part of the International Association for the Evaluation of Educational Achievement. Mary looked at a sub-sample of the original project in Ireland, and sought to investigate the attitudes of both Pre-School Officers and Supervisors regarding the Regulations. Her findings indicated an improvement of the structural components of quality in pre-school services over the decade and further illustrated the interface between training and the quality of provision. However, Mary's paper ends with a caveat with respect to the remuneration of pre-school personnel.

Dr. Brian Murphy commences his paper by arguing that the 1971 Primary School Curriculum (Curaclam na Bunscoile) placed a high emphasis on play in the Infant Classes. He then briefly traces the implementation of the primary school curriculum, its assessment and impact from 1971 to 1999 when the Revised Primary School Curriculum was introduced. Having stated that the New (1999) Primary School Curriculum encompasses the broad philosophical thrust of its 1971 predecessor Brian goes on to say that "the identification of and engagement with issues pertaining to early childhood/Infant education and the resulting labelling of the area as a 'key issue' of primary education marks a significant change between the 1971 and 1999 curricula." The paper continues with a presentation of findings of a nationwide questionnaire which elicited the views of three hundred randomly-selected Senior Infant Teachers with respect to resources, teaching methods and attitudes to the 1999 Primary School Curriculum.

Mary Dineen considers quality experiences in the early years for children with "special needs". She highlights the importance of involving the multi-disciplinary team as early as possible, involving parents and integrating such children (where possible) into 'normal' provision. She makes the important point that "In the past, false assumptions about the potential abilities of children with "special needs" have led to them being denied the social and educational opportunities they needed. We now know they can benefit from participating in a normal playgroup experience." Mary continues by concentrating on play, language and social skills. She concludes by saying that despite their developmental delays children with "special needs" require a high quality environment which, in an ideal world, would involve the expert advice of teachers, psychologists and speech and language therapists.

In a very thought-provoking paper Stefane Corbett and Dr. Anna Ridgway describe and evaluate the introduction of supervised placement in the UCC BA Degree in Early Childhood Studies. This paper investigates the role of the student on placement and the role of the mentor and concludes by highlighting the strengths and weaknesses of the present system. Their paper makes an excellent conclusion to this section on "Aspects of Quality".

Section Two – Parents

In the first paper in this section Dr. Rosaleen Murphy describes the Parent and

Family Involvement (PFI) Project, for which she was awarded a Government of Ireland Post-Doctoral Scholarship in October 2003. This research aims to develop a conceptual framework for parent and family involvement in early years services in Ireland; to develop a model for the training of early years educators in implementing programmes of parent and family involvement; and to put together a resource file for early years educators and tutors. Having explored the background to parent and family participation in Early Childhood Education and Care Rosaleen describes in detail the methodology that she is using in the PFI Project, the PFI training workshops, and concludes with a discussion of the key issues and concerns which have emerged to date.

Edel Conway presents a study which highlights the health information support needs in the South East of Ireland from ante natel to the pre-school years. This research formed part of the 'Child Health Information Service Project (CHISP) which aimed to increase service planning and to provide an understanding of the child health information needs of parents and carers of pre-school children. Her fieldwork, which consisted of consultation with ten focus groups, yielded interesting findings with respect to participants' perceptions, needs and recommendations. She concludes by stating that "A Central conclusion was that quality information and effective communication empower the parent and are linked with improved health. Furthermore, quality information provision is not just a bi-product of the service provision but requires active management in its own right."

Section Three – Disadvantage and Special Needs

Jacqueline Fallon presents the findings and recommendations of an 'Audit of Services Targeting Disadvantage and Special Needs among children aged birth to six in Ireland.' This audit was carried out as part of the brief given to the Centre for Early Childhood Development and Education (CECDE) by the Department of Education and Science. The CECDE has assembled a data base of approx. 1,400 services. Moreover, the CECDE has committed itself to basing all its policy recommendations on research. Thus evidence-based policy becomes the driving force of the CECDE which, as Jacqueline points out, is a somewhat different approach to that adopted by Ireland in the past. Her paper discusses the diversity of services for children with "special needs" and the resultant difficulties for those endeavouring to co-ordinate them. She concludes by giving the CECDE recommendations which have been drawn from this audit of services.

Dr.Maire Mhic Mhathuna discusses the needs of young newcomer children learning English as an additional language in Early Years settings in Ireland. Recent arrivals of children in Ireland come from Poland, Lithuania, Latvia, the Philippines and the Ukraine in that order. Asylum seekers come mainly from Nigeria with a smaller number coming from Romania, the D.R.Congo, Moldova, and the Czech Republic. Maire examines the 'needs' from 'Social' and 'Language' perspectives. With the latter she explores the relationship between English and their home language and the advantages and disadvantages of both for the child. Considering the role of the Early Years Educator, Maire highlights the importance of attitude and methodology. Finally, she concerns herself with the relationship between the Educator and the parents of these children.

Rosaleen Dempsey's paper brings to our attention the plight of parents whose preschool children have been diagnosed with a visual impairment. Tracing the provision of educational and support services from past through present to future requirements, her work is incisive and constructively critical. She concludes with a poignant reminder of the fact that attitudinal change in preschool children, as a result of their experience with the visually impaired, is positive and empowering for all involved.

Section Four – Play
Margaret Kernan chronicles the development of playgrounds in Dublin. These playgrounds which were founded in the 1930s by the Civics Institute of Ireland sought to improve public health, morals and safety. In her concluding remarks Margaret makes the interesting point that Dublin Corporation, which took over the playgrounds from the Civics Institute, has not yet achieved any of these three objectives in their entirety.

Carmel Brennan's paper, based on research involved in the IPPA Quality Improvement Programme, focuses on the 'competent' as distinct from the 'needy' child. In this context, she relate play to 'meaning making'; play to problem solving; play as 'scaffolding'; play to 'the zone of proximal development'; play as a means of identifying with each member of the community; play as a means of making friends; play as a community of players; play as a community of pioneers and explorers; play as a community of professionals; and finally, play as a community of phantasmagorical characters. Carmel concludes by saying that: "To guide children's participation in any community of practice, the adult must be more expert and/or a co-learner. This view of learning has major implications for childcare practice and the 'communities of practice' that suggests ways of understanding and assessing children's learning within the context of family and community and of guiding their participation in the larger community."

Marlene McCormack presents a small scale study which looked at the effectiveness of IPPA training as perceived by three groups of participants. Although each group undertook a different training programme, each was similar with respect to methodology, levels of support to participants, underpinning philosophy and ethos of the tutors. The results of the study indicated that that effective training is supportive, empowering, facilitates dialogue, promotes reflection, promotes critical thinking and develops pathways.

Section Five – Spirituality

Dr. Mary Daly argues that spiritual development is a vital area which receives little recognition. In essence it involves looking inwards in search of meaning and purpose while seeking an understanding of what truly matters. In her article, she claims, that the search for meaning is one of the primary motivators in children's lives and argues that if this deep need for meaning is unmet then their lives come to feel shallow and empty. Mary then continues with a discussion concerning the Spiritual Quotient (SQ) vis a vis IQ (Intelligence Quotient) and EQ (Emotional Quotient). She argues that these three intelligences work together. Having shown that spiritual development is not necessarily connected to organised religion, Mary concludes her paper by providing an appendix which indicates the types of activity that can be used by practitioners to enhance spiritual development in young children.

In his paper, Dr. Francis Douglas contends that every human being is part of a much larger, integrated system with a multitude of feedback loops which link together living and non-living systems. In exploring this concept he traces social systems theory through culture to family, highlighting their role as part of this living system which is dynamic and ever changing. Next, he considers the family and pre-school provision as part of this 'living system' before moving on to the young child as a 'social scientist'. Finally, he looks at the integrated world in the light of the above. He concludes that the pre-school child has to have a sense of 'something beyond' which requires a) A Deeper Social Reality. b) An Awareness of the Mythological, Archetypal or Religious dimensions of our situation. c) Some More Profound level of Truth or Beauty and d) An attunement to a Deeper, Cosmic sense of Wholeness, a sense that our actions are part of some greater universal process.

Conclusion

It is with delight that we present these research papers which represent sixteen further contributions to our growing knowledge of and insight into Early Childhood Education and Care in Ireland. They all represent the heartfelt desire to improve conditions and enhance the development of those who lack the political power to speak for themselves. We are particularly grateful to the Katharine Howard Foundation for its generous donation of one thousand Euro which went towards publishing these 'proceedings'.

Mary Horgan
Francis Douglas
Department of Education, UCC.
February, 2005.

Section One
Aspects of Quality

Welfare and Wellbeing:
Impact of Social Policy
on Early Educational Practice in Ireland

Nóirín Hayes

Pangúr Bán

So we find by degrees
Peace in solitude
Both of us, solitaries,
Have each the trade

He loves: Pangúr, never idle
Day or night
Hunts mice; I hunt each riddle
From dark to light.

[trans: Eavan Boland]

Introduction

There is general agreement that many different systems interact dynamically across time and context to influence the development and education of young children. Within the bio-ecological framework of development a strong case has been made for recognising the impact of social policies on the way in which services are provided and practices influenced and the consequent influence they have on the development of individual children (Bronfenbrenner & Cecci, 1994; Bronfenbrenner & Morris, 1998).

Over the last number of years there have been enormous policy changes in the field of early childhood care and education in Ireland including the publication of the National Childcare Strategy (Ireland, 1999a); *Ready to Learn*, the White Paper on Early Childhood Education (Ireland, 1999b), the National Children's Strategy (Ireland, 2000a) and *Towards a Framework for Early Learning* (NCCA, 2004). This increased interest in early education has afforded ample opportunity for considering how young children in Ireland are considered within this policy activity and, like the poet above, I have spent many hours hunting the riddle. This article is an attempt to put some shape on the musings. It is necessarily tentative and I look forward to the discussion I hope it provokes.

Role of language in early childhood education policy
Although something of a truism it is impossible to overstate the importance and influence of language on our thinking and our behaviour. In 1956 Benjamin Whorf captured the importance when he wrote:

> We cut nature up, organise it into concepts and ascribe significances as we do *largely because we are parties to an agreement to organise it in this way*, an agreement that holds throughout our speech community and is codified in the patterns of our language [emphasis added].

There is an expectation that, generally speaking the words we use will be understood as they are intended by those who are listening. However, it is a false expectation and one which could lead to a dangerous complacency.

The subject of the words we use and the meaning we ascribe to them deserves careful attention in the field of early education. There are many examples of words meaning different things to different populations. For instance, some time ago while attending a parent-teaching meeting the teacher introduced parents to the primary school curriculum. She pointed out that the curriculum is child-centred and explained that this meant that everything in the classroom and school was directed at the child. This understanding of the term child-centred is not untypical but it is at odds with the general understanding in early educational circles where child-centred means being responsive to the interests of the child. Such is the potential for confusion with the term child-centred that many in the field have stopped using it preferring to talk, instead of curriculum and practice as child-sensitive.

Similarly, in his paper on senior infant classroom practice Murphy (2004) has illustrated the differing understanding of the term play by primary teachers when compared to the understanding of the term by others working in early education and points to the differing impact on practice.

Within the National Children's Strategy the 'whole child' approach is identified as a central guiding element. This approach is elaborated as referring to the complex dimensions of development within the individual child that need attention as a whole. This characterisation of the concept falls short of acknowledging the importance to development of the child in context – a central element of the 'whole child' approach in contemporary thinking in child development and early educational literature (Greene & Moane, 2000)

In recent publications (Hayes, 2001; 2002) the case has been made that the language of policy documents in Ireland relating to services for young children actually fragments rather than integrates the policy area. At the moment two different policy strategies, the National Childcare Strategy and the White Paper on Early Childhood Education, from two different government departments, that of Justice, Equality & Law Reform and Education & Science respectively, are being implemented as separate policies despite the fact that they relate, in large measure, to the same population of children. The language of the two policies differ – one focusing on 'childcare' and the other on 'early childhood education' – and this difference in language perpetuates the myth that these two concepts refer to two different services. In fact they do not; increasingly it is recognised that early childcare *is* early education (OECD, 2000, 2002). The distinction that is maintained between childcare and early education is not benign in its impact on either children or adults and it has been argued that the characterisation of early childhood teaching as akin to caring and mothering has acted to maintain a lower professional status for those working in early education and to dis-empower early years practitioners from claiming their identities as professionals, as teachers (Dalli, 2003)

Children in policy
Over the last decade there has been a noticeable shift in the use of language describing children in policy documents. This change reflects a changing view of childhood that is beginning to take account of the rights as well as the needs of children (Hayes, 2002). The shift has been driven, in large part by the growth of the rights discourse and the post-modern spotlight on the limitations of the traditional child development approaches in considering children.

In 1992 Ireland ratified the UN Convention on the Rights of the Child (UNCRC). It took some time before this led to discernible differences in the language of policy. The National Childcare Strategy (1999a), a strategy which emerged from a strong consultative process, was one of the first policy document to take children's rights as a starting point and most of the child related policy document published since then make reference to children as active participants in the policy process. This recognition of children as active participants – reflecting Article 12 of the UNCRC – was most evident in the consultation which took place with children in the development of the National Children's Strategy (Hayes 2004; Ireland, 2000; National Children's Strategy, 2000).

From Welfare to Wellbeing

One trend in the language of policy documents that is particularly noticeable is the increased reference to child wellbeing alongside child welfare. To what extent does this development reflect a recognition and respect for the rights of children and an engagement with them on policy issues affected the language and action of policy?

Has the change in language led to a shift from the traditional, protectionist child welfare approach to policy and legislation towards an approach that responds to the active child and is child wellbeing led? Simply recognising that children have rights and should be considered as active participants in policy and actions impacting on them does not necessarily lead to change in practices or in the way services and supports are developed and delivered. Indeed one of the weaknesses of the rights discourse is the lack of clarity in the language used to outline rights allowing for a number of degrees of interpretation.

A review of Irish policy documents has found that, while the rights of children are acknowledged, the language continues to be protectionist; focusing on protecting children [a welfare approach] rather than focusing on protecting their rights, including their right to protection (Hayes, 2002). This is a weak, welfare dominated form of commitment to the rights of children and continues to portray children as passive. The danger with this approach is that policymakers and practitioners working with children and their families take the idea of the 'best interest of the child' and determine what is best for the child from an adult rather than a child perspective. This limitation constrains what can be done with and for children and, at its worst it can 'legitimate practices in some cultures which are positively damaging to children' (Parker, 1994).

It is the argument of this paper that committing to the rights of children through such actions as ratifying the UNCRC and the establishment of an Office of Ombudsman for Children requires more than simply a change in written language, it requires a change that is also reflected in changes in thinking, in action and in resource allocation. At the moment it appears as if a change in language is emerging although strong commitment to the rights based approach continues to be resisted in some areas –most recently evidenced by the fall of the Disability Bill (2003).

Child welfare versus child wellbeing

The increasing use of the term wellbeing in policy documents could be seen as reflecting a positive shift in thinking. A wellbeing approach to children and childhood would break through 'the web of paternalistic protectionist constructions that emphasise children as powerless dependents separated off from adult society and effectively excluded from participation in shaping their own destiny' (Woodhead, 1997).

Can it be said that there is a significant and clear distinction drawn between the two terms? By certain dictionary definitions welfare and wellbeing are seen in terms of each other; that is welfare is defined as wellbeing and vice versa. However, through usage it is the argument of this paper that the two terms carry different weight and, in respect of children significantly different potential in terms of impact for policy and practice. The distinction between what the two terms imply can be seen in a number of ways. For example:
(i) A welfare approach focuses on a problem that needs to be addressed whilst a wellbeing approach is strength focused. In the field of early education the difference can be seen in how one addresses in practice issues of safety. A welfare approach would focus on the protection of children from harm and might lead to a very safe but unchallenging environment. A wellbeing approach would recognise the development necessity of children taking risks and address the safety issue in terms of sufficiently well trained staff present in sufficient numbers for the number of children present.

(ii) A welfare view of children considers the child in deficit terms – from the perspective of what the child cannot do – whilst the wellbeing approach looks to the competencies of children. Thus an early years curriculum, from a welfare perspective, would aim to teach or train children to achieve what they are not able to do, whether that is to sit still, eat with a knife and fork or know letters. A wellbeing approach would, on the other hand look to a child's interests and where a child is at in a particular time and context. It would provide opportunities and time for children to acquire the skills which might include sitting, eating or reading in a way that is meaningful and relevant to them.

(iii) A welfare view of children reflects a traditional and rather static view of development, one that views children as following a series of well-established milestones with each building on the last. Where a child has not achieved an expected level then there is a need for intervention to bring him or her to the expected level. A wellbeing approach would recognise development as a more dynamic and complex process with milestones merely a guide to what one might expect rather than a fixed point on a developmental path. The welfare approach in this context sees development in a linear way as opposed to the wellbeing approach where the 'toing and froing' of development as a function of the child's own experiences and background is seen as critical and as an important component in decision making.

(iv) Finally it could be argued that the welfare approach considers the child as an isolated individual rather than as a child-in-context. It is more concerned with progressing the individual child towards the next development step than a wellbeing approach which takes the child as a he or she is in the here and now. Paradoxically, this wellbeing approach allows for a more respectful engagement with the individual child as it takes account of wider influencing factors both within and around the child.

The development of early education services in Ireland is driven by two main policy agendas that of educational disadvantage and labour force equality (Hayes, 2001). An issue of great concern to education policy in Ireland is meeting the commitment to combating educational disadvantage. The attention to early education from the Department of Education & Science, as evidenced from their various documents, is specifically in terms of this focus. Early education is considered largely as an intervention, a service to those children who need it, a compensation for some lack that they have in themselves or that is present in their environment. This reflects a strong welfare approach. Were policy makers to address the issue from a child wellbeing approach they would be looking to wider issues such as the extent to which the school curriculum is appropriate to young children, the extent to which the school environment, the culture of the school, reflects their own culture and is welcoming. One of the elements of the early education policy approach to educational disadvantage that appears to be moving in this direction is the commitment to include parents in the process. The language of the commitment, however, tends towards being both patronising and welfare driven – the aim being to teach the parents about what their children need to experience in order to succeed at school rather than about partnering with parents in the education of children.

Where the development of early education is seen as an equality issue it is driven by the requirement to meet the needs of parents to access work and/or training. In this context the child is seen as needing to be cared for while the parent is at work or education and the focus is very much on early education/childcare as child protection with a predominantly health and safety focus. This approach is evident in the language of the preschool regulations and the inspection criteria used. While there is detail on issues of health and safety there is little mention of the development and education of the young child and no requirements regarding the qualification of staff providing centre-based services.

In both the above cases the child is characterised as a dependent recipient of a service rather than as a competent and active participant in the process. Notwithstanding the use of the rights discourse in policy documents the welfare model continues to predominate over a wellbeing approach.

The wellbeing approach in practice
Canada recently drafted an Early Childhood Development Agreement (Canada, 2000, 2001) which committed to the development of policy 'driven by child wellbeing'. The rationale for this move was based on the recognition of the dynamic and interacting factors that impact on young children's development. The framework for progressing the Agreement is based on a scientific analysis of development that recognises the integration of elements across the life course. Wellbeing is considered holistically across the physical, cognitive and socio-emotional domains and it is the strength of the children within these domains that guides policy and action.

Specifically the Agreement notes that children are shaped by the world around them and the many environments that affect their development. Healthy children are recognised as emerging from healthy families who are supported by healthy communities and what happens in the first five years of life is seen as setting the stage for how children will fare in the future.

Taking the child as the primary focus the Agreement identified the domains of wellbeing as including: physical health and motor development; emotional health; social knowledge and competence; cognitive learning and language communication. While these domains map on to different dimensions of child development they are somewhat removed from the more traditional developmental approach in the way in which they are characterised – they capture, in the wording, the active participation of a competent human being.

Furthermore, the Agreement explicitly commits to the importance of early childhood as the core of its policy and implementation. In elaborating on this it also uses the language of wellbeing rather than welfare. The Agreement emphasises that it is during the early years that the foundational strengths for future wellbeing such as the development of problem-solving skills; emotional regulation and physical safety are established. To this child-focused end the importance of high quality early educational opportunities is stressed. In addition the 'value added' of supporting high quality early education to wider society is acknowledged through a recognition that investment in early education is an investment in the future. The present wellbeing of the individual child positively influences later wellbeing and – by extension – society.

This is a recent policy agreement in Canada and has yet to be evaluated. It is presented here as an illustration of what a policy document development from a wellbeing focus might look like. The language is strengths focused and child sensitive and recognises the immediate value to the child of early educational investment while acknowledging the other positive aspects from the point of view of, for instance, combating educational disadvantage and also facilitating parents to access educational and employment opportunities. Unlike Irish policy, however, the driving force is the child and the wellbeing of the child.

Conclusion
This paper is presented as a series of musings on the direction in which Irish policy making is going in Ireland with respect to young children and early

education. It argues that there is a significant difference between approaching policy development from a wellbeing, as opposed to a welfare approach.

Child policy documents in Ireland are beginning to use the language of child wellbeing. The rights discourse and contemporary developmental knowledge are supporting a competency view the child – even the very young child – as an active participant in his or her own development. It has been argued that changing the language of policy is only the first step. It is now necessary to become proactive in ensuring that policy moves from the rhetoric of child wellbeing within a welfare framework to action in support of child wellbeing in a rights framework.

Language is a powerful tool. In any sector those of the sector must own and be comfortable with the language being used. In early education – where early childcare is recognised as early education – it is important to clarify and refine language and terminology so that it can be used to influence policy in the direction best suited to overall child wellbeing. This will lead to an increased likelihood of attaining the high quality services necessary for young children, their families and society. The shift from characterising children as passive to competent, coupled with a move towards a wellbeing, rather than a welfare framework will require attitudinal and behavioural change. A change in language is a first step – but a change in action is the important step.

Bibliography

Bronfenbrenner, U & Ceci, S.J. (1994) 'Nature-nurture in developmental perspective: A bio-ecological theory' *Psychological Review* 101: 568-586

Bronfenbrenner, U. & Morris, P. (1998) 'The Ecology of Developmental Processes' in W. Damon & R.M. Lerner (eds.) *Handbook of Child Psychology Volume 1: Theoretical models of Human Development* (5th edition) (New York: John Wiley & Sons) pp. 993 – 1028

Canada (2000) *Early Childhood Development: Government of Canada Backgrounder* (Ottawa: Government of Canada)

Canada (2001) *Early Childhood Development Agreement: Report on Government of Canada Activities and Expenditures 2000-2001* (Ottawa: Government of Canada)

Dalli, C. (2003) 'Professionalism in early childhood practice: thinking through the debates' Paper presented to the 13th Annual Conference of the European Early Childhood Education Research Association (EECERA), Glasgow, Scotland

Greene, S. & Moane, G. (2000) 'Growing up Irish: Changing Children in a Changing Society' *Irish Journal of Psychology*, Vol. 21, 3-4, 122 – 137

Hayes, N. (2001) 'Early Childhood Education in Ireland: Policy, Provision and Practice' *Administration* Vol. 49, 3, 43 – 67

Hayes, N. (2002) *Children's Rights – Whose Right: A Review of child policy development in Ireland* Policy Paper (Dublin: Policy Institute, TCD)

Hayes, N. (2004) Children's Rights in Ireland: Participation in Policy Development. In D. Crimmens & A. West (eds.) *Having Their Say: Young people and participation – European experiences* (Lyme Regis: Russell House Publishing)

Ireland (1999b) *Ready to Learn: White Paper on Early Childhood Education* (Dublin: Government Stationery Office)

Ireland (1999a) *National Childcare Strategy: Report of the Partnership 2000 Expert Working Group on Childcare* (Dublin: Government Stationery Office)

Ireland (2000) *Our Children – Our Lives: The National Children's Strategy* (Dublin: Government Stationery Office)

Ireland (2003) *Disability Bill* (Dublin: Government Stationery Office)

Murphy, B. (2004) Irish Senior Infant Classroom Practice – a case for imaginary play?' Paper presented to the OMEP (Ireland) Annual Conference, Dublin, April 24th

National Children's Strategy (2000) *Report of the Public Consultation* (Dublin: Stationery Office)

NCCA (2004) *Towards a Framework for Early Learning* (Dublin: National Council for Curriculum and Assessment)

OECD (2000) *Starting Strong: Early childhood education and care* (Paris: Organisation for Economic Co-operation and Development)

OECD (2002) 'Strengthening Early Childhood Programmes: A Policy Framework' in *Education Policy Analysis* (Paris: Organisation for Economic Co-operation and Development) pp. 9 – 33

Parker, S. (1994) 'The best interests of the child. Principles and problems' in P. Alston *The Best Interest of the Child* (Clarendon Press/Oxford University Press)

Woodhead, M. (1997) 'Psychology and the cultural construction of children's needs: Postscript' in A. James & A. Prout (Eds.) *Constructing and Reconstructing Childhood* (London: Falmer Press)

Talking About Quality
Report of a Consultation Process on Quality
in Early Childhood Care and Education

Maresa Duignan

Introduction

In 2001 the Minister for Education and Science invited the Dublin Institute of Technology (DIT) and St. Patrick's College, Drumcondra to jointly establish the Centre for Early Childhood Development and Education (CECDE). The CECDE was launched in October 2002 to complete a comprehensive programme of work in pursuance of the objectives of the White Paper 'Ready to Learn' (DES, 1999).

Our remit is comprehensive, focusing on all care and education settings for children from birth to six years of age, bridging many of the traditional divides between education and care and between the early years settings and the formal education system.

Within this context, the objectives of the CECDE (CECDE, 2001) are:

▸ To develop a quality framework for early childhood education;
▸ To develop targeted interventions on a pilot basis for children who are educationally disadvantaged and children with special needs and
▸ To prepare the groundwork for the establishment of an Early Childhood Education Agency as envisaged by the White Paper.

The core function of the Centre is to produce a National Framework for Quality (NFQ) for ECCE in Ireland. Within the NFQ, three distinct elements can be identified. First of all, a set of standards will define what we understand by quality for children in the Irish context. Secondly, a system of inspection or assessment will be devised to ensure that quality is achieved and maintained. Last of all, an infrastructure will be devised and implemented to support all those working in the ECCE sector to accomplish the quality as prescribed in the standards.

Three key strands of research are involved in the devising of the NFQ.

1. 'A Conceptual Framework on how Young Children Develop and Learn in Ireland' (CECDE, Forthcoming) reviews current research on child development and learning and distills implications for the NFQ.
2. A review of national policy, practice and research, focusing on quality and an examination of the international context for quality through review of a range of selected countries, will distil best policy and practice nationally and internationally in relation to the development of an NFQ.
3. National consultation with stakeholders in ECCE regarding the development of the NFQ will draw on the wealth of experience and expertise related to the promotion of quality in ECCE that exist in Ireland.

This primary objective of this research is to provide a solid foundation on which to build our National Framework for Quality. This paper briefly outlines the rationale, methodology, findings and implications of the national consultation process with ECCE stakeholders.

Rationale

> Consultation with stakeholders will be a crucial part of the process of developing quality standards. (CECDE, 2001: 4).

The CECDE is fully committed to consultation with all interested stakeholders at all stages of our work and this is not only because we wish to draw upon the wealth of experience and expertise that exists within the ECCE sector in Ireland on this issue. It is also because the development and implementation of a National Framework for Quality in Ireland is a potential catalyst for change. Review of the literature on change management reveals a general consensus, which is well articulated by the following:

> Informed change is political, just like any other change and people will not commit to it without engagement in its invention. (McTaggart, 2001: 5)

We not only want to develop a national framework for quality that meets the criteria laid down in our work programme; we want a framework that has relevance and, in fact, is owned by those who will directly implement and benefit from it.

We seek to build future growth and development in the ECCE sector in Ireland on the collective wisdom and knowledge regarding effective policy and practice. This perspective necessitates the adoption of research methodologies that are collaborative and inclusive of all stakeholders in the future of the ECCE sector. These stakeholders include parents and families, teachers and carers, children, policy makers and practitioners from a wide range of professions and disciplines.

The rationale for our commitment to consultation is grounded in the bio ecological theory of child development proposed by Bronfenbrenner (Bronfenbrenner, 1979). See figure 1 below. This proposes a theory of child development as a process which is influenced by multiple variables that exist in the child's environment. This environment is conceptualised as a series of systems that are distinctive yet interrelated (see figure 1 below). The characteristics and interplay of these systems are experienced individually by each child. Therefore if we are to develop an NFQ in ECCE in Ireland, which will ultimately impact on the well being of children, we must take account of the nature of these systems in the Irish context.

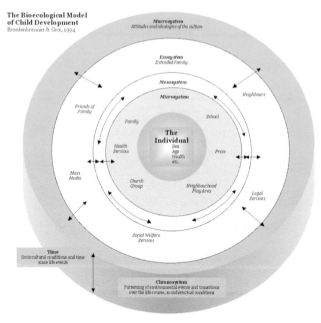

Figure 1: The Bio-ecological Model of Child Development

On the basis of this model Bronfenbrenner has outlined five critical processes for positive development (Bronfenbrenner, 1997). These relate to the systems outlined above. They are not proposed as a hierarchy, rather they reflect the 'nested' nature of the bio ecological systems model. Of particular relevance to our rationale for consultation are propositions four and five that articulate the optimal nature of relationships and conditions within the exosystem and macrosystem:

> Proposition 4 – "The effective functioning of child rearing processes in the family and other child settings requires establishing ongoing patterns of exchange of information, two way communication. Mutual accommodation and mutual trust between the principal settings in which children and their parents live their lives. These settings are the home, childcare programs, the school and the parents' place of work." (Bronfenbrenner, 1997:38)

> Proposition 5 – "The effective functioning of child rearing processes in the family and other child settings requires public policies and practices that provide place, time, stability, status, recognition, belief systems, customs and actions in support of child rearing activities not only on the part of parents, caregivers, teachers and other professional personnel, but also relatives, friends neighbours, co-workers, communities and the major economic, social and political institutions of the entire society." (Bronfenbrenner, 1997:38)

Putting these propositions into the content of developing an NFQ for ECCE therefore requires that ECCE policy and practice be embedded in a common set of understandings regarding the nature of quality. Furthermore these must be relevant for and to, the society in which the child is growing and developing, and also must take account of the dynamic nature of systems which continue to evolve and change over time.

A further dimension to the complexity of establishing an NFQ is the fact that quality itself is an abstract concept, which is very difficult to define. Some of the possible perspectives include:

- Quality as perfection – the achievement of consistent, flawless outcomes – attainable by all.
- Quality as exceptional – something special or distinctive – relative to notions of excellence and unattainable by most.
- Quality as fitness for purpose – meeting specific needs or desires.
- Quality as value for money – giving a good return on investment.
- Quality as a transformation – change and improvement *e.g.* in terms of service provision or professional practice
- Quality as accountability – *e.g.* ensuring child welfare, safety. (DJELR, 2002)

It is very probable that stakeholders in ECCE and therefore participants in the consultation process, bring one or more of these perspectives to this research. The opportunity to engage in discussion regarding this complex issue will hopefully support the resolution of these differing perspectives towards a consensual view of quality that places the child at the centre of policy, provision and practice.

Methodology

Theoretical Framework
It has been argued that:

> Outcomes (of research) that are consistent with existing knowledge are more easily accepted by the existing community of knowledge creators ... (Fannin, 2002: 6)

Our objective of accessing the accumulated knowledge within the ECCE sector regarding the development of national quality standards could only be met if our approach to information gathering elicited relevant knowledge in all its dimensions.

Our search for research methodologies congruent with our constructivist perspective led ultimately to the adoption of an Action Research (AR) approach. This approach, which has gained status within the social and educational research community in recent times has been defined as "...a systematic, reflective, collaborative process that examines a situation for the purpose of planning, implementing and evaluating change." (Garner, 1996 cited in Borgia and Schuler, 1996: 1).

AR also 'fits' with our view that we are co constructors of knowledge leading towards the development of the national quality standards for ECCE rather than presenting ourselves as 'expert' in the knowledge creation process. AR is premised upon the conceptualisation of research as the means by which 'communities of practice' (Lave and Wenger, GET REF) can "..mobilise information and knowledge resources as one part of their broader strategies for community empowerment." (Sohng, 1995: 2).

The key characteristics which distinguish AR from other forms of research include:

▸ Collaboration between researcher and practitioner;
▸ Solution of practical problems;
▸ Change in practice; theory development;
▸ Publicising the results of the inquiry
  (Adapted from Zuber-Skerritt, 1992: 14).

Within the paradigm of AR there are a number of different approaches or methodologies (Dick, 1997, Kemmis and Mc Taggart, 2000, Mc Niff, 2002). We have taken what has been described as a practical or participatory approach. This type of AR involves the researcher and practitioner coming together in order to identify potential problems, underlying causes and possible solutions or interventions. The researcher encourages participation and self-reflection of the practitioner (Hatten et al, 1997:3)

Our objective for this program was primarily to tap into the accumulated knowledge of stakeholders in ECCE regarding the development of national quality standards. Additionally, we hoped to use the occasion of the seminars to disseminate information regarding the work of the CECDE and provide a forum at which the diverse perspectives and opinions of participants could be voiced, shared and discussed.

Method
A total of six public consultation seminars were held during the months of October and November 2003 in Dublin, Cork, Galway, Athlone, Monaghan and Carraroe. The final seminar was conducted through the medium of Irish while all documentation was provided in both English and Irish at all seminars.

In addition to these events, a facility was established on the Centre's website (http://www.cecde.ie) to allow stakeholders who were not able to attend the seminars to complete and submit the information template on-line. Additionally, the information templates devised to gather the data during consultations were distributed to members of our Consultative Committee to be completed by members of the organisations they represent and returned by post. Students in the final year of the BA in Early Childhood Care and Education in the Dublin Institute of Technology also participated in the research.

Publicity

The CECDE's databases and personal contacts were utilized to publicise the consultative seminars and draw attention to the web facility. Flyers were distributed to umbrella and representative organisations nationally, to be further disseminated to members. Advertisements were placed on appropriate local radio stations and staff members also gave interviews on news and current affairs programmes. Information on the seminars was placed in a number of pertinent educational magazines. All infant teachers in primary schools in the environs of the last three seminars received a flyer and information on the consultation.

Initially, a finishing date of December 5th was set for the consultation process, but this was extended until January 5th to allow more stakeholders to participate by using the website and posting back the information templates that were distributed.

Seminar format

Each seminar was conducted in the evening to facilitate participants unavailable during the day due to work or family commitments. Refreshments were served during the registration process and this time afforded an opportunity for networking and sharing among participants. Participants were purposefully assigned to mixed groups (delegates from different professional backgrounds) to enhance the discourse.

The seminars then opened with two brief presentations; the first relating to the origins and progress of the CECDE and the second describing the rationale and format of the evening. Delegates then moved into their pre-assigned discussion groups; each with a briefed facilitator to ensure all participants had an opportunity to voice their perspectives. Information templates were distributed and the discussion was preceded by the completion of background/demographic data.

After initial introductions the group discussion focused on three main questions:

1. What does the term '*quality*' in early childhood care and education mean to you?
2. In your opinion, what are the most effective ways of *assessing quality* in early childhood care and education?
3. What *supports* do you need to receive in order to achieve and maintain quality in early childhood care and education?

Approximately twenty minutes per question was allocated and participants recorded their thoughts and insights on the information template during this time and in the time allotted at the end of the discussion session. The facilitator for each group then provided feedback to the whole audience, highlighting the important issues raised within their respective groups. The seminar concluded with participants completing an evaluation on the consultative seminar as a whole, providing valuable information for the CECDE in the planning of future consultations. The information templates gathered as a result of the consultative seminars were coded and analysed by Red C Research.

Findings

The results of the analysis of the information template are not cumulative in nature due to the fact that participants were encouraged to give multiple responses under each question. The findings foreground the actual voices of participants in the consultation process to reinforce their ownership of this information. Where possible therefore the findings have been illustrated with actual quotations from the participants' feedback.

Profile of Participants

A total of 387 delegates participated in the consultative seminars. There was a great diversity of people in attendance. The majority of participants were female (95%) while a good provincial and urban: rural balance (56%: 40%) was achieved. The greatest attendance was in the urban areas of Dublin (26%), Cork (18%) and Galway (15%) (Galway City and Carraroe), while 11% of the respondents completed the information template online.

Delegates included practitioners/teachers (43%), students (29%), parents/guardians (28%), adult educators (15%) and policy developers (11%). Consequently, these delegates represented an extensive array of settings and contexts for ECCE. The pedagogical approach/philosophy utilised by the greatest proportion of participants was the Montessori method (20%), followed by a play-based curriculum (17%) and High Scope (15%). 29% of respondents did not state a pedagogical approach/philosophy.

Many participants commented on the value of the seminars in terms of listening and sharing experiences and perspectives with others from diverse backgrounds, often for the first time. This greatly enriched the feedback on the information templates and it was encouraging to note the levels of agreement and the commonalities on many of the core issues.

Defining Quality
The challenge of defining quality resulted in a great diversity of responses as is illustrated by the statements of respondents below:

> "Quality is a somewhat nebulous concept which changes and evolves as the early childhood care and education sector continues to develop, it can be difficult to define and difficult to claim as achieved."

> "Quality should cover all areas of a setting from the structure and staff to the broad range of individual needs of the child and their parents."

Thematic analysis ultimately led to the establishment of eleven overarching categories as represented in Figure 1.

As the chart illustrates, there was a great deal of consensus on indicators of quality. A consideration of the top five of these here reveals that participants have considered the issue of defining quality in some detail and have very definite view on this key issue.
The Environment of the child was the predominant response, highlighted by 229 (66%) of all delegates. This includes a number of elements in the immediate

environment, relating to both static and dynamic variables. Many respondents cited the provision of a safe, clean and warm space for the child. The availability of appropriate adult-child ratios also featured prominently within the responses. The advantages of an outdoor play space and of a suitable atmosphere were also commonly cited by delegates. The highest percentages of references to the environment emanated from parents and practitioners, while it was less of an issue for researchers and people more removed from the childcare setting.

There was a strong feeling that regulation and introduction of quality standards should not limit the child's potential for discovery and freedom.

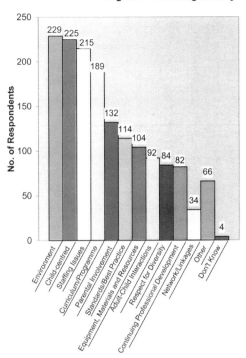

Figure 1 - Defining Quality

> "Quality is also in this instance, about providing an environment that complements and supports the home, safety yes, but important that there are opportunities for risk – not sanitised."

The second most common element in defining quality among respondents related to the service being child-centred (225/65%). This relates to the recognition and the valuing of each child as an individual and the need to work towards the realisation of these needs. The development of all aspects of the child, including the physical, intellectual, emotional and social elements is of paramount importance. Such settings allow for the full potential of the child to be realised at their individual rate of development.

Staffing Issues accounted for 215 (62%) responses. This relates to the training and qualifications of staff working with children at all levels. The characteristics of staff were also seen as being of pivotal importance in the care and education of children.

"Cáilíochtaí cuí i gcúram leanaí a bheith ag na Stiúrthóirí."

The Curriculum or Programme featured prominently within the responses, cited by 189 (55%) delegates. This includes the use of defined routines, structure and methodologies implemented within the setting, which evolve according to the changing individual needs and capabilities of children.

Parental Involvement was raised as an aspect of defining quality by 132 (38%) respondents. This involved accommodating the needs of families through real and consistent partnership.

Assessing Quality

The matter of Assessing Quality also generated lively debate at the seminars and a wide array of responses were forthcoming in this regard. Following thematic analysis, the responses were classified and generated ten all encompassing categories as represented in Figure 2.

Once again the opinions of participants coalesced on a number of issues. The four most popular are considered here. The largest number of respondents (178/46%) focused on External Advice and Support in relation to the assessment of quality. This category includes the existing preschool inspections in operation but there was a focus on the

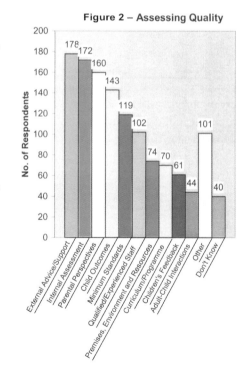

Figure 2 – Assessing Quality

support as opposed to the inspection element of such services. There was great emphasis placed on the suitability of the personnel supplying the external supports, with wide experience and qualifications in the ECCE sector being cited as essential selection criteria. Another prominent characteristic of responses was the call for the inspectors to look beyond the physical environment only and to focus on the quality of the care and education also. Such external advice and supports would be with a view to suggesting improvements for the setting and the sharing and dissemination of evolving developments in policy and practice.

> "A robust and informed external inspection system can play a critical role in assessing and raising the quality of early childhood care and education. This system should have an evaluative and advisory function rather than a 'policing' function."

Internal Assessment was cited by 172 (44%) delegates. This relates to regular ongoing assessment and self-assessment within services. This involved the discussion, planning and evaluation of assessment in a cycle of reflective practice among all members of staff. Participants noted the time needed to implement this form of assessment and the necessity to develop self-evaluation tools within settings.

The viewpoint of the stakeholders within the service, such as Parental Perspectives was noted by 160 (41%) respondents. Delegates cited this form of assessment in relation to the willingness of parents to use the service and based on the happiness of the child. In addition, parents could be asked to complete evaluation forms regarding the service from which alterations and modification might be made.

> "Sástacht agus meas atá ag an tuismitheoir leis an t-ionad atá an gasúr ag freastail air."

Child Outcomes was mentioned as a form of assessment by 143 (37%) delegates in the process of conducting the seminars. This involves regular assessment and evaluation of the rate of development of each child, which is documented and recorded on an ongoing basis. This relates to all aspects of the development of the child, including physical, social, linguistic, cognitive and emotional aspects. Some mention was also made of the use of formal standardised tests and assessments within the early years settings.

> "Children differ in terms of abilities, cultures, life experiences and learning styles. Knowledge of and sensitivity to difference and individual interests on the part of practitioners is essential for quality care."

It is interesting to note that children's perspectives were also cited as another possible assessment mechanism. This is a positive reflection of the growing recognition and commitment to inclusion of children's voices in decision-making pertinent to their daily lives.

It is also noteworthy that participants found the issue of assessing quality the most difficult to frame a response to.

Supporting Quality

Feedback from participants on the theme of Supporting Quality reveals very strong consensus around a number of core issues. Following thematic analysis, the ten categories shown in Figure 3 below were produced. Many delegates pointed out that a support infrastructure was crucial for the successful implementation of the NFQ:

> "A framework alone is likely to enable limited improvement in the quality of provision. Supporting structures and mechanisms should accompany the framework. These supports could take the form of financial assistance, professional development, opportunities for local networking and sharing practices and mentoring."

The main support cited by respondents at the consultative seminars regarding quality was Funding and Financial Support, mentioned by 224 (58%) delegates. Respondents proposed a number of ways in which this could be facilitated, including direct funding for childcare, capital grants, capitation grants, tax breaks and tax credits for parents. Such funding was seen as essential to allow staff wages to reflect the onerous task they fulfil, and to support the training and continuous professional development of

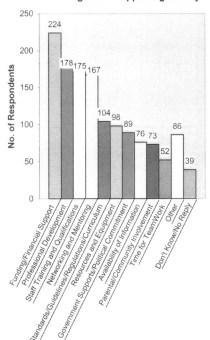

Figure 3 - Supporting Quality

practitioners to provide the infrastructure to allow the sector to develop and prosper.

Professional Development was proposed as a support by 178 (46%) respondents. This involved access to ongoing training and development for practitioners, which dovetailed with their work and personal commitments. This could include release time from work as well as the provision of modular or part-time courses. There were calls within this for ongoing training for management to support them in their role and also for specialist training, regarding special needs and diversity.

Closely related to the theme of Professional Development, and cited by 175 (45%) delegates, was the issue of Staff Training and Qualifications. This comprised access to training opportunities for staff at pre-service level and the provision of courses leading to accredited and standardised qualifications. There were calls for an increasing professional identity for the sector, which may be facilitated by improved access to training and qualifications. Such a training infrastructure would permit a career path to be created, attracting and retaining young practitioners and strengthening the emerging identity of the sector.

The provision of Networking and Mentoring was viewed by 167 (43%) respondents as an important element of supporting quality. This involved the sharing and dissemination of information among organisations at a local and national level. In addition, this networking was proposed to cross the traditional professional and sectoral divides, to include all the stakeholders in

ECCE. The inspectors and regional support workers were seen as important elements within this support framework, offering advice and support to practitioners in addition to performing their inspection role.

"Build on the organisations that are already in existence – help and support them. They have already started the quality process."

Implications for the development of the National Framework for Qualifications

The consultation on questions of quality in ECCE revealed that there is a valuable pool of experience and expertise which can support and inform the development of the NFQ. Participants in the seminars were articulate, informed and constructive in their comments and expressed a general welcome for the need for and development of a NFQ.

Synthesis of responses under the three main questions of quality reveals a number of core elements of quality under which development activities should be focused. This secondary analysis resulted in a number of cross-cutting themes. These are presented below with specific recommendations for the development of the NFQ. These elements are not ordered hierarchically. They are interrelated and interdependent and must each be accorded equal attention.

Multiple perspectives

It is evident from analysis of the feedback templates that a broad range of opinions, views and advice was shared in this consultation process. This breadth and depth of perspective is a valuable asset to early childhood care and education in Ireland and should not be lost in the process of developing and implementing the NFQ.

Recommendation 1

Quality in ECCE in Ireland exists within a huge diversity of perspectives, philosophies and practices, which are also dynamic and evolving. This necessitates that quality indicators or standards must contain sufficient flexibility to accommodate these characteristics.

Environment

The majority of responses under this heading refer to the immediate environment where the child is present. Comments encompass the physical spaces in terms of space, layout, design, comfort, safety, and hygiene, indoor and outdoor. It was agreed that the environment should be aesthetically pleasing, welcoming, and balance the need for safety and hygiene with the opportunity for children to experience 'safe risk' in support of their optimal development.

A clear set of minimum standards relating to the nature of the environment in ECCE settings should be developed to apply to all situations where children (Birth-6) are present. They should be firmly grounded in research and best practice in relation to child development, encompass all current and relevant legislation and guidelines and embrace existing best practice as exemplified in established quality assurance programmes in ECCE.

Child-centred

This heading refers to the strong consensus that the best interests of the child must inform all policies and practice in ECCE. Participants clearly endorsed the need to consult with and listen to children's views when developing policies and services directly related to them. In light of this consensus the following recommendations are made:

The NFQ must support the well-being and development of all the children (Birth-6) of Ireland. This child centred focus must inform all elements of the NFQ including standards, assessment and support structures.

Mechanisms and protocols must be developed to facilitate the voices of children to be heard on all aspects of the development, delivery and assessment of quality in ECCE. Guidelines for consulting with young children should also be inherent to the NFQ.

Staffing

This heading refers primarily to the staffing issues in centre based ECCE settings. It includes:

▶ Concerns regarding the need for adequate ratios of staff to children in order to facilitate the optimal levels of support and interaction for children and also to facilitate essential activities such as child observation, record keeping, supervising students, engaging with parents etc;

- The need for managerial staff with appropriate management qualifications and expertise;
- The need for allocation of time and resources to teamwork/team building and networking and liaison with other professionals and agencies. This time should be within usual working hours.

On the basis of this consensus the following recommendations are made:

The NFQ should give clear guidelines on adult-child ratios based on research evidence and best practice. It should also provide guidelines for practitioners in centre-based settings on supporting essential activities such as teamwork, team building and reflective practice.

Education, Training and Qualifications

This heading reflects a wide range of consensus amongst participants including:

- The positive relationship between quality of provision in ECCE and the qualifications of staff;
- The need for standardised and accredited education, training and qualifications, both pre-service and in-service;
- The need for infrastructure to afford all practitioners access to accredited education, training and qualifications wherever and whenever they require it;
- The importance of continuing professional development and need for specific training programmes related to changing nature of ECCE practice *e.g.* diversity, special needs, quality assurance.

On the basis of this consensus the following recommendations are made:

The NFQ must articulate the important relationship between quality of ECCE and the qualifications of practitioners. It must articulate well with and support developments regarding standard setting for qualifications, mechanisms for access, transfer and progression and quality assurance procedures currently being undertaken by the National Qualifications

Authority of Ireland, the National Awarding bodies and all institutions involved in the development and delivery of education and training in ECCE. It must make provision for education and training associated with the implementation of the NFQ.

Parental Involvement

This heading refers, in the main, to the necessity for the NFQ to recognise parents as the primary carers and educators of the child. There was a strong consensus on the necessity of parental involvement in ECCE. Perspectives on this involvement varied along a continuum from asking parents to give satisfaction ratings to services, through to full partnership in the day-to-day operation, management and development of services. It was agreed that facilitating parental involvement was often difficult to achieve and that the NFQ must be able to support and develop this important dimension of quality.

On the basis of this consensus the following recommendation is made:

> The NFQ should support the development of infrastructure to facilitate the representation of parents' perspectives in the development of policy and practice in ECCE. In addition it should provide guidelines for practitioners regarding supporting and developing parental involvement in service provision.

Curriculum/Programme

As is evident from the heading a number of different terms were used by participants to refer to the need for some sort of overarching national guidelines in relation to everyday practice in ECCE settings with children aged birth to six years. It was agreed that such guidance needed to have a high degree of flexibility to take account of children's needs, support the autonomy of practitioners and accommodate the broad range of existing curricula, programmes and methodologies that exist in ECCE in Ireland.

On the basis of this consensus the following recommendation is made:

> The National Council for Curriculum and Assessment (NCCA) is presently engaged in the development of 'Towards a Framework for early Learning.' This initiative will provide overarching curriculum guidelines for all adults working with children birth to six years and may resolve

concerns expressed by participants in this consultation. The NFQ should support the development and dissemination of this initiative.

Standards
It was clearly acknowledged that standards were an essential element of the development of quality in ECCE. The role and nature of such standards attracted the following consensus:

▶ They should support the harmonisation of existing regulations, standards and guidelines;
▶ They should be applicable to all settings where children aged birth to six are present and be flexible enough to have relevance to a wide variety of practice;
▶ They should be based on a clear set of values and principles, which should emerge from the consensus of stakeholders in ECCE;
▶ Implementation materials should be developed that are easy to administer and facilitate regular review of practice.

On the basis of this consensus the following recommendation is made:

Clear, standardised guidelines in relation to the development of policies, procedures and practice in a wide variety of ECCE settings should be included in the NFQ. In addition any assessment materials developed should be uncomplicated, straightforward and easy to complete.

Adult-Child Interactions
This heading refers to the consensus that emerged regarding the critical importance of positive adult child interaction in the development of quality in ECCE. It also highlights skilled and purposeful child observation as a key tool for the development of such positive interaction.

On the basis of this consensus the following recommendations are made:

The NFQ should take account of the literature regarding the role of adult child interaction in the development and provision of quality in ECCE.

Observation is a valuable tool in the assessment of quality in adult child interactions and the NFQ should include clear guidelines and policies on this important issue.

Respect for Diversity
This heading refers to the significant consensus that ECCE provision must be guided by a fundamental respect for diversity in society. This loosely translates into two key perspectives. The first is that all children and families must be treated with respect regardless of their circumstances. Secondly, that the recognition of the individuality of children should result in policy and practice that avoids uniformity and instead supports difference.

On the basis of this consensus the following recommendation is made:

> Respect for diversity is a key issue, which must be central to the development of the NFQ. A review of literature and best practice on this issue should underpin this development process.

Networking, Linkages and Information
This heading refers to the consensus that emerged regarding the necessity for the establishment of networks at local, regional and national level, which would facilitate the sharing of information and best practice amongst ECCE practitioners. It was emphasised that these networks should build upon established infrastructure and a number of practical suggestions related to the nature of a networking infrastructure were made, including a national clearinghouse for research and information, mentoring systems for practitioners at all levels, discussion groups and telephone help lines. A separate theme emerged out of this heading related to the need for promotion and profile raising of ECCE itself within society in general.

On the basis of this consensus the following recommendation is made:

> The NFQ should facilitate the development of infrastructure to support networking and meet the information needs of the broad range of stakeholders in ECCE. This should build upon existing infrastructure and expertise and should be accessible at national, regional and local level.

Assessment

This heading refers to the consensus regarding assessment mechanisms in ECCE. It is divided under two clear sections that of external and internal assessment. External assessment referred primarily to existing inspection systems that operate within ECCE. Comments stated the need for:

▸ Inspectors and assessors qualified in ECCE;
▸ Formative and supportive assessment;
▸ Consideration of the more dynamic variables of quality;
▸ Standardisation, coordination and consistency of external inspection.

Internal assessment can be conceptualised as a continuum from the individual practitioner through to the team within a centre and ultimately to the wider community of practice involved in ECCE. It generally involves review and reflection on practice towards the development and improvement of same. It was viewed as essential to the development of quality.

On the basis of this consensus the following recommendations are made:

The NFQ must take account of the variety of established approaches to the assessment of quality and be able to accommodate, support and where necessary develop current practice to achieve the desired levels of consistency and co-ordination.

Assessment of quality must have relevance and involve all stakeholders in the provision of ECCE. The NFQ must acknowledge and support the importance of internal assessment at all points along this continuum.

Government Support, Commitment and Funding

This heading reflects the unequivocal consensus that quality in ECCE in only achievable if strong Government support is present. This support can be realised by clear and coordinated policy across all Departments. Financial support emerged as a major issue for participants and it was widely viewed that exchequer support for ECCE was essential for the sustainability of growth and development. Funding was identified as necessary under a variety of different headings including, development for infrastructure, capital investment in service provision, adequate terms and conditions of employment for staff and support for parental choice of ECCE.

On the basis of this consensus the following recommendations are made:

Government support for ECCE in Ireland must be clearly evidenced by the publication of strategic, coordinated policy and adequate allocation of financial support to realise and sustain these policy commitments.

Conclusion

The premise upon which this consultation process was conducted was that the formation of the National Framework for Quality should be based upon wide ranging consultation with all stakeholders in early childhood care and education in Ireland. The CECDE would like to reiterate its appreciation to all those who participated in the consultative process and who consequently have played an integral role in the development of the NFQ.

The wealth of data generated during the consultative seminars outlined in this report provides invaluable insights from a diverse array of stakeholders. This complements other elements of the CECDE's work in developing the NFQ. It is now envisaged that these elements will be amalgamated and synthesised to produce the core elements of the NFQ, *i.e.* a set of national quality standards, and mechanisms for implementing and supporting achievement of these standards in early childhood care and education in Ireland.

The CECDE is committed to ongoing consultation in the development of the NFQ and we look forward to further collaboration and partnership with the sector in the process of developing and implementing the NFQ.

Bibliography

Borgia, E. and Schuler, D. (1996). *Action Research in Early Childhood Education*. ERIC Digest. [Accessed at http://www.ericfacility.net/ericdigests/ed401047.html. 16/01/04]

Bronfenbrenner, U. (1979). *The Ecology of Human Development: Experiments by Nature and Design*. Harvard University Press. Cambridge, Mass.

Bronfenbrenner, U. (1997). Ecological Models of Human Development (in) Guavain, M. and Cole, M. (Eds.). *Readings on the Development of Children* (2nd edition), pp. 37-47.

Centre for Early Childhood Development and Education (2001). *Programme of Work.* Dublin. Centre for Early Childhood Development and Education.

Centre for Early Childhood Development and Education (Forthcoming). *A Conceptual Framework on how Young Children Develop and Learn in Ireland.* Dublin: Centre for Early Childhood Development and Education.

Department of Education and Science (1999). *Ready to Learn – A White Paper on Early Childhood Education.* Dublin: The Stationery Office.

Department of Justice, Equality and Law Reform (2002). *Quality Childcare and Lifelong Learning: Model Framework for Education, Training and Professional Development in the Early Childhood Care and Education Sector.* Dublin: The Stationery Office.

Dick, B. (1997). *A Beginner's Guide to Action Research* [On line] Available at http://www.scu.edu.au/schools/sawd/arr/guide.html, Accessed 16/01/04]

Fannin, M. (2002). *Collaborative Research Methods in Regional Science: What have we Accomplished? Where do we go from here?* Paper presented at the 41st Annual Meetings Southern Regional Science Association, Arlington, VA, April 13, 2002.

Garner, B. (1996). *Using Action Research: Challenges and Opportunities for the Beginner.* Paper presented at the Greater St. Louis Sixth Action Research Collaborative Conference, St. Louis. MO.

Gummesson, E. (1991). *Qualitative Methods in Management Research.* Newbury Park: Sage Publications.

Hatten, R., Knapp, R. and Salonga, R. (1997). "Action Research: Comparison with the concepts of 'The Reflective Practitioner' and 'Quality Assurance'" (in) Hughes, I. (Ed.). *Action Research Electronic Reader,* The University of Sydney, on-line http://www.behs.cchs.usyd.edu.au/arow/Reader/rmasters.htm (Accessed 16/01/04).

Kemmis, S. and Mc Taggart, R. (2000). "Participatory Action Research" (in) Denzin, N. and Lincoln, Y. (Eds.) *The Handbook of Qualitative Research* (2nd Edition). London: Sage.

Mc Niff, J. (2002). *An Action Research Update: Progress and other Stories.* A paper presented at the Research Forum, Centre for Research in Teacher Education and Development, University of Alberta, 24th October 2002.

Mc Taggart, R. (2001). *The Mission of the Scholar in Action Research.* http://www.scu.edu.au/schools/gcm/ar/w/McTaggart.pdf [Accessed: 16/01/04]

Santrock, J. (1996). *Adolescence: An Introduction – 6th Edition.* Madison:

Brown and Benchmark.

Sohng, S. (1995). *Participatory Research and Community Organizing*. A Working Paper presented at the New Social Movement and Community Organizing Conference, University of Washington, Seattle, WA, November 1-3, 1995.

Zuber-Skerritt, O. (1992). *Action Research in Higher Education. Examples and Reflections*. London: Kogan Page.

A Study of the Impact of Child Care (Pre-School Services) Regulations (1996) on the Quality of Early Childhood Services in Ireland:
The IEA PrePrimary Project Revisited

Mary O'Kane

Introduction

The first legislative control over early education services in Ireland came into place in 1996, in the form of the Child Care (Pre-School Services) Regulations (Department of Health). The research hypothesis of this study was that the implementation of the Regulations would have had an impact on quality of early childhood care and education (ECCE) services in Ireland. It was also acknowledged that other related factors, such as increased level of investment and improved levels of training, may have affected quality of provision.

Baseline data, gathered in 1994 and 1995 as part of the International Association for the Evaluation of Educational Achievement (IEA) Preprimary Project in which Ireland took part, was used to investigate the changes in quality. This was a large cross-national study into early childhood care and education conducted over three phases. The present study focused on data from Phase II of the project, which investigated the experiences of four-year-olds in early childhood care and education. Full details of the Irish aspect of this Phase can be found in Hayes, O'Flaherty and Kernan (1997) *A Window on Early Education in Ireland: the First National Report of the IEA Preprimary Project*. Use of this data allowed comparison of both structural and process elements in ECCE provision before the implementation of the Regulations, and six years after their implementation in 2002.

The methodology of the present study involved revisiting a sub-sample of the original IEA Preprimary Project national sample, and undertaking structured observations and administering questionnaires to teachers and supervisors. The study also sought to investigate the attitudes of both Pre-school Officers and Supervisors towards the Regulations.

A number of key issues emerged from the research. Improvements were found in the quality of the pre-school provision in the present study as compared to that of the original study although it is not clear the extent to which these improvements relate directly to the Regulations. This paper concentrates on how the findings relate to two of the themes identified: interaction between structural and process aspects of quality, and training.

The Child Care (Pre-School Services) Regulations 1996

Since 1980s, policy documents relating to ECCE in Ireland had been calling for some form of regulation and co-ordination of the area (Dept of Labour, 1983; Dept of An Taoiseach, 1985; Dept of Health, 1985; Dept of Equality and Law Reform, 1994). Calls for regulation of ECCE were also coming from the voluntary organisations working in this area. The Irish Pre-School and Playgroups Association (IPPA), The National Children's Nurseries Association (NCNA), An Comhchoiste Reamhscolaíochta Teo, and the Montessori organisations, all operated codes of best practice during this period (Dept of Education & Science, 2002). However, Hayes (2002) reports that during this time "despite the variety of reports and recommendations there was a very limited response at a political or practical level." (p.66.)

Finally, in 1996, the Child Care (Pre-School Services) Regulations came into force, under the Child Care Act 1991. The Regulations cover various types of preschool provision including community playgroups, day nurseries, crèches, naíonraí, or any similar service catering for children under six years who are not attending school. They cover areas such as: Development of Child; First aid; Adult/child ratios; Premises and facilities; Sanitary accommodation; Equipment and materials; Food; Safety measures; and Insurance. The Regulations also include an Explanatory Guide to Requirements and Procedures for Notification and Inspection.

Some areas of particular interest are as follows. Features such as adult/child ratios and adequate space have different recommendations for four different types of category. For example, Full Day Care services must have an adult-child ratio of 1:3 for 0-1 year; 1:6 for 1-3 years; 1:8 for 3-6 years. Sessional Services must have an adult-child ratio of 1:10 for children from 0-6 years. Health Boards will also specify on an individual basis the number of preschool children that may be cared for in any particular facility. It is also important to note that the Regulations do not require that preschool teachers have specific training.

The Child Care Act 1991 imposed a statutory duty on Health Boards to inspect preschool services to ensure that they were adhering to the Regulations. Health Boards must also provide information on preschool services to parents. Providers are obliged to notify Health Boards of their existence, and to conform to the regulations. (Department of Health, 1996) There are certain providers who are exempt from the Regulations, these include relatives caring for preschool children and childminders taking care of limited numbers of children in their own home.

Once a service has notified the Health Board of its existence an inspection is arranged. The Health Board also decides from the application form if the provider needs to take further action to comply fully with the Regulations. The Explanatory Guide section of the Regulations advises that the Health Boards will provide information and support as necessary to assist providers to reach the required standards. The Explanatory Guide also states that the first inspection should take place three months after notification, and then on an annual basis. If a service does not comply with the Regulations they should receive notice in writing of any issues identified, and should be given a set time period to rectify these problems, after which they will have another inspection. Any service refusing to comply with the Regulations can be brought to the District Court under Section 57(b) of the Child Care Act.

The Regulations are seen by many as a positive step in the attempt to formalise and regulate the childcare industry, however they have been criticised as not being far reaching enough (Dept of Justice, Equality and Law Reform Expert Working Group on Childcare, 1999). These were the first regulations imposed on preschool services, and allowing for the fact that they cover such a broad spectrum of services, should be seen as a positive first step in an ongoing process of development. They focus very much on the structural aspects of settings and do not regulate quality in terms of process variables such as relationships and adult-child interaction. However it should be noted that these aspects can be very difficult to regulate (Hayes, 2002).

In October 2001, the Minister for Children, Mary Hanafin, announced that the Regulations were to be reviewed at national level. The first meeting of the Review Committee took place in January 2002. The group includes representatives from the Departments of Health & Children; Justice, Equality and Law Reform; and Education. It also includes a parent representative; representatives from various Health Boards; and representatives from various Childcare Voluntary Groups. A report on the Regulations was expected end 2003 but has not yet been published.

Measurement Instruments

For the purpose of this study, the effect the Pre-School Regulations have had on both the structural and process aspects of quality in pre-schools was investigated. The instruments used reflect the emphasis on both types of variables.

Quantitative research methods in the form of structured interviews were used to measure the effect the Regulations have had on the more structural input aspects of quality. An adapted version of the "Provider Survey" used in Phase II of the IEA Preprimary Project was used to collect data of a structural nature. Firstly a questionnaire was administered to the Supervisor of each of the 10 pre-school facilities. It focused on the characteristics of the setting, including its physical description, enrolment characteristics, and materials and equipment available. A survey was also completed by the teachers at each setting examining teacher characteristics. In total 23 teachers completed this survey.

Observation methods were used for the measurement of the process-orientated aspects of quality. The Management of Time (MOT), Child Activities (CA) and Adult Behaviour (AB) observation systems were specifically designed for the IEA by the National Research Committees of the IEA Preprimary Committee, under the direction of the International Co-ordinating Committee.

The CA observation focused on the activities and interactions of one Target Child. The purpose was to record the types of activities the child engaged in, and the amount of time spent on any given activity. This observational measure also recorded the groupings in which the child spent their time. Observations took place on two non-consecutive days, for 20 minutes per day, divided into two ten-minute sections, conducted at different times of the child's day. The activities of the Target Child were recorded at thirty-second intervals; this resulted in a total of eighty observation episodes per child. With the sample of 40 children, this produced a total of 3200 child behaviour observation episodes.

The AB instrument focused on the behaviour of the lead teacher in the particular setting. The purpose was to note the general behaviour of the teacher and their interaction with the children, for example supervising or actively participating with the child. This observation used the same time sampling format as the CA observations, producing a total of 800 adult behaviour episodes.

The MOT observational instrument looked at how the teacher in any given setting organised the children's time. The instrument was used to record the type of activities proposed by the adult, the length of time spent at any given activity, and the group structure of each activity. The process lasted for between two and two-and-a-half hours each day, and was carried out on two non-consecutive days. The three observation instruments have been shown to be valid, reliable and stable measures of quality through cross-national analysis of the data from the IEA Preprimary Project.

Supervisors, and a small sample of Preschool Officers, were also questioned about their views on the implementation of the Regulations and their experience of working with them. However the results from that aspect of the study are not reported on in this paper.

Sample

The sample for the present study represented a subset of the original IEA Preprimary Project. It was decided to draw the present sample from the original Dublin, Meath, Louth, and Kildare sample. In the original study 20 pre-schools from this region were included in the full sample of 54 pre-schools. However, for the present study it was decided to limit the sample number to 10 pre-schools, as this figure was within the travel limitations and budgetary constraints of the study.

The sample of children was randomly selected from those who had received parental permission to take part in the study. A total of 40 children were studied in 10 settings, as compared to the original sample of 193 children in 54 settings.

Questionnaire Findings

Generally speaking improvements were found in the quality of the structural characteristics examined in the present study as compared to that of the original study. Some of the findings from the questionnaire data are presented below.

When the issue of teacher training was reported on in the original study, it was found that 48% of teachers had not attended any pre-service training. 58% of services reported that in-service training was available to staff. The results from the present study show an increase in pre-service training, with all 10 of the teachers reporting that they had attending some form of formal teacher training. Teachers were asked how long they had attended this training for, and the mean length reported was 20 months. Although these figures would suggest that teachers in 2002 are less reliant on in-service training, the study also found a positive increase in this area, with seven out of 10 services reported that in-service training was available to staff.

Group sizes in the original study were on average 14.5, with the smallest group being four, and the largest being 36. In 28 of the pre-school groups studied there was a second adult, and sometimes a third, present. In the present study, the average group size was 14.4, the smallest group was six, and the largest was 20. There was a second adult available in nine of the 10 settings, and in five of the 10 settings there were three or more present.

The average adult-child ratio in the original sample was 1:7, however this figure included a minimum ratio of 1:2, and a very high maximum ratio of 1:36. In the present study, the average adult-child ratio had changed to 1:6, with a minimum ratio of 1:3, and a maximum of 1:10.

In terms of availability of a separate room for adult use only, half of the pre-schools in the present study reported having this facility, this shows no increase over the 50% reported in the original study. The Regulations do not specify that such a room should be available, however they do state that a service should keep a first aid box; keep a register of pre-schoolchildren; maintain records on attendance/staff rosters etc. The Regulations do not specify where such items should be kept, however a separate room for adult use only would also be an ideal area to store such items.

Supervisors were given a comprehensive list of items of equipment (33 in total) and asked if these items were present in their setting, and if present, how often the equipment was used. Generally speaking levels of equipment were found to have risen, with the present sample reporting high levels of materials and equipment in all areas, audio-visual equipment being a notable exception.

Teachers were also asked if their classrooms were divided into special play areas, figures here had increased from 92% saying yes, to 100%.

In the original study a lack of record-keeping in pre-school settings was noted. Figures for record-keeping are shown in Table 1 below. These show a significant improvement in settings maintenance of records. The increase in maintained records of evaluation was particularly significant.

Table 1: Percentages of Settings Keeping Records

Record Type	1997 Data N = 29	2002 Data N = 10
Attendance	100%	100%
Medical	61.5%	90%
Developmental Tests	6%	40%
Evaluation Records	22.5%	80%

Observation Findings

These findings throw light on the process characteristics from the study. These are the relationships and interactions taking place within the settings, as relationships between educators and children are recognised as being crucial to children's ability to benefit from the educational environment.

1. Management of Time Observations

Teachers in the original study proposed that children spent the largest amount of time (29.5%) involved in Mixed Activities. Teachers in the present study also proposed Mixed Activities for the majority of the time (30.5%). Mixed Activities were defined as times when the adult proposes several simultaneous activities from which the children can choose, or when they are asked to rotate through a selection of activities. In both studies this was followed by Free Activities (19% in the original study, and 25% in the present study). Free Activities are defined as time when the children are free to use any available materials and are encouraged to make their own choices of activities. For both studies, this was followed by Personal/Social activities at 12.5% in the original study, and 15% in the present study. Preacademic Activities were proposed for 11.5% of the time in the original study, as compared to 9% in the present study.

Each observation was categorised as to whether the teacher intended the children to Listen/Watch or to Participate/Do. In the original study teachers proposed that children Participate/Do for 96% of the time, in the present study this figure had dropped slightly to 90% of the time. These finding would seem to indicate that the majority of teachers in preschools intend that the children take an active part in classroom activities rather than a passive/watching role.

For each observation the type of group structure proposed for that activity was noted. For example, did the teacher propose the activity to be undertaken by the whole group or a sub-group of children. Teachers in the original study proposed that children spend 70% of their time in whole group activities, this was followed by 28.5% in part group structure. Teachers in the present study also proposed whole group activity for 70% of the time, with part group structure for 19% of the time. It is interesting to note that teachers in both studies proposed so much time to be spent in whole group activity when in most of these settings there is at least one other adult present. However it should be noted in both studies much of the free activity time is coded as whole group activity (97% in the original study, and 100% in the present study) as the teacher proposed that the whole group should have the freedom to make their own choice of activity. In these circumstances although the activity is proposed for the whole group, in reality children are working in smaller groups, with the teacher, or alone.

2. Child Activities Observations

Like the MOT findings, it was interesting to note how similar in general the CA results from the present study were in relation to the results from the original study.

This observation looked first of all at how children were spending their time in the setting. In the original study children were observed in Physical Activities more frequently than any other activity, at 26% of the time. This was closely followed by Personal/Social Activities at 21.5%, and Expressive Activities at 18.5%. The overall pattern of child activities in the present study was very similar to the original study. Children were observed in Personal/Social Activities for 25.5% of the time. This was closely followed by Physical Activities at 24%, and Expressive Activities at 17%. The MOT findings showed that adults had proposed Mixed and Free activities for the majority of the time, this suggests that the children played some part in choosing the above activities to take part in.

Each line of observation was categorised as to whether the child was actively participating or watching an activity. Children were found to be Participating/Doing for 81.5% of the time in the original study. In the current study, the figure had dropped to 71.5% of the time. This suggests that although teachers intend that children take an active part in classroom activities, for some of this time children are actually taking a more passive/watching role. When looking at these figures however, it must be noted that children in the present study were only found to be "Not Actively Engaged/Waiting" for 5% of the time, so although they were in a passive role for 18.5% of the time, they were listening and/or watching rather than sitting inactively and unoccupied.

Each child activity observation was also categorised in terms of group structure. The results of the original study found that children in pre-schools spent 39% of their time in a small group with an adult present. The next most frequent categorisation was 22.5% of time spent in a large group with an adult present. This was closely followed by time spent alone with an adult at 21.5% of their time. The present study found that children were most likely to spend their time in pre-school in a large group with an adult present, at 30% of their time. This was closely followed by time spent in a small group with an adult present, at 29% of their time. These findings appear to be in conflict with the teachers proposals in both studies that children spend 70% of their time in whole group activities. However, this could be explained by the fact that Free Activities were often proposed for the Whole Group, however in reality the children had the free choice of both activity and who to interact with during this time.

3. Adult Behaviour Observations
The relationship and interaction between the children and the adults who care for them are acknowledged to be important factors influencing quality in ECCE. The findings from these observations found a change in adult behaviour. The original study found that adults spent most of the time in Participation/Shared Activities (27%) followed by Routine Activities (24%).

Participation/Shared Activities are ones in which the adult is a full participant in the child's activity. Routine Activities are ones related to programme operation and smooth operation of the setting. Figures had changed in the present study with 38.5% of time being given to Teaching behaviours. Teaching behaviours are ones defined as giving/receiving information, giving demonstrations, eliciting information from the child, eliciting an action or behaviour, offering choices to the child, encouraging the child's activities, providing assistance or clarification, suggesting solutions, or providing feedback. (Teaching behaviours were observed in 20% of cases in the original sample). This was followed by 24.5% spent in Participation/Shared Activities; 15.5% spent in Routine behaviours; and 12% in spent Child Management. These findings would support the Social Origin of Activity findings above, where activities which were adult directed had risen from 19% to 33.5%. However, this needs to be considered in conjunction with the MOT findings in which Preacademic Activities were proposed for such a small time, with the primary focus on Mixed and Free Activities. This reinforces the fact that Teaching Behaviours not only include giving/receiving academic type information, but also include offering choices to the child, encouraging the child's activities and providing assistance or clarification. So although levels of teaching behaviours have increased, these behaviours are not necessarily used to promote preacademic type activities.

For each adult behaviour observation, the degree of involvement that adult had with the children in the setting was recorded. There were five categories: non-participation; supervision; specific and short intervention (where the adult moved in and out of children's activities offering support); direction; and participation.

Teachers in the original study spent the majority of their time (42%) actively participating with the children. In the present study the figure for participation had dropped to 33%. Teachers in the present study in fact spent more time using Short and Specific Interventions, at 54% (25.5% in the original study). These findings tie in with the above findings on general adult behaviour and child social origin findings. The adults in the present study appear to spend less time actively participating in the children's activities, but spend more time moving in and out of the children's activities, offering support to them.

Discussion

Training

Findings from the current study suggest that the level of pre-service training in Irish pre-schools has increased compared to pre-Regulation figures. Although the present sample is small (23 teachers), these figures suggest that the need for pre-service training is becoming more widely understood in the ECCE sector. Findings from various aspects of the research added weight to the suggestion that these trained staff were having an impact on classroom quality. The rise in the number of evaluations and assessments being undertaken by services could well be linked with the increase in pre-service training, as there should be greater awareness within this group of the need to monitor and assess the activities and progress of the children. Increases in availability in all six of the categories of materials and equipment could also reflect the increased levels of teacher training undertaken, as the resources that a teacher makes available for children reflect her expectations for their development. However, this could also be linked to increased levels of funding.

The observation findings from the study showed an increase in "teaching behaviours" among teachers. However, it was noted that teaching behaviours not only include giving/receiving academic type information, but also include offering choices to the child, encouraging the child's activities and providing assistance or clarification. So, although levels of teaching behaviours have increased, these behaviours are not necessarily used to promote traditional preacademic type activities but could also be promoting general cognitive skills. There may well be links between these changes in teaching style and the increase in pre-service training. It would be interesting to explore this area further.

This link is reinforced by the findings related to the degree of involvement of adults with children in the settings. These suggested that the present sample of teachers are managing their time differently to their counterparts in the original sample. The teachers in the present study spend more time moving in and out of the children's activities, offering support to them. This may also be in some part related to the fact that six of the services have been recently trained to use the High/Scope curriculum. Within this curriculum the role of the teacher is to facilitate and support the child's active learning. In this way, the teacher would spend more time observing the children's experiences to see what key experiences should be encouraged, and to extend the children's thoughts and actions.

Interaction of Structural Variables and Process Variables in Quality Provision: A large body of research has shown that structural characteristics can significantly affect the quality of settings. From a practical point of view, these characteristics can serve as useful markers for monitoring quality in pre-schools as they are more easily regulated than the more subjective characteristics such as the interactions between adult and child. It has also been widely accepted that structural variables also have an influence on the classroom dynamics that affect process quality. We have seen above the links between increased levels of staff training and developments in adult-child interactions in the classroom. This interaction between structural variables and process variables in quality provision became apparent in the analyses of the findings.

Group size and adult:child ratio are two related setting features in which the structural and process aspects of quality are very much linked. Many studies have shown these two variables to be predictors of classroom quality, however most researchers would agree that they also serve as an indicator of process quality in terms of classroom dynamics. The group sizes and adult:child ratios recommended by the Regulations, are intended to provide an environment which facilitates high quality interactions between the adults and the children, and it is these interactions which have a positive effect on the child's development. The results of this study in terms of the drop in largest group found from 36 children to 20 children; and the drop in maximum adult:child ratio found from 1:36 to 1:10 are two areas in which the Regulations have impacted on structural quality. These reductions in class size and adult:child ratio will then have a further impact on process quality in terms of adult:child interactions. The issue of whether the reductions are linked with the changes in adult degree of involvement with children could warrant further research. It is possible that these smaller group sizes and ratios are required for teachers to increase levels of short and specific interventions, identified in the observations, whereby they are moving in and out of the children's activities offering support.

The organisation of the physical environment is another area where structural and process variables interact. The results from this study found that the number of teachers reporting they had special play areas had increased. The establishment of different areas is encouraged to facilitate choice and decision making, active involvement with the environment and different levels of adult-child and child-child interactions, which is intended to improve the quality of the pre-school experience for the child.

The availability of a separate room for adult use is another area in which structural and process aspects of quality are linked. No increase in availability of such a facility was found. This is a pity as it could play an important part in the development of adult relationships. This could indicate a lack of valuing staff, and a lack of support for staff in their role as professionals. From a staff development perspective a separate room could be used for staff meetings, seminars or discussions.

The amount and characteristics of the equipment and materials available to children is also of relevance in both structural and process terms. The Regulations state that each child should have "suitable means of expression and development ... .having regard to his or her age and development" (Department of Health and Children, 1996, p8). This statement is very much open to individual interpretation. This links back to the issue of training, as an individual with a sound knowledge of child development, and an understanding of the subjects in the early years curriculum, would be the best equipped to provide equipment which interested, challenged, stimulated, and provided enjoyment for the children.

Conclusion

In conclusion, generally improvements have been found in quality in the pre-schools in the present study as compared to those in the original study. Some improvements were found to relate directly to the Regulations. Findings suggest that the Regulations may be directly responsible for the fall in the maximum group figure. They may also be responsible for the slight reduction reported in average ratio size. It is highly likely that they are responsible for the reduction in the maximum group size figure. Many studies have shown these variables to be predictors of classroom quality, and it is suggested that they help to facilitate high quality interactions between the adults and the children. The fact that the Regulations appear to have had a positive influence in this area confirms that the regulation of structural variables can affect quality in ECCE settings.

It is not clear however that improvements all relate directly to the Regulations themselves. As predicted, increased awareness of training for ECCE professionals appears to have had an effect on quality. Findings from various aspects of the research suggest that increases in training are promoting positive changes in teacher behaviour, and teacher-child interactions in the classroom. If the increase in training noted in the study has either directly or indirectly had an impact on the quality of these services, then making training accessible to all staff in ECCE services is a key issue. The DIT/NOW Early Childhood Project (OMNA Team, 2000) developed a proposed qualifications framework for ECCE, and facilitated access to the system by developing a system of Accreditation of Prior Learning (APL) making training more accessible to ECCE workers. In 2002, the National Co-ordinating Childcare Committee developed a Model Framework for Education Training and Professional Development in the Early Childhood Care and Education Sector (Department of Justice, Equality and Law Reform, 2002). It is hoped that this model, which sets out the occupational profiles of ECCE workers, will "inform the development of education and training programmes leading to nationally awarded/recognised qualifications" (p.5).

If we continue to work towards raising the standards of training undertaken by our ECCE workers, and raising the ratio of staff trained to degree level, a "provider focused" approach to regulation could be possible in Ireland. Gormley (2000) noted that this approach is being adopted in France and Germany where well-trained staff are trusted to self-regulate in many ways, while the emphasis of pre-school officers is on providing technical assistance and support. However, to achieve this, appropriate remuneration and working conditions for ECCE staff across the sector must be provided. To recruit and retain staff trained to degree level it is necessary to ensure that a career in ECCE is seen as being respected and financially viable. Initiatives which support centres in increasing the amount they pay teachers would in turn effect the level of teacher they could attract and the length of service, which would in turn influence the quality of care that children experience.

Bibliography

Department of An Taoiseach (1985) *Working Party on Women's Affairs and Family Law Reform.* Dublin: The Stationery Office.

Department of Education and Science (2002) OECD *Thematic Review of Early childhood Education and Care: Background Report.* Ireland., Unpublished.

Department of Equality and Law Reform (1994) *Working Group on Childcare Facilities for Working Parents.* Dublin: The Stationery Office.

Department of Health (1991) *The Children Act 1989: Guidance and Regulations.* Volume 2, *Family Support, Day Care and Educational Provision for Young Children,* London: HMSO.

Department of Health (1985) *Report of the Committee on Minimum Legal Requirements and Standards for Day Care Services.* Dublin: The Stationery Office.

Department of Health (1996) *Child Care (Pre-School Services) Regulations,* Dublin: The Stationery Office.

Department of Justice, Equality and Law Reform (2002) *Model Framework for Education Training and Professional Development in the Early Childhood Care and Education Sector.* Dublin: The Stationery Office.

Department of Justice, Equality and Law Reform Expert Working Group on Childcare (1999) *National Childcare Strategy: Report of the Partnership 2000 Expert Working Group on Childcare,* Dublin: The Stationery Office.

Department of Labour (1983) *Working Party on Child Care Facilities for Working Parents, Report to the Minister for Labour.* Dublin: The Stationery Office.

Gormley W (2000) Early Childhood Education and Care Regulation: A Comparative Perspective, *International Journal of Educational Research,* 33, 55-77.

Hayes N, O'Flaherty J and Kernan M (1997) *A Window on Early Education in Ireland: the First National Report of the IEA Preprimary Project,* Dublin: Dublin Institute of Technology.

Hayes N (2002) *Children's Rights – Whose Right? A Review of Child Policy Development in Ireland.* Studies in Public Policy No.9. The Policy Institute, Trinity College Dublin.

OMNA Team (2000) OMNA-DIT/NOW *Early Childhood Project 1995-2000.* Dublin Institute of Technology.

Irish Senior Infant Classroom Practice – A Case of Imaginary Play?

Brian Murphy

Curaclam na Bunscoile – Primary School Curriculum (1971)

The introduction of a new curriculum *Curaclam na Bunscoile* (An Roinn Oideachais 1971) into Irish primary schools in 1971 heralded the beginning of a new era in Irish primary education. In sharp contrast to its subject-centred, prescriptive predecessor, which had endured for a period of nearly fifty years, the 1971 curriculum was clearly grounded in child-centred ideology and practice with the stated overall aim of the programme being "to enable the child to live a full life as a child and to equip him to avail of further education so that he may go on to live a full and useful life as an adult in society" (Curaclam na Bunscoile 1971, Part 1, pg. 12). Consequently, the curriculum was structured in a sufficiently flexible manner to allow each child to progress at an appropriate pace and to achieve success at his/her own level.

In attempting to achieve its overall aim the curriculum emphasised the processes of active exploration and discovery learning, incorporating methodologies such as the use of concrete materials, verbal discussion and first-hand experiences of subject matter. These curricular aspirations were clearly rooted in an acknowledgement of difference between individual children and the pedagogical imperative to give precedence to the learning process rather than the product to be learned. Although the curriculum was to be regarded as "an integrated entity, involving linguistic, mathematical and artistic organisation of the child's knowledge and experience" (Curaclam na Bunscoile, Part 1, pg. 20), its various aspects were arranged under the subject headings of Language (Irish and English), Mathematics, Social and Environmental Studies, Art & Craft Activities, Music, Physical Education and Religion. Wherever possible, integration between different areas would allow these subject barriers to be penetrated.

At Infant level, all learning was to be organised around play activities. The potential of play to enhance the child's cognitive, linguistic, social and creative development was to be exploited. In the cognitive domain, encompassing the areas of concept formation including literacy and numeracy development, the role of play was clearly given prominence. The central importance and methodological implications of Piaget's ideas on the role of activity and play in concept formation were emphasised:

> According to Piaget, the child forms mathematical concepts as a result of his actions with objects and not from the objects themselves ... Passivity has no place in this process ... It is essential that the child be afforded every opportunity of discovering for himself mathematical relationships in the environment. The use of discovery methods of learning not only leads the child to an understanding of a particular mathematical concept but gives him a training in organising his intellectual powers as efficiently as possible. (Curaclam na Bunscoile 1971, Part 1, pg. 126)

Consequently, the syllabus at Infant level was to be structured around free play and experimentation using concrete materials and apparatus. Such free play, exploration and make-believe activities would also foster the necessary language and discussion skills to advance the pupils' understanding and active construction of knowledge. This reality was explicitly acknowledged:

> Many of the activities of the junior classes, such as mathematics, art and craft work and, indeed, play will involve much oral language. This is particularly true where children are formed into groups or where activity and discovery methods of learning are used. Here, group and individual exploration and experimentation lead to a fruitful exchange of ideas between the pupils themselves and between pupils and their teacher. Discussing the subject in hand helps the child to understand it and to place his ideas in order. (Curaclam na Bunscoile 1971, Part 1, pg. 83).

Play and small group work were also recognised in term of their potential of promoting social development, as a means of promoting respect, tolerance, co-operation and group cohesion at a proximate level. At a more general level, the child's social maturation and conceptual development was also to be fostered through observation and investigation of natural phenomena. To this end, it was suggested that pupils be taken outdoors frequently to observe plants and animals in their natural surroundings. In this way they would come "to appreciate that living things are dependent on one another and on their environment and are continuously changing" (Curaclam na Bunscoile 1971, Part 2, pg. 19). The concern of the 1971 curriculum to foster the full and harmonious development of the child was also evident through its stated promotion of the child's creative development through activities in the art and craft, drama, and music areas. The curriculum clearly envisioned a holistic, developmentally appropriate, activity-based child-centred classroom practice. It remained the official primary school programme until 1999.

From Curaclam na Bunscoile (1971)
to the Primary School Curriculum (1999)

In the context of calls for a review and an assessment of the impact and implementation of the primary curriculum of 1971, Minister Mary O'Rourke established the Review Body on the Primary Curriculum in 1987. When the Review Body reported in May 1990 (Ireland 1990), it endorsed the underlying child-centred philosophy and principles of the 1971 curriculum, while suggesting that:

> The curriculum requires revision and re-formulation in its aims scope and content, in the manner in which it is implemented and in the way in which pupil progress is assessed and recorded and the way the overall effectiveness of the system is evaluated (Ireland 1990, pg. 97).

In 1991, in light of the Review Body report, the Minister for Education invited the National Council for Curriculum (NCCA) and Assessment to conduct a formal revision of the primary curriculum. In its brief however, the NCCA was still to retain the basic child-centred curricular principles and approaches adopted in 1971, the official importance of which were again highlighted by the Green Paper (Ireland 1992) Education for a Changing World:

> Emphasis on the child and the child's needs is the central feature of the system. This together with the delegation to teachers and schools of the responsibility for meeting the individual needs of children, activity and guided discovery methods of learning and

an integrated approach to teaching will remain the basis for curricular reform in the future. (Ireland 1992, pg. 87)

By 1995 the NCCA had carried out its review of all elements of the primary school curriculum. In the intervening years between 1995 and 1999 work proceeded on the development of the revised programmes in each of the six curricular areas through a host of committees comprising representatives of the principal partners and interests in primary education. The revised child-centred curriculum, heralded by Minister for Education Micheál Martin as "an exciting opportunity for change and renewal in primary schools" (Primary School Curriculum Introduction 1999, pg. vi), was formally introduced as the official programme for all primary schools in September 1999.

The New Primary School Curriculum 1999

The new Primary School Curriculum (Ireland & National Council for Curriculum and Assessment 1999) encompasses the broad philosophical thrust of its 1971 predecessor. Thus the programme content and methodologies are once again explicitly child-centred, clearly recognising the importance of developing the full potential of each child. The focus is once again on the child as active learner, with each subject area encouraging active learning processes, which are enjoyable and captivating. It therefore aspires that the child is directly engaged in the learning process, cognitively, physically, emotionally and creatively and consequently he/she is enabled to internalise and to gain ownership of what is learned.

While encompassing the broad philosophical thrust of Curaclam na Bunscoile (1971), the Primary School Curriculum 1999 is however a revised curriculum. It clearly constitutes a detailed interpretation of the recommendations of the aforementioned Review Body on the Primary School Curriculum (Ireland 1990). Moreover, it reflects the thinking and aspirations of the significant educational policy documents, which preceded its publication including the Report on the National Education Convention (Coolahan 1994), the White Paper on Education (Ireland 1995) and the Education Act (1998). It thus claims to incorporate "current educational thinking and the most innovative and effective pedagogical practice" (Primary School Curriculum Introduction 1999, pg. 2).

The curriculum begins by endorsing but redefining the aims of primary education with respect to the child. The principles of the Curaclam na Bunscoile 1971 to promote the full and harmonious development of the child and to make due allowance for individual difference, are redefined in the broader concepts of "celebrating the uniqueness of each child and ensuring the development of the child's full potential" (Primary School Curriculum Introduction 1999, pg. 8). The pedagogical principles of the 1971 curriculum dealing with the importance of activity and discovery methods, the integrated nature of the curriculum and the importance of environment-based learning are also expanded and developed. These three pedagogical principles are subsumed into a wider range of fifteen learning principles, which are deemed "to characterise more fully the learning processes that the revised curriculum envisages" (Primary School Curriculum Introduction 1999, pg. 8). Such principles range from a recognition of the importance of the immediate environment as a context for learning, to an acknowledgement of the centrality of linguistic, social, emotional and aesthetic factors to a child's learning.

Specific identification of and engagement with issues pertaining to early childhood/Infant education and the resultant labelling of the area as a 'key issue' of primary education marks a significant change between the 1971 and 1999 curricula. The overall thrust of the curriculum as well as the Infant education programme itself, is however deemed to be as equally appropriate to the developmental and learning needs of young children, as was its predecessor. This is evident in its outline of the curriculum for Infant classes as:

> ... based on the uniqueness of the child and the particular needs of children at this stage of development. The informality of the learning experience inherent in it, and the emphasis it gives to the element of play, are particularly suited to the learning needs of young children. It stresses, too, the centrality of language in early childhood learning and the importance of activity and the manipulation of a variety of materials in promoting motor and sensory development. (Primary School Curriculum Introduction 1999, pg. 30)

The programme also acknowledges the reality that children at Infant level perceive and experience learning in an integrated way. Consequently it affords teachers at this level a more flexible time frame to implement the requisite approaches to teaching and learning through its incorporation of discretionary curriculum time into the envisaged weekly time allocation.

The 1999 Primary School Curriculum also incorporates new content and embraces new approaches and methodologies. In terms of content and subject areas, it responds to changing child and societal needs and circumstances through new programmes in science, and social, personal and health education. Arts education in the form of visual art, music and drama receives a renewed emphasis, stemming from an acknowledgement that it "contributes uniquely to the child's conceptual development and to the expansion and refinement of their view of the world" (Primary School Curriculum Introduction 1999, pg. 52).

Aims of and Background Information to the Questionnaire Survey

Explicitly child-centred curricula have thus been a consistent feature of primary education in Ireland for over thirty years. The degree of implementation of the play-based curriculum principles and methodologies into infant classroom practice has however been less clear. In order to ascertain a general sense of the views and practices of infant teachers with respect to the implementation of the child-centred curriculum, a nationwide questionnaire survey of three hundred randomly selected Senior Infant teachers was conducted covering questions of resources, teaching methods and attitudes to the 1999 Primary School Curriculum.

The questionnaire was completed and returned by 62% of the three hundred Senior Infant practitioners. One hundred percent of the respondents were female, being indicative of reality that the gender composition of infant teachers in Irish primary schools is almost exclusively female. Just over half (51%) of respondents came from teachers teaching Senior Infant classes in rural areas, with the remaining 49% from either urban or suburban school settings, predominantly outside the Dublin area, since response rate from urban Dublin schools was particularly low. 47% of respondents taught a single class group of Senior Infant pupils, with a further 22% teaching an infant class combination of Junior and Senior Infants. The remaining 31% was almost evenly split between teachers teaching the various multi-class combinations of Junior Infant, Senior Infant, First and Second classes. 89% of respondents were teachers of mixed Senior Infant classes in terms of gender. This would not be entirely indicative of the relatively high number of single-sex schools in the country. However, the figure can be explained by the reality that many of these mixed Senior Infant classes were in fact located in single-sex girls' schools that maintained a co-educational composition to the end of the junior cycle of the primary school. 8% of the teachers taught classes of girls only, with the remaining 3% of teachers teaching Senior Infant classes containing only boys.

In terms of age profile, just over half (51%) of the respondents were aged in their twenties or thirties, being evenly split between both age brackets. Many of these younger teachers had been teaching infant classes since the commencement of their teaching careers. A further 17% of teachers were in the forty to forty-five age bracket, with the remainder of the respondents (32%) indicating that they were over the age of forty-five. Many of the older teachers indicated that they too had taught infant classes for long periods of time ranging from five to thirty five years. The age composition of the respondents was directly correlated to the data gathered with respect to the teaching qualification held. Over 68% of respondents (those up to the age of forty-five years old) held the Bachelor of Education degree, with the remainder usually holding the National Teacher Diploma, predating the introduction of the degree programme as the basic teaching qualification over twenty-seven years ago. One percent of the respondents indicated that they held no formal teaching qualification. A large majority (79%) had received their initial training in Irish training colleges or colleges of education, with a further 8% indicating that they had been trained abroad, predominantly in the United Kingdom. Some 9% held higher degrees, usually a Masters in Education. A mere 15% had completed a specialist course of any kind in Infant/Early Childhood Education, the majority of these indicated to be either specialist pedagogical options taken during initial training or week-long in-career development courses for infant teachers run by the Department of Education and Science.

The average class size of the Senior Infant teacher respondents was twenty-seven pupils, with pupil-teacher ratios ranging from 14:1 to 36:1. Most teachers felt that there should be positive discrimination in favour of the infant classes with respect to pupil-teacher ratio. Whereas a pupil-teacher ratio in or around 25:1 was thought adequate in senior primary classes, a very large majority (88%) favoured a pupil-teacher ratio of less than 20:1 at Senior Infant level, with 40% outlining a preference for a ratio of under 15:1.

Availability and Frequency of the Use of Equipment in Senior Infant Classrooms

Respondents to the questionnaire indicated that in spite of the play-curriculum and the consequent resource requirements, many infant classrooms remain very poorly resourced and still lack very basic play equipment. Equipment for water play, science, music, home corner play and even basic visual aids were indicated to be available in between half and three-quarters of classrooms and even where such apparatus were available in classrooms, it was indicated that they were used infrequently *e.g.* music, science and water play equipment were indicated to be used frequently or very frequently by under 11% of respondents. Basic equipment comprising structured materials (*e.g.* pegboards, jigsaws), materials for art and crafts and books and children's stories were indicated to be available in over 90% of the respondents' classrooms and used frequently or very frequently in each case in over 70% of situations.

The findings with respect to the availability and frequency of use of literacy resources indicated a more positive picture and perhaps a nationwide trend that purchase of classroom equipment has been weighted very much in favour of aids, which directly support curricular subjects. With the exception of computer software at 85%, in each case the figure for availability was significantly over 90%, comprising equipment indicative of the interactive model of literacy development outlined in the 1999 Primary School Curriculum *e.g.* phonic resources (99%), flashcards (98%), big books (91%), library books (98%), word games (95%). However frequency of use of the materials indicated a more traditional classroom methodological practice with the flashcards, phonic resources and library books being prioritised and used frequently or very frequently by 72% of teachers, while the newer type resources of big books, word games and computer software being used sometimes, seldom or never in anything between half and three-quarters of surveyed Senior Infant classrooms.

Availability and variety in mathematical equipment was indicated to be quite high across the surveyed Senior Infant teachers. Resources spanning the number, measurement (length, weight, capacity, time, money), shape and space (two and three-dimensional shapes), and data (*e.g.* visual representations, games) strands of the 1999 curriculum, incorporating mathematical games and computer software were available in over three-quarters of all surveyed practitioners' classrooms. Surprisingly, despite the emphasis on number and arithmetical operations in numeracy activity at Senior Infant level, availability of number equipment appeared to remain scarce beyond the basic unifix cubes and counting materials, which were indicated to be available in over 97% of classrooms. Traditionally accepted basic aids to the development of number concepts including Dienes' blocks and Cuisenaire rods were available in only 23% and 28% of surveyed classrooms respectively. Furthermore, despite the stated opinion of the teachers that use of concrete material is an essential pre-requisite feature of numeracy development at all primary levels, but particularly at infant level, use of concrete mathematical equipment rarely, if ever, was a feature of the numeracy activity within their classrooms. Respondents indicated that each mentioned piece of mathematical equipment (with the exception of unifix cubes) was used either seldom or never by over 40% of teachers, with an approximate further 30% indicating use of such material 'sometimes'. Such figures and practices, signalling a limited use of concrete materials in primary infant classrooms would seem to be indicative of an enduring traditional teaching of numeracy concepts at Senior Infant level.

Thus in terms of the availability and frequency of use of basic classroom equipment, essential requisites of a play-based, child-centred curriculum, curricular implementation would thus appear to be somewhat removed from the principles, methodologies and classroom practices envisaged not only in the Primary School Curriculum (1999), but also in its 1971 predecessor, Curaclam na Bunscoile.

Teaching Methods and Strategies Employed at Senior Infant Level

Whole-class, large-group, parallel instruction, being used 'frequently' or 'very frequently' by 85% of the surveyed teachers, is clearly the methodology most employed by Senior Infant teachers. The engrained nature of this traditional didactic teaching in the Irish practitioner psyche can be further gauged by the fact that, even under ideal classroom conditions, 61% of surveyed teachers indicated that they would continue to use such a teaching approach 'frequently' or 'very frequently'. Group teaching, usually on the basis of ability, was indicated to be currently used 'frequently' or 'very frequently' by 32% of teachers, but this figure increased to 54% when teachers were asked to indicate how frequently they would use this teaching method under ideal conditions. This would seem to indicate that in many cases teachers desire to afford more attention to addressing individual pupil difficulties but feel constrained by the realities of current classroom conditions, particularly due to large class size and lack of appropriate resources.

It is perhaps the above situational constraints, which can also explain the relatively low 22% of teachers who indicated that they facilitated child-directed activities 'often' within their classrooms. Under ideal conditions it was indicated that this figure would increase to 51% of teachers. This statistic can also however be interpreted as being quite low, especially in the context of a distinctly child-centred curriculum. It may suggest perhaps that the teaching force remains a little sceptical regarding the desirability or feasibility of fully implementing the play-based methodology, as envisaged by both Irish curricula spanning the past thirty years. When specifically and directly asked to indicate how often they used structured and unstructured play activities however, 61% of teachers said they used such approaches either 'frequently' or 'very frequently'. What this would seem to signal is perhaps a classroom practice where play appears to be treated as a separate classroom activity rather than an all-pervasive methodology, as outlined in the curriculum. The historical origins of this practice could perhaps be traced back to the foundation of the state in 1922, when the Froebellian kindergarten practice was deemed as a separate school subject, rather than an overriding curriculum philosophy. This distinction would thus appear to indicate a continuing fundamental misunderstanding of the term 'play' among the surveyed Senior Infant teaching force, and may point to a need for the 'play' topic to be redressed at in-career development seminars for infant teachers.

Attitudes of Teachers

Table 1 Teachers' Attitudes to Curriculum
and Methodological Approaches at Senior Infant level

KEY					
SD	=	Strongly Disagree	D	=	Disagree
NO	=	No Opinion	A	=	Agree
SA	=	Strongly Agree	NS	=	Not Stated

Statement	SD	D	NO	A	SA	NS
1. The 1999 revised primary curriculum has impacted greatly on classroom practice	2%	29%	23%	27%	18%	1%
2. The 1999 curriculum takes adequate cognisance of the needs of Irish children	4%	11%	29%	46%	9%	1%
3. Children's problem-solving skills are best developed through play	0%	6%	4%	49%	40%	1%
4. Intellectual development is best advanced through play activities	0%	11%	14%	48%	24%	3%
5. The Senior Infant teacher should guide the child in those activities the child wishes to do	7%	43%	12%	32%	5%	1%
6. The Senior Infant teacher should allow the child to initiate and direct his own activity	7%	56%	15%	18%	1%	3%
7. Children's problem-solving skills are best developed through teacher instruction	8%	46%	12%	27%	4%	3%
8. The Senior Infant teacher should initiate and direct the child's activities	1%	14%	7%	57%	18%	3%
9. Workbooks have a vital role to play in the Infant classroom	15%	31%	13%	32%	8%	1%
10. Social interaction is an essential activity for the holistic development of Senior Infant pupils	2%	11%	3%	41%	42%	1%
11. Adequate learning materials need to be provided if the Senior Infant programme is to be effectively implemented	1%	1%	0%	11%	86%	1%
12. Implementation of the S.I. programme is dependent upon provision of in-service courses	1%	11%	5%	35%	47%	1%
13. Effective implementation of the S.I. programme is dependent upon improvement of the P/T ratio	0%	2%	3%	24%	70%	1%
14. Principal teachers expect Senior Infant teachers to adhere to timetables and schemes of work	13%	35%	19%	23%	9%	1%
15. The Senior Infant teacher should comply with parents' wishes to develop the basic skills in S.I.	29%	45%	9%	9%	6%	2%
16. The primary function of the infant programme is to prepare the children for more formal first class work	26%	48%	7%	14%	4%	1%

It immediately appears that the jury seems to be out among Senior Infant teachers regarding the degree of implementation, to date, of the new 1999 curriculum (statement 1), with only 45% of teachers indicating that the curriculum had impacted greatly on classroom practice, coupled with a high 23% of teachers who indicated that they held no opinion on the particular statement. Indecision was also high on the issue of whether the curriculum takes adequate cognisance of the needs of Irish children (statement 2), with 29% of Senior Infant teachers signalling themselves to be of no opinion and just over half (55%) of the surveyed teachers agreeing the curriculum to have adequately embraced Irish children's needs. These figures serve to highlight the long road, which lies ahead to full acceptance and implementation of the new curriculum and the reality that many teachers appear to remain unconvinced or sceptical towards many elements of practice advocated therein.

The next cluster of statements (statements 3-8) examined the teachers' attitudes towards a play curriculum in general and how they saw the teacher's role within such a curriculum. While there was overwhelming agreement regarding the value of play activities for cognitive development (72%) and for the development of problem solving skills (89%), the understanding and format of such play activities was quite far removed from the understandings of such a methodology, as envisaged in the international literature or in the 1999 curriculum itself. The reality that 50% of teachers disagreed with the concept of guided instruction, 63% disagreed with child self-initiated and self-directed activity, and 75% of teachers agreed that the Senior Infant teacher should initiate and direct the pupils' activities is a clear illustration of this. These statistics also serve to re-emphasise the previously outlined findings of the questionnaire study with respect to overall methodological practice, which appeared to indicate a teacher-focused Senior Infant classroom practice, with little opportunity for any child-initiated activity.

Statements 9-16 (as outlined in Table 1) examined the perceived impact of various external and environmental constraints on the process of curriculum implementation. There was unanimous agreement among the teachers regarding the urgent and immediate need for the provision of adequate resources (97%), for a reduction in the pupil-teacher ratio (94%), and for provision of in-career development courses (82%), if successful implementation of the 1999 curriculum was to be ensured. There was also consensus among the practitioners with three-quarters of the respondents rejecting any narrowing of approach, which might arise from pressure of compliance with parental demands regarding the development of literacy and numeracy skills and preparation of infant pupils for first class, as well as possible school management pressures with respect to time allocation to and preparation of class work. Opinion was evenly split however, regarding the relative importance of textbooks within the overall child-centred programme. In contrast, opinion regarding the important role of social interaction was clearly not in dispute with 83% of surveyed teachers indicating its central role in the holistic development at this level.

Overall Picture of Infant Classroom Practice Emerging from Questionnaire Survey

In spite of over thirty years of child-centred curricula, opinions gleaned from the nationwide survey of Senior Infant teachers would appear to indicate that practice in Irish infant classrooms remains traditional and teacher-focused. A large lacuna between curriculum theory and practice appears to exist. Certain identified features of Irish primary education appear to be militating against a more faithful implementation of the child-centred practice envisaged in 1999 curriculum *i.e.* lack of availability of appropriate equipment and resources in the infant classroom coupled with a high pupil-teacher ratio, which appears to make provision of child-centred activity significantly less realistic. A further reason for this failure to implement the principles stated in the curriculum appears to be that the teachers' assumptions and understandings about play and child-centeredness differ from those upon which the curriculum is constructed. Many teachers appear to see play as a discrete classroom activity rather than an all-pervasive methodology. In other words, teachers' instructional practices appear to be influenced by their deeply ingrained personal beliefs and understandings rather than by the principles of the curriculum. This raises interesting questions for Irish educational administrators and policy-makers. In particular it highlights the reality that educational change cannot be achieved simply by producing new curriculum statements. It would seem that the starting point for increasing child-centred approaches to the ways in which learning is organised in Irish infant classrooms is to help teachers to re-construct their own understandings of child-centeredness through professional development programmes, which allow for reflection and discussion. Such in-career development, in conjunction with improvements in resourcing of classrooms and in the pupil-teacher ratio should go some way towards ensuring a more child-centred classroom experience for our all pupils.

Bibliography

An Roinn Oideachais (1971), *Curaclam na Bunscoile – Primary School Curriculum, Cuid 1 agus 2 – Parts 1 and 2*, Dublin: The Stationery Office

Coolahan, J. (ed.) (1994), *Report on the National Education Convention*, Dublin: National Education Convention Secretariat

Ireland (1995), *Charting Our Education Future: White Paper on Education*, Dublin: The Stationery Office

Ireland (1992), *Education for a Changing World: Green paper on Education*, Dublin: The Stationery Office

Ireland (1990), *Report of the Review Body on the Primary Curriculum (The Quinlan Report)*, Dublin: Department of Education

Ireland and National Council for Curriculum and Assessment (1999), *Primary School Curriculum*, Dublin: The Stationery Office

Providing quality experiences for children with special needs

Mary Dineen

Providing quality experiences in the early years for children with special needs requires an understanding and knowledge of child development. The first thing to emphasise is that a child with special needs has all the same needs as any other child, that is to have all their basic needs met, to be loved, talked to and to be played with so that the child feels comfortable and emotionally secure. From this base they will be ready to explore and learn about the world with confidence. [Maslow, 1968; Kellmer Pringle, 1975.]

The components of a quality Early Intervention Programme is; to begin as early as is possible; to include parents and families as full participants in their child's programme; and to involve the multi-disciplinary team in the assessment and planning of each child's individual education. Schools should provide an encouraging and stimulating play environment to promote all areas of the child's development. They should provide the facility of a pool of professionals that are equipped to meet the needs of the child and family. They should provide a supportive and caring environment where parents' queries and concerns may be discussed. They should provide an environment whereby parents can meet and support one another, and they should help the parents to understand and optimise their child's developmental pattern by providing them with concrete and appropriate developmental activities.

Children should be assessed through the collecting of data from families and therapists and an observation period within the pre-school programme – parents and team members should be consulted when these programmes are being devised. Children should be encouraged to attend their local community pre-schools and special pre-school programmes should be forwarded to these pre-schools.

Children with special needs are not just generally delayed, or going along the same developmental pathway as other children but at a slower speed, they have a specific profile of learning difficulties so early intervention activities need to be targeted to overcome these. These specific difficulties cause their development in different areas to go at different speeds and so progress in one area will not allow the teacher to predict what she might expect in another area in the way she might with a typical child. For example, the child's language development is usually more delayed than their motor or social skills but not always. Some children have two-word speech before they walk, while others are early walkers but very late talkers. This means that we should be very cautious about predicting a child's future development in the early years. We should simply assess the stage the child has reached in each area of development, that is social, physical, cognitive, linguistic, emotional, spiritual and creative, and suggest activities to help the child reach the next step in each area. The activities chosen will need to take account of the child's abilities in other areas but the only way to find out what a child is capable of learning is to give them the opportunity to learn. The teacher should set up situations designed to enable the child to learn through play or exploration, to teach by practising small steps using prompting and thus enabling the children to see how to complete the task successfully. In the past false assumptions about the potential abilities of children with special needs have led to them being denied the social and educational opportunities they needed. We now know they can benefit from participating in a normal playgroup experience.

Like all children, children with special needs show a wide range of development. Some progress faster then others. Teachers should design activities for the next step in the child's development, the teacher will be going at the right pace for each individual child.

Play has been described as children's work, (Froebel, 1782-1852) (Brierley 1987) and this can be quite a useful way of thinking about it. All children in their early years are busy learning about their world and the people in it and much of this learning takes place through play, some of their play is solitary, some play is with adults and some with other children. All these forms of play are equally important in all children's development. When adults play with children they are often showing them how to do something new with the toys or an activity. Psychologists describe this as scaffolding children's learning and most parents do this quite naturally. (Vygotsky 1978) (Montessori 1952). So playing with the child provides many opportunities to help the child to learn in a natural way. Children also learn a great deal from play with other children, where they need to know how to get on with one another and where they learn by copying the other children. Playing alone gives children the opportunity to explore and experiment. It also allows them to go over things they have learned and play out what they have seen in the real world consolidating their learning.

Many children with special needs require help with learning to talk, ideally, every child should be offered the advice of a speech and language therapist from the first months of life. Communication begins with eye contact, smiling and babbling. The language development of children has received a lot of attention from researchers and most children show a similar pattern of difficulties to varying degrees. With special needs children their language progress is usually more delayed than other areas of development and usually language is more delayed than their non-verbal cognitive development. Being able to use words to communicate usually lags behind the child's understanding of speech. This is one of the reasons for using a total communication approach to help the deaf child that is using signs and speech together.

Social skills are very important because interaction with ones' peers facilitates inclusion, language development and early socialisation. Pre-school activities teach the child pro-social behaviour *i.e.* taking turns in conversation with another child and also taking part in motor activities and also promotes listening skills. Many children are returning to special schools because of their lack of social skills and feelings of isolation. Social skills are more important than academic skills in the early years. Some children with good language skills and poor social skills experience school failure. Social skills are equally as important as language skills.

A communication notebook would be of great benefit containing information such as what the child did in school today. A child may be unable to tell his parents what he has done during the day, child care staff should make sure he or she takes pictures, craft work or other items so that his family can enjoy his activities and build up a picture of the school day. If the parents are unaware of the child's experience in school activities such as painting etc., the child with special needs who has especially poor communication skills will not initiate the conversation so a chance for sharing their experience is lost. The parents are usually only told about what the child ate and toileting arrangements. It is very important to work with the child's parents because although professionals in many fields have invaluable contributions to make to our understanding of conditions which affect children, it is the parents who must mediate between professional services and the needs of the child. If they are to do this successfully, their expertise must be respected and their work supported within the group.

This can only happen if staff and parents work together in genuine partnership for the sake of the child, sharing each other's strengths and knowledge and supporting each other's weaknesses. This can mean a new approach on the part of the staff. They have to be willing to share knowledge and expertise, and also to learn new skills and fresh approaches. Changes in expectations and in working patterns can be a source of valuable stimulus and challenge to adults, but can also be stressful. On-going training, both within and outside the group, will give staff the confidence and satisfaction which come from extending skills and understanding, and will at the same time support them in making changes to their approach to both children and adults.

The high adult:child ratios in pre-schools make it possible for an individual response to children; the ongoing training systems mean that adults' skills and knowledge are constantly updated, and the active participation of parents sets a pattern for partnership.

Special needs children must have the opportunity to be with children of the same age so that they can learn about the social world of childhood. This is really important. Special needs children will learn from talking to and playing with other children. Children with special needs will benefit from attending an ordinary playgroup. They need age-appropriate role models and the other children will 'scaffold' their learning. They also need to learn how to make friends, how to share, take turns and be part of a group. In other words they need exactly the same social experiences and opportunities as all other children.

Because children with special needs need more one-to-one adult-child help with learning than the typical child, it is even more important that they also learn to be in a group and cope without one-to-one support as they get older. They need to move on to become independent adult learners. If all of their early learning has been supported by an adult and they have received no social group experience, this can cause difficulties for them and their teachers when they start school.

Above all, pre-schools are part of their local community, and they should focus on community involvement and support. The ideal pre-school model of society, in which all members have something to offer and in which all members can find the level of support they need, will provide an inclusive approach to the needs of all children.

All children benefit from growing up with clear and consistent guidelines for their behaviour and children with special needs are no exception. However, developmental delays can lead to frustration and a limited repertoire of self-initiated play for some children, so they are more likely to be difficult at times. Some particular behaviours, such as running away, may be more common but whatever the difficult behaviour is, it needs controlling quickly and effectively if possible. Most difficult or distressing behaviours can be changed with a consistent approach. This is often made easier if the teacher consults the educational psychologist who will be able to help the teacher to design a programme and support the teacher in maintaining it until the teacher succeeds. It will take time to change a behaviour that has become a habit and it will often get worse on a behavioural programme before it gets better. So patience and consistency are essential. Punishment is not appropriate for children with special needs, as children with special needs do not have the same reasoning processes as other children. Adults in charge of children with special needs should be aware of this, and have sufficient knowledge of the disorder or special need to enable them to react appropriately when the child exhibits difficult behaviour.

Children with chronic medical conditions like all other children need a pre-school environment within which they can enjoy the fun and satisfaction of exploring and developing to their full potential in company with their peers and with friendly, supportive adults. In a setting with an inclusive approach, the environment will be adjusted as necessary to ensure that all children have the opportunity to be included in all activities. The adult acts as a facilitator: the child acts as an active engaged learner. The adult is responsible for building an environment in which children are safe, yet able to explore, make mistakes, and learn from trial and error. Adults are responsible for supporting children during this process in ways that enhance self-esteem, assist children in relating to each other, and help children learn self-control. (Wolery and Bredekamp, 1995).

The structuring of a responsive environment is important for all children but is critical for those in the early stages of learning. The child can gain a response through their interactions with people or objects in their environment. The child with good communication and motor skills will be able to elicit a response from their environment without too much difficulty. The child who has very limited movement and does not yet engage in intentional communication will need a highly sensitive environment that is structured to enable an immediate response. Generally, rewarding responses at this level will be of a sensory nature, making full use of whatever sensory preferences may have been identified for the child. For example, if the child seems attracted to noise, crinkly paper could be placed close to his or her hand so that any slight movement will create a sound. If interest in the visual environment is noticed or even suspected, an unusually attractive mobile might be placed so that a slight turn of the head brings it into immediate view.

The teacher can further ensure a responsive environment by becoming familiar with the likely responses of each child in various situations. Some responses can be quite subtle, and a general policy of being alert for possible responses is critical. It is also important for all adults to be aware that some children may need quite a lot of time to respond and some may need a distraction-free environment, especially when new activities are being introduced. Response can be by expression, action or vocalisation. While new concepts may need to be introduced in a distraction-free environment, children should gradually be encouraged to become acclimatised to coping with an environment with reasonable distractions. Routines are important in helping children to make sense of their day, but it is also essential to enable them to cope with change and unexpected events. As children become more established in their responses, it is important to structure situations that challenge them to initiate activities so that they can become more independent in their interaction with objects and people. This should include gradually reducing the prompts and assistance given to the child, increasing the level of difficulty of tasks, consciously not doing something that the child is expecting the adult to do, or deliberately leaving something just out of the child's reach.

As a child becomes adept at acting on the immediate environment, he or she will need to establish a means of communication that can be understood by all those with whom he or she may wish to communicate. At first, this may be by looking, using facial expression, using body movements, using gestures and/or vocalising. These can gradually be shaped and refined, for example by expecting more accurate and sustained eye, hand or finger pointing or by encouraging the child to increase his or her range of vocal tones. Children may use objects of reference, hand-signs, pictures, symbols or words. The use of technology may offer increased opportunities for intentional and functional communication.

The importance of early intervention is to provide these protective factors of quality physical and emotional care that promote self-esteem and self-efficacy. These factors are the keys to a positive outcome for children in any intervention programme, whether it be for the disabled or non-disabled (Rutter, 1988; Kolvin, Miller, Scott, Gazonts & Fleeting, 1990.) Once these elements are in place, they appear to provide individuals with the life-long skills they need to face and deal with various kind of adversity (Vaillant & Milofsky, 1990; Werner & Smith, 1992.)

To conclude, it is clear that children with special needs benefit from all the same early experience as other children, and like other children their progress will be influenced by the quality of their early environment and the learning opportunities provided for them. However, they also need extra help to overcome their specific developmental difficulties, especially with learning to talk. They are not able to learn by themselves as readily as other children and will not make the progress that they are able to make without sensitive structured learning.

In an ideal world there would be an early intervention service. This service would provide the expert advice of a teacher, psychologist and a speech and language therapist. This would be a most valuable source of support for parents as well as for the child. Most parents also find that it is helpful to meet other parents and to join a local parent's support group.

Bibliography

Brierley, J., (1987) *Give Me A Child Until He Is Seven*, Brain Studies & Early Childhood Education. Falmer Press London.

Dare, A., O'Donovan, M. (1997) *Good Practice In Caring For Young Children With Special Needs*. Pub. by Stanley Thornes Ltd., London.

Froebel, F., (1954) Cited in *The Educational Value of the Nursery School.* Isaacs. S. Association for Early Childhood Education, London.

Kellmer Pringle, M., *The Needs of Children.*(1975) Pub. by Routledge, London.

Kolvin, I. *et al, Continuities of Depravation. The Newcastle 1,000 Family Study.* (1990) Aldershot, England.

Maslow, A.H., *Toward A Psychology of Being.* (1968) Van Nostrand, New York.

Montessori, M., *The Discovery of the Child.* (1948) Kalakshetra Publications, Madras-41 India.

Rutter, M., *Epidemilogical Approaches to Developmental Psychology – (1988) Archives of General Psychology.* 45, 486-495.

Salvia, J., Ysseldyke, J.E. (2004) *Assessment In Special and Inclusive Education.* Pub. by Houghton Mifflin Co., New York.

Vygotsky. L., (1978) *Mind In Society – The Development of Higher Psychological Processes.* Cambridge Mass: Harvard University Press.

Werner, E.E., Smith, R.S. (1992) *Overcoming the Odds.* Pub. by Connell U. Press.

Wolery, M., Bredekamp, S. (1995) *Developmentally Appropriate Practices And Young Children* With Disabilities. Pub. by Journal of Early Intervention 18 (4) 331-341.

Students' Experiences on Practice Placement During their B.A. Degree in Early Childhood Studies in UCC

Stefane Corbett & Anna Ridgway

Introduction

This paper is the first in a series of papers, which set out to look at the experiences of students while on practice placement during their B.A. Degree in Early Childhood Studies at University College Cork. The students of the B.A. Degree in Early Childhood Studies undertake 800 hours of unpaid practice placement. This is made up of two placements, each of 400 hours, during their second and third years as undergraduates. The placements are done in blocks of ten to twelve weeks, beginning in February of second year when students begin a Social Studies/Child Health placement. This is followed by an Education placement the following September, as they begin their final year of the degree.

Six third year students, ten percent of the class group, were interviewed about their experiences on each of their two placements. A semi-structured interview was conducted and each student was asked a series of questions. The questions ascertained factual information about the agencies where the students worked and, more importantly focused on details of their experiences there. Particular reference was made to the role of both student and Mentor and, to the ways in which the placement is assessed. To give breadth to the study, a Questionnaire was administered to the second year students. This was completed by 50% of the students in that class.

Aims and Principles of Practice Placement

With the development of the new childcare profession in Ireland the highest standards of professionalism will have to be achieved (Government of Ireland, 2002), therefore, the need for high quality practice placements is paramount. The B.A. Degree (ECS), in order to be recognised as a professional qualification in the future, *must* have supervised placement practice.

> The placement provides opportunities for progressive, professional development where the student can reflect on,

analyse and evaluate professional practice and it also offers the student opportunities for putting theories, ideas and activities generated in the taught elements of the course into practice (Douglas 2003, 1).

Supervised practice placements are seen to be a fundamental core principle of the B.A. Degree in Early Childhood Studies. The principles underpinning this element of the course are threefold (Douglas 2003),

1. All placements are selected and monitored by UCC Placement Coordinators.
2. UCC Placement Coordinators, in partnership with agency staff, supervise all students on placement.
3. Students will only graduate if they are deemed to be satisfactory in both the academic and professional practice areas of the course.

Two fulltime Placement Coordinators work on this Degree course. The role of the coordinators is to find appropriate placements for approximately sixty students each term. Initially students are asked to identify the areas in which they would like to work and, where possible, an appropriate agency is found. New agencies are continually being sought and these are visited and assessed before students are sent there on placement. The Agency Manager agrees to work in partnership with the student and his/her Placement Coordinator, to provide a successful learning experience for the student. Ideally, each student should be assigned a Mentor, by the Agency, at the beginning of the placement period, with whom he/she would work on a daily basis. This Mentor should nurture the student's learning and provide opportunities for growth and learning. This is a difficult role for a Mentor to assume, particularly as the Mentor is usually involved in the very time consuming and stressful position of working with very young children. All of the students on placement work with children under eight years of age. A large variety of agencies take the students on placement, including National Schools, Montessori Schools, Crèches, Hospitals, Family Centres, Gárda Siochaná Juvenile Liaison Scheme and a range of Special Needs providers. A successful placement will involve challenges for the student, which will be overcome with the help, support and guidance of an experienced Mentor. The Mentor completes monthly assessment forms for each student together with weekly time sheets. Each student is visited twice by the Placement Coordinator to discuss his/her progress. The Placement Coordinator, Mentor and student sit down together at this time to ensure a full and frank discussion of the student's progress and any issues arising from the placement. The report, which is generated from these open and frank discussions, are signed by all parties. Likewise, it is envisaged that all assessment forms would be completed after lengthy discussions between student and Mentor.

Role of the Student while on Placement

Students on placement may assume any of the non-teaching roles defined in Circular 7/02, Department of Education and Science. This circular refers to the role of Special Needs Assistants in National Schools and the duties specified are within the remit of the B.A.(ECS) students. In many cases the students assume rather more responsibility than this, but they should always be under the supervision of a qualified staff member. Ideally, students should negotiate their role with their Mentors, which might include planning appropriate activities to do with either individual children or groups of children. These activities are an important part of the student's learning, but they must always be carried out under the supervision of the Mentor. Students on placement are required to keep a daily diary of their experiences. This diary should describe the daily activities in detail but should provide a forum for students to reflect on key issues. This diary informs the portfolio that students submit at the end of the placement. The portfolio is a highly reflective piece of work where students develop three key areas of their learning while on placement. Students often engage in small research projects while on placement, which provides a focus for their portfolios. These research projects are always carried out with the school Principal's or Agency Manager's permission and may focus on such issues as school lunches, physical education, school transport or other issues of interest to the student.

Mentoring

University College Cork, through the Placement Coordinators, has endeavoured to provide a forum for Mentors to come together to discuss issues relating to the placements. This has taken the format of informal gatherings in the College and the development of a Newsletter, *Mentors' Forum*, (Ridgway and Corbett, 2003b. 2003c) which is issued several times per year. It is recognised that it is not easy for many of the Mentors to come to regular meetings, therefore, informal discussions take place during the two supervisory visits paid to each student, by the Placement Coordinator, while on placement. The provision of this Newsletter ensures that all Mentors are kept informed and right up to date with all matters pertaining to placement. It is envisaged that this publication will develop further into a very useful resource for Mentors.

Research – The Experiences of Students while on Placement

It must be stressed that prior to the appointment of the two Placement Coordinators currently working on the Degree, students found their own placement settings and, were supervised by Agency staff only. The students interviewed for this paper found both placements for themselves. The first placement was not supervised by UCC staff, but each student was visited at least *once* during the second placement. They were the first group to work with the Placement Coordinators. Each student was asked questions to elicit information on the following:

1. Factual information pertaining to the Agencies
2. Attitudinal information regarding other aspects of the Placement including:

    i.   Role of the Mentor
    ii.   Role of the Student
    iii.   Challenges perceived and overcome
    iv.   Identification of the Student's skills/competencies
    v.   Bridging of Theory and Practice
    vi.   Assessment of the Placement

The students surveyed worked in a variety of agencies in both advantaged and dis-advantaged areas. These included:

    i.   National Schools in Ireland and overseas
    ii.   Family Resource Centre
    iii.   Special National School
    iv.   Justice Project (Gárda Siochána J-LO Scheme)
    v.   Pre-School
    vi.   Residential Care setting
    vii.   Activation Centre

The following extracts are taken from the responses of students to the questions stated. (Note that the questions and answers only are italicised).

Q. Did the Agency have a written Mission Statement?
R. Only ONE of the twelve Agencies DID NOT have a written Mission Statement.
This was significant in that the Mission Statement is one of the core documents that students use when describing the Agency in their Daily Diary/Portfolio.

Q. How many staff members did the Agency have?
R. Staff numbers varied from 1 to 120
It was interesting to note the variety of experiences the students had in such diverse placements, yet they often encountered the same difficulties in writing up their experiences.

Students were asked a number of questions concerning their own role in the Agency and that of their Mentor.

Q. Was a Mentor assigned to you immediately?
R. A Mentor was assigned immediately in 10 of the 12 Placement settings. Two students were not aware of any one person in the Agency to whom they should report, as they were given assignments with different class/groups of children.

This indicates poor communication between students and Mentors and this is one area that the Placement Coordinators have focused on this year. It has become clear to us that Mentors sometimes wait for students to ask questions, while students wait for direction. One of the aims of the meetings with Mentors throughout the year has been to agree a set of guidelines for Mentors and students detailing the role of both during the placement. The students who responded to the questionnaire also identified this need and we are working on producing these guidelines at the moment.

Q. What did you initially understand to be the role of the Mentor?
R. All of the students stated that they expected the role of Mentor to include, giving direction and support, assisting with problems and conflict and giving specific information about the needs of the pupils. Some students found that they were not informed of specific learning difficulties of pupils in some National Schools. This information would have really helped them in their role with these pupils. They also

stated that they would have liked to do some research on some of the learning difficulties they had not encountered in lectures.

This raises questions around confidentiality and the level of involvement students should have in any agency. Again, guidelines clarifying the student's role are paramount here; we must remember that a student on a practice placement is not in the same privileged position as an employee, with regard to access to confidential information about pupils/clients needs.

Students also stated they expected their Mentors to help them to fuse theory and practice – this key issue has been addressed with Mentors and it has become clear that most of the Agencies would like to see the students begin their placements with more practical ideas for working with children. They would like to facilitate them in working with these ideas, but they do not see their role as identifying these for students. In the forthcoming year it is hoped to include practical workshops for students so that they may begin placement with a greater understanding of the practice underpinned by the theory they have learned.

Q. What role did the Mentor actually have in your Placement?
R. Responses varied enormously here. One student said the Mentor 'gave her more leeway than expected'. Another stated that her Mentor was 'too busy' to have contact with her, although students from other courses (Social Care) who were on placement were given lots more attention. Other students stated that their Mentors demonstrated good practice for them and discussed elements of good and bad practice.

Q. What level of interaction did you have with your Mentor?
R. In 10 of the 12 placements the student met his/her Mentor daily. However, one student never met her Mentor and had to come to UCC staff for help with any problems that developed. Mentors met the students expectations in 8 of the 12 settings. In some cases the Mentor who was assigned to the student was not actually working in the same location, which made interaction difficult if not impossible.

Q. What was the most challenging aspect of this Placement?
R. Students responded in a variety of ways to this question as seen in the following

Table 1

	Challenges	How they were overcome
1	Keeping your patience with children	Received help from Staff
2	Adapting to the routine of the National School	Requested additional work
3	Being afraid of making mistakes	Read books and consulted Staff
4	Worried about not being *perceived* as professional	Tried to emulate Staff
5	Adapting to working with children and adults with special needs	Asked for advice from co-workers
6	Lack of understanding of the procedures involved in solving difficulties for children	Observed Mentor carefully
7	Dealing with severe behavioural problems	Learned distraction methods by observation
8	Large Staff numbers	Worked hard at interacting with the group
9	Classroom Management	Classroom teacher modelled good practice
10	Working with parents	Worked at interacting with parents and did some additional research with some parents for the Portfolio

It is interesting here that the main difficulties the students experienced were overcome by a mixture of observation and research. None of the students indicated that they had discussed these matters with their Mentors, or that they received any particular advice from their Mentors. This perhaps reflects the general lack of clarity around the role of the Mentor rather than an unwillingness to help. It also emphasises the urgent need for role clarification as discussed earlier.

Q. What skills or competencies did you bring to the Placement?
R. Responses to this question varied from:

Openness
Creativity
Knowledge of the Developmental stages of children
The ability to plan appropriate activities for children

However, two students replied '*NOTHING*' which is a cause for concern particularly as the students spend a considerable number of hours in Skills Labs which are designed to help them to identify what they bring to the placement setting.

The majority of students who responded to the questionnaire identified the need for more practical preparation for placement. These students were commenting on possible future course content of the Skills Labs. It is interesting to note that students would like to have more time at these Skills Labs to design, plan and carry out activities that they could use while on placement. The Skills Labs could provide a forum where students could discuss these activities and receive peer and tutor feedback on them. This is a key point, which has been identified by both Mentors and students throughout the year. We hope to incorporate practical workshops into the course in future.

Q. What skills or competencies did you gain while on this Placement?

R. Students found it much easier to answer this and although some stated that they did not enjoy their placement, nevertheless they gained ...

Confidence
Assertiveness
Understanding of the benefits of Reflection-in-Action (Schon 1983)
Practical activities,
Communication skills
N.B. Fusion of theory and practice

This finding reiterates the need for the type of personal development focused on in the Skills Labs, which students have found to be invaluable. Students are given quite a lot of help and support to prepare themselves, both personally and professionally, for placement. They work on building up their confidence, self-esteem and assertiveness in preparation for the challenges of working with young children. However, the preceding questions also highlight the need for increased practical preparation as well.

Conclusion

The role of the student and his/her Mentor is clearly in need of clarification to ensure that students have a successful learning experience during placement. Collaboration and partnership between students, Mentors and the Placement Coordinators in UCC is crucial to developing this partnership. The role of the Placement Coordinator is essential to this work. It is a dynamic role, one that we are developing throughout our first year in consultation with all the stakeholders. The development of the Mentors' Forum, through its monthly meetings and Newsletter will ensure greater communication levels between the Agencies and the University. We also endeavour to connect and build relationships with all those involved in the provision of early childhood care and education. This paper is the beginning of a series documenting the developing role of the Placement Coordinators, together with the experiences of students and Mentors involved in the Placement Programme at UCC.

Bibliography

Douglas, F. G. 2003. Supervised Work Practice: Guidelines in *B.A.(ECS) Degree Placement Handbook* 2nd Edition, compiled by Ridgway, A and Corbett, S. UCC 2003.

Government of Ireland, 2002. *Model Framework for Education Training and Professional Development in the Early Childhood Care and Education Sector.* Dublin: Department for Justice Equality and Law Reform

Government of Ireland 7/02, Department of Education and Science

Ridgway, A., Corbett, S. 2003a. *B.A.(ECS) Degree Placement Handbook* 2nd Edition. UCC.

Ridgway, A., Corbett, S. 2003b. *Mentors' Forum*, Vol. 1, Issue 1, March 2004. UCC, Department of Education.

Ridgway, A., Corbett, S. 2003c. *Mentors' Forum*, Vol. 1, Issue 2, May 2004. UCC, Department of Education.

Schon, D. A. 1983. *The Reflective Practitioner: How Professionals Think in Action.* N. Y. Basic Books

Section Two
Parents

The Parent and Family Involvement Project:
Skills for Early Years Educators

Rosaleen Murphy

The Parent and Family Involvement (PFI) Project began in October 2003. It was inspired by the wish expressed by many people working in early childhood settings for more support and training in working with families. It has as its goals

▶ To develop a conceptual framework for parent and family involvement in early years services in Ireland
▶ To develop a model for the training of early years educators in implementing programmes of parent and family involvement
▶ To put together a resource file for early years educators and tutors.

The importance of parent and family participation in education is well documented. Research internationally has shown that it is particularly important in the context of early intervention programmes, in programmes designed to counter educational disadvantage, and that it is vital to establish a climate in the early years where parents and families see a role for themselves in their children's education. A recent update by Anne Henderson and her colleagues (2002) added a further fifty one studies to the sixty-plus already included in her 1994 synthesis, almost all of which underlined the fact that children whose families are interested in and involved with their education do better both in the short and in the long term. Family support has been identified as one of the most effective ways of improving the long-term outcomes for children, and early years services are a vital element in this. See for example Dunst and Trivette (1990), Gilligan (1995), Higgins *et al.* (1998), McKeown (2000), Murphy (1996), Pithouse *et al.* (1998), Pugh *et al.* (1994) and Yoshikawa (1994). The principles of parent involvement are a fundamental part of the philosophy and good practice guidelines of IPPA the Early Childhood Organisation, the National Children's Nurseries Association, Childminding Ireland, and other early years organisations, as well as of the Department of Education's Home School Community Liaison Scheme.

However, there is very little support material available to practitioners wishing to improve their practice in respect of parent and family involvement, nor is there much debate on what this means in practice. The dearth of support materials is all the more surprising given the general acknowledgement of the necessity for family involvement and indeed the rights of families to be involved. Pre-schools, nurseries and crèches are not just a service to the community- they are often a vital element in creating a sense of community, of helping parents of young families to build up formal and informal support networks. Two years ago, I suggested at an OMEP conference that it was time to re-think our approach to parent and family involvement (Murphy, 2002). This project is an attempt to give practitioners the tools to do just that.

People working in early years settings are being confronted daily with new challenges. However, it appears that people currently working in the field of early years care and education can feel unprepared for and somewhat daunted by the demands being made on them. Irish society has undergone huge changes in a comparatively short time – mothers of young children are now more likely to be in the workforce, families using early years services are likely to be from a wide variety of ethnic and cultural backgrounds. In the course of the current research it has become apparent that there is an increasing emphasis being placed on services catering for children from birth to three as well as those generally regarded as "pre-school", *i.e.* those services which cater for children aged three to five in the year(s) immediately before they begin primary school. As many of these new services are full day care, service providers need to think of parent and family involvement in a different and more structured way to the traditional one which relied largely on informal daily contact between carer and parent at hand-over time.

Preparing early years workers for these new challenges is in itself a challenge. Ideally, this preparation would be incorporated into initial training and integrated with other subjects and with work experience with families and communities. While parent and family involvement should be and is integrated with all of the other subjects (child health, social studies, early years education etc.), I would suggest that in my experience it is necessary, indeed vital, to devote time specifically to this topic in order a) to ensure that students are conscious of its importance relative to other aspects and b) that they are able to develop specific skills and knowledge in this area. The skill s they need include communication, empathy, conflict resolution and specific skills in sharing their own knowledge and convictions with parents and families. Recent research (Murphy 2001) found that while early years educators are very conscious of the importance of participation by parents and families, they would like to know more about how to go about implementing it. In some cases, they felt that while their training prepared them very well for direct work with children, they lacked the skills and knowledge to work with the family as a whole. The aim of the PFI Project therefore is to help early years educators to meet some of these challenges. The PFI project tackles this in two ways- firstly by asking people to reflect on their current practice, on the needs and requirements of the families they serve, and secondly by providing them with a file of ideas and resources which they can explore further and adapt to their own situation. There are however no easy answers – rather the project aims to give people the tools they need to find their own solutions.

Methodology

The objectives of the PFI project are to develop a training module in the skills necessary to promote parent and family involvement in early years services and to assemble a resource file for practitioners. In the process, a theoretical model would be developed, suited to Irish conditions, which will allow practitioners to evaluate their own practice and implement new initiatives suited to their own particular service. Throughout the project, the emphasis has been on reflective practice, on shared experience, on developing self-assessment skills, and on meeting the needs of participants. The suggested resources – case studies, books, posters, websites, links with support organisations – are starting points which people can follow up and use according to their own circumstances and needs, rather than prescribed methods of working. Flexibility and diversity are paramount, both in the project itself and in how the resulting resources are used.

The approach adopted in this project was very much a collaborative one. As the principal researcher, I would like to acknowledge the valuable contribution of all those who took part, and in particular the Togher Family Centre who hosted the workshops and which is itself an exemplar of good practice in family and community participation. Since October 2003, experienced practitioners and support workers from a variety of early years settings have taken part in a series of workshops, discussions and interviews. All of these are also parents, and in some cases grandparents. A separate group of parents have also contributed. Between them, they have helped to shape the project and ensured that it is grounded in the everyday realities of working in an early years service.

The conceptual framework underlying this project was grounded in Bronfenbrenner's ecological view of development, in which the child is seen as developing not in isolation but in the context of family, neighbourhood, community and society. The care and education of young children is a matter for the whole of society, not just for the individual parent. The development of "family-centred" early educational programmes owes its origin to this ecological social systems perspective (Burton-Maxwell and Gullo, 1995). Key assumptions are that families provide the central context for children's learning and development, that supporting the formal and informal support networks available to families will benefit children and that families' own needs and interests should guide the activities that serve them.

The PFI Workshops

While this ecological perspective underlies the whole project, a functional approach was adopted in order to give a practical and action-oriented focus to the workshops. The topics addressed in the workshops were initially based on the work of Epstein (1995, 1997, 2001) but Epstein's framework of six types of involvement (parenting, volunteering, communicating, learning at home, decision making, collaborating with the community) was adapted and considerably expanded. Through reflecting on their own experiences and beliefs, participants helped to identify the most important additional areas that needed to be addressed. These included equality and diversity, special needs, the impact of full day care on children and families, promoting continuity and managing the transitions in a child's life. Parent, family and community involvement is implicit in each of these topics; the workshops made this aspect more explicit.

Issues were explored through discussion, reflecting on people's own experiences, through considering case studies and scenarios, and through contributions from people with particular experience or expertise in different areas. For example, two parents who have served on management committees contributed their experience and insights on that topic, a crèche manager shared her experiences of running multi-cultural events, pre-school workers who were implementing the IPPA Quality Improvement programme told how they used video and photographs to share children's Learning Stories (Carr, 2001; IPPA 2004) with parents. At each workshop, points raised in discussion were recorded, written up and then sent to participants for comment.

Workshops were also used to identify and share resources and ideas for practical activities. Examples included copies of newsletters and parent handbooks, ways of sharing ideas about learning and learning activities with parents and other sources of material which could be adapted to individual and group needs.

The topics addressed in the workshops were

- Defining parent, family, community.
- What does partnership mean? What are the factors that help or hinder partnership proneness? (based on the work of Pugh and De'Ath, 1989)
- Effective communication and its contribution to partnership with parents and families
- Parent involvement in decision-making and management in early years services.
- Parents as volunteers.
- Exploring the role of families' involvement in their children's learning. Identifying ways of helping families to help their children become effective learners. Parents' input into an early years curriculum.
- Equality and diversity – what does this mean in practice in early years services?
- Children with special needs and their families- implications for practice.
- Enhancing continuity and managing transitions: from home to pre-school and from pre-school to formal schooling, from one service dealing with the child to another, managing transitions within the day.
- The impact of full-day care on children and families.
- Sessional care as a support service for family carers and childminders as well as for parents.

During the first workshop, participants explored what the words *parent* and *parenting* meant for them. The response to this varies according to people's own life experience- their own experience of being parented, whether or not they have children of their own or experience of looking after young children. There are many styles of parenting, and in order to work effectively with a diverse group of parents, it is a valuable exercise to examine our own assumptions and beliefs on the subject. Support for parents and carers includes access to child care, access to information, and providing them with emotional, psychological and practical support in their parenting role. Pre-school centres provide these in different ways, depending on the needs of the families they serve and the resources they themselves command.

Involvement or participation was explored next. One can hardly better Gillian Pugh's definition of partnership as "a working relationship that is characterised by a shared sense of purpose, mutual respect and willingness to negotiate. This implies a sharing of information, responsibility, skills, decision-making and accountability" (Pugh and De'Ath, 1989, p.33). Defining what this means in practice is in a sense what the whole project is about. It is closely related to the next topic-effective communication. The two-way sharing of information between home and pre-school is fundamental to a partnership approach. While informal contacts are the everyday bread and butter of communication, a more formal approach is needed to ensure that all parents are kept informed, not just those who have the time and make the opportunity for a regular chat with the staff of the preschool. General information – activities, schedules, fund-raising etc- can be shared through posters, newsletters, notice boards, word-of-mouth and, where appropriate, by phone, e-mail or text messaging. However, specific times need to be set aside for meetings with individual parents where they can discuss their child's progress, share any concerns, and learn more about the work of the pre-school and how it is helping their child's development. A related skill is the development of inter-personal and conflict resolution skills – effective communication does not always mean the absence of conflicting viewpoints.

While a strong case can be made for all these aspects of parent involvement, families' role in supporting children's learning is of fundamental and long-lasting importance. The project participants reported that in their experience parents, given the opportunity, are very interested in helping their children to learn. Groups are looking at innovative ways of doing this, and some of them are engaged in developing specific programmes in this respect. The work of Margy Whalley and the Pen Green Centre team (1997, 2001) has been hugely influential in this, as has the work of Margaret Carr (2001) in New Zealand. Some of the participating groups in the PFI project are taking part in the IPPA Quality Improvement programme and they spoke about their experiences of helping pre-schools to document children's learning using video and photographs and to share these with the children's parents.

Some pre-schools run courses on early learning for parents, either designed in-house or brought in from outside. The structure and design of the course is important; participants felt strongly that hands-on experience of play should be included. Many parents have had very little opportunity to play in their lives and need to experience it first hand to appreciate its relationship to learning. Funding – or rather its absence- may pose a barrier to providing courses; the cost of speakers and materials for workshops may be prohibitive. It may be possible to link with local adult education schemes – family literacy programmes are one promising example.

The informal contacts that take place every day in a pre-school setting were also identified as a valuable means of sharing knowledge about how children learn. If staff are conscious of the value of sharing their knowledge about how children learn, they can draw the parent's attention to moments when learning is happening and explain how and why this is so. However, early years services need to take positive steps to ensure that they are reaching all of the parents and not rely solely on chance encounters. A sample page from the draft PFI manual featuring a list of suggested ways to share children's learning experiences is to be found at the end of this article.

Some further areas of concern which arose in discussion were issues relating to equality and diversity, to the integration of children with special or additional needs into mainstream services, and the management of transitions. Each of these areas is complex in nature and will be treated in detail in the PFI resource materials. Changes in Irish society are reflected in the challenges faced by early years workers. Children attending pre-school services increasingly come from many different cultural and ethnic backgrounds, including those where English or Irish are not the language of the home. Early years professionals need to adapt the way they work with parents and families to take account of these differences and work in partnership. The area of work with children with special needs has a longer history, and is perhaps the area in which parent and family involvement has always been most crucial. The trend towards the integration of children with special needs into mainstream services means that services need to be able to access information on how best to meet the specific or additional needs of children with disabilities.

A further area of concern at transitions in children's lives and the roles of the family and the childcare service in maintaining continuity and minimising disruption. Transitions occur at various points the child's life, as the child goes

- from care by parent to care by others
- from parent to childminder, nursery or preschool
- from one carer to another
- from one pre-school service to another
- from one class/group to another, e.g from baby room to toddler room
- from pre-school to primary school.

Very few of these transitions, apart perhaps from the transition to primary school, have received much attention in the research literature until very recently. Each of these transitions brings with it changes in the people the child encounters, in the physical environment, in the scale of the setting, in the limits on the child's movements within it and in the expectations on the way the child behaves. This has implications also for the way in which services are organised- a realisation of the importance for children's well-being of continuity of caregiver has led to the introduction of key worker systems in nurseries for example.

Practitioners often find it difficult to take time to research, locate and evaluate material that is relevant, informative and useable. The resource file being assembled in the course of the project is one of the aspects on which participants have commented most favourably- it allows them to research further those areas which are of particular or immediate concern to them and to meet the needs of the children in their care.

Conclusion

The consultation process, case studies, workshops and other research conducted so far have identified a number of interlinked areas of concern. All of these impinge on the role of the early years educator as someone who works with families as a whole, not just with the child in isolation, and who therefore needs preparation for this role.

Some of the most important issues to emerge from the present research are:

- Parenting- understanding and providing support for parents and caregivers.
- Coping with change and helping others, parents and children to cope with changes in their lives. This also includes understanding that children have a very different childhood experience from that of their parents and carers.

- Issues relating to the management of services and the involvement of parents and families in decision-making.
- The importance of consultation with parents and families on their needs and preferences.
- Issues relating to the professional role and the training of early years educators.
- Preparing early years educators for the challenge of working with parents and families whose home environment and culture differs from the majority one.
- Considering how to foster continuity of care for young children and help them and their families to cope with the necessary transitions in their lives.

Other areas which participants have mentioned include the role of the practitioner in the holistic development of the child, access to funding for parent involvement activities, breaking down barriers to parent involvement, and the role of men in childcare programmes.

Participants in this initial stage of the PFI project were already widely experienced in working with young children, their families and in a variety of early years settings, and they have contributed valuable insights as well as taking the opportunity to review their own practice and extend their range of skills. It is intended to incorporate their contributions into a comprehensive handbook on parent and family involvement. It is planned to make this available as a training module/resource file for use in courses, for self-evaluation, and as a resource for practitioners. The final manual will include suggestions and exercises for using this approach with students at the beginning of their careers-integrating it with experience on placement, using role play and case studies to explore issues and situations. It is hoped that the availability of this resource will help early years workers in their work with parents and families.

Appendix: From the draft manual for the PFI Project

Some ideas on helping parents to be more aware of how their children learn:

▸ Share with parents the topics that the children are interested in at pre-school- and vice versa- find out what their interests are at home.

▸ Parent and toddler sessions are an opportunity to share ideas about how children learn in an informal, play-based setting.

▸ Include ideas for supporting learning at home in newsletters and handbooks. Include as many ideas as possible that are free or very low cost.

▸ Develop shared concepts on learning with parents – for example Pen Green uses the concepts of *schemas* and *levels of involvement* to help parents observe and understand their children's learning (Whalley, 1997, 2001). Montessori, High Scope etc. each have their own structure and underlying concepts- share these with parents.

▸ Get parents involved in providing for play- helping to develop an outdoor play area, fundraising for new equipment. This often makes them more aware of the learning potential of such play.

▸ Draw up a *Wish List* of ways parents can help the pre-school and let them know about it. This might include collecting cereal boxes and other materials for junk art, helping with the newsletter, accompanying children on outings, or whatever is appropriate to your particular setting. It should include a range of items and activities, many of which are free or do not require a lot of time or a long-term commitment.

▸ Invite parents into the pre-school for an hour or two to share a learning activity with their children – *e.g.* planting bulbs in the garden or in window boxes, baking, playing a game, making a book.

▸ Include the words of the songs and rhymes that the children are doing in the weekly newsletter – parents may have forgotten or never learned these.

▸ Have tapes of songs and rhymes available for parents to borrow.

▸ Learning kits- for children to use at home, before they start or over the summer holidays- crayons, safety scissors, ideas for activities.

▸ Share examples of children's work with parents and families- open days, exhibitions, photographs and videos of children at play (made with permission from parents), portfolios of children's work.

▸ Have a weekly hour when parents are invited to drop in to share story-time and to see children's work for the week.

▸ Posters, talks, workshops on learning through play and everyday activities.

- Have several copies of the children's favourite storybooks to lend so parents can read them at home with their child.
- Lend books on child development and learning through play.
- Collaborate with local Family Learning initiatives and adult education schemes.
- Many parents now have access to e-mail- why not use e-mail to share news and ideas with them as well as notices and printed handouts and newsletters?
- Be aware that parents may have different views on how children should be learning – they may think that a more formal or academic approach should be used. Help parents to become more aware of the social and emotional aspects of learning, and that play and active exploration of the environment is valuable both in itself and as a foundation for later learning.

Acknowledgements

The PFI research project was undertaken while Dr. Rosaleen Murphy was the holder of Government of Ireland Post-Doctoral Fellowship at the Department of Education, UCC. The Fellowship was awarded in 2003 by the Irish Research Council for the Humanities and Social Sciences.

Bibliography

Bronfenbrenner, U. (1979). *The Ecology of Human Development.* Cambridge, MA: Harvard University Press.

Burton-Maxwell, C. and Gullo, D.F. (1995). "Negotiating family-centered early education: a multi-dimensional assessment of interests and needs". *Early Child Development and Care*, Vol. 113, 45-58.

Carr, Margaret (2001). *Assessment in Early Childhood Settings: Learning Stories.* London: Paul Chapman Publishing.

Epstein, Joyce L. (1995). "School/Family/Community Partnerships. Caring for the Children We Share." *Phi Delta Kappan*, Vol. 76, No. 9, 701-712.

Epstein, J. L. (1997). *National Network of Partnership Schools: Epstein's Six Types of Involvement.* http://scov.csos.jhu/p2000/sixtypes.htm

Epstein, Joyce L. (2001). School, Family and Community Partnerships: Preparing Educators and Improving Schools. Boulder CO. and Oxford, UK: Westview Press.

Henderson, Anne T. and Berla, Nancy, (1994). *A New Generation of Evidence. The Family is Critical to Student Achievement.* Washington, DC: National Committee for Citizens in Education.

Henderson, Anne T. and Karen Mapp (2002). *A New Wave of Evidence. The Impact of School, Family, and Community Connections on Student Achievement.* Austin, Texas: Southwest Educational Development Laboratory. Website www.sedl.org/connections/

IPPA (2004). *Power of Play: A Play Curriculum in Action.* Dublin: IPPA The Early Childhood Organisation.

Murphy, Mary Rosaleen (2001). *Parental Involvement in Early Years Education and Care in the Cork Area.* PhD thesis, NUI-Cork.

Murphy, Rosaleen (2002). "Rethinking Parental Involvement in Early Years Education and Care". Proceedings of the OMEP Ireland Conference, *Lessons for the 21st Century: Research, Reflection, Renewal,* DIT, Aungier St, Dublin, 20 April 2002.

Pugh, G. and De'Ath, E. (1989). *Working Towards Partnership in the Early Years.* London: National Children's Bureau.

Whalley, Margy and the Pen Green Centre Team (1997). *Working with Parents.* London: Hodder and Stoughton.

Whalley, Margy and the Pen Green Centre Team (2001). *Involving Parents in Their Children's Learning.* London: Paul Chapman Publishing.

A study of parents, carers and providers of child health information support needs in the South East, from ante natal to the pre-school years

Edel Conway

Background

The genesis for this research as a part of the Child Health Information Service Project (CHISP) is to increase service planners and providers understanding of the child health information needs of parents and carers of pre school children. This includes an understanding on information needed on allied social support services. Furthermore, it aims to contribute to on going development of a best practice approach to quality child health services within our health board, as recommended by Denyer *et al.* (1999).

The literature identified empirical information allied to the consumers' information needs and the gaps, which then drove the methodology. In addition, evidence of best practice by providers in furnishing quality information and achieving effective communication was highlighted in the international, national, and regional literature. The methodology was complimented by a brief engagement with service providers, to glean an overview of current child health and related information they impart. Additionally the formats used for imparting this information and the issues and concerns identified by service providers. For a comprehensive examination of the broader aspects of information support needs of parents, as well as providers' perspectives, refer to the report in the South Eastern Health Board by Conway (2003). This report is distilled down to the abridged version in this paper, which affords an overview of the qualitative study conducted by the Child Health Information Service Project in the South Eastern Health Board. For a copy of this full report contact conwaye@sehb.ie

Purpose of engagement with parents and carers

To explore the information needs of parents and carers from ante natal to the pre school era in relation to their child's health and well being, from their perspective, with a view to developing appropriate quality information and systems to meet these needs.

Methods

Ten in-depth focus groups, incorporating 74 parents/carers from the ante natal to pre school years were conducted. These were transcribed verbatim and thematic analysis was used to examine the data. In addition, contact or links with a range of 47 service providers furnished an overview of the existing child health and related support service information currently supplied.

Literature review on information as a support for parents
Information support is one of the key aids that parents required in order to assist their parenting role (Best Health for Children, 2002; Ryland, 1995). This should be supplied at "the birth of a first baby" and when "children are under school going age and childcare and rearing demands are at their most intensive" (Commission on the Family, 1998). The rationale is that all families face difficulties and challenges in raising their children in Ireland in the 21st Century (Lyons *et al.*, 2001; Commission on the Family, 1998). The provision of identified universal information in various formats to parents goes towards addressing their information support needs (Conway, 2003).

The rationale for furnishing quality child health and related support services information is to empower parents by offering informed choice and ultimately promoting the health and well being of the child (Department of Health and Children, 2001, Denyer *et al.* 1999; Commission on the Family, 1998). As such, the provision of quality information, that is identified and acted on by the parent, results in a more effective and informed use of the services and improved health status (Best Health for Children, 2002; Department of Health and Children, 2001; International Year of the Family Committee, 1994).

The context for targeting parents is at the core of a series of strategies, policy documents, and research papers drawn from an international, national, and regional perspective (Best Health For Children, 2002; Clavero, 2001; Commission on the Family, 1998; Department of Health and Children, 2001; Hall, 1996; International Year of the Family Committee, 1994; South Eastern Health Board 1999). For instance, the 'Supporting Parents' Strategy (Best Health For Children, 2002) has an objective of mapping out a sustainable framework for assisting parents and advising Health Boards on how they can fulfil their responsibilities in relation to the identified needs of parents. Another illustration is the current health strategy that proposes, "the health system must focus on providing individuals with the information and support they need to make informed health choices" (Department of Health and Children, 2001, p 20). National research by Riordan (2001) had a broad aim to address the current lack of knowledge by service providers about the general support needs of parents. Denyer *et al.*, (1999) argued that the provision of health information, especially to first time parents was an area that supported parents.

Major elements of these documents endorse the rationale and indicate the importance of targeting and supporting parents in terms of furnishing quality information. The principles underpinning these perspectives relate to making the rights and well being of children a priority; supporting parents as individuals and facilitating assess to information and related support services.

Literature review on Communication of Quality Health information

The concept of information as a service is a fundamental notion. There is literature to suggest a positive relationship between communication of the information and clinical outcome (Cortis and Lacey, 1996; International Year of the Family Committee, 1994; Sweetland, 2000; Wagner and Greenlick, 2001). Moreover, there is evidence to indicate that if people are equipped with the relevant information, it encourages the appropriate and effective use of services by the seeker (International Year of the Family Committee, 1994). Tailoring this information to what the consumer wants is a key issue identified in the communication process with parents by Cullen, *et al.* (2002).

The literature shows a range of international, (Saunders, 1999; www.parentlineplus.org.uk) national (Commission on the Family, 1998; www.icdb.ie), and regional (FitzGerald, 2001; Mid Western Health Board, 2001) perspectives on how child health information and related support services are developed and provides exemplary evidence in supporting parents, including information support.

What is highlighted is that the key to success lies within listening to the problem from the client's perspective and communicating in a fashion tailored to meet the needs and preferences of the parent (Conway, 2003). New skills, suitable management systems, communication training for a range of service providers and a change in the mindset are required by the service providers in order to overcome barriers and empower families through information provision.

Literature review on Parents/Carers Information Support Needs

With the notable exception of the laudable national based survey of generic parents support needs by Riordan (2001) and the review of antenatal education in Sligo/Leitrim by the North Western Health Board, (2000) literature was not identified which linked what professionals thought parents of young children needed and what parents *actually* needed.

From the parents perspective, studies identified topics of child health information needed, such as details on child sleep pattern; new-born care; a crying baby; discipline; toilet training; normal development and early learning by the child (Riordan, 2001; Young, *et al.* 1998). Riordan (2001) also recommends the need for improved access to quality information on child development and behaviour, nutrition, and childcare issues.

A majority of parents reported using multiple sources to access information on child development and rearing (McKeown, 2000; Young *et al.*, 1998). The foremost sources of health information that adults' approach in the Irish context, within the statutory sector included the General Practitioner and the Public Health Nurse (Ruddle *et al.*, 2002; Garavan, Winder and McGee, 2001; Friel, Gabhainn and Kelleher, 1999). Within the informal area, there was strong preference expressed for Family, peer led support, and word of mouth as highly rated sources of information (Riordan, 2001; Roche, 2000: Young *et al.*, 1998).

Difficulties by parents in trying to find information on basic topics relevant to parenting and caring for children is argued by Dempsey, (2001) and Riordan, (2001). Parents were dissatisfied with the information received if there is a general difficulty in obtaining the information, or, if they are given insufficient information to suit their needs (Fisher, 2001). In relation to general needs of asylum seekers, very basic problems found included accessing and understanding information on entitlements, rights, and services embracing health and welfare (Fanning, Veale and O'Connor, 2001; Kennedy and Murphy-Lawless, 2001).

Barriers to seeking or receiving informational support include attaining the information too quickly and receiving inaccurate information (Brazy, *et al.* 2001; Fisher, 2001; Smith and Daughtrey, 2000). There also appears to be a lack of research and awareness of the father's experiences and issues around specific information needs (McKeown, Ferguson and Rooney, 1998; Henderson, and Brouse, 1991). Low literacy skills were also highlighted nationally as a barrier to good health, as this barrier limits access to health information and related health services (National Adult Literacy Agency, 2002; Department of Health and Children, 2000).

In summing up, one of the key issues noted within the available literature reviewed is that apart from a few notable exceptions, most of the research studies examined that focused on the parents child health information needs, were conducted outside Ireland. While this does not negate the results, the fact that there are fundamental differences in health care systems and cultures in each country must be highlighted. Also, of the major studies reviewed, the community-based domain was not a key area researched by many authors' and the hospital and acute setting took dominance in many instances. Gaps then emerge in relation to the child health and allied information support needs of expectant women, their partners, and parents and main carers of children under five in the Irish context. This paper will explore these needs in the south eastern region of Ireland.

Methods

This section contains two parts:
(a) Procedure for identification of current child health and related support service information furnished by providers.
(b) The methodology for the focus groups with parents/carers in relation to their child health and related support service information needs.

(a) Current Child Health Information and Related Support Service Furnished by Service Providers

The focus of this research was to identify the child health information needs of the parent/carer. The providers' perspective was first sought though in order to establish what was currently available, thus putting the parents needs in that context. Moreover, considerable care must be afforded when consulting adults about their information requirements. It cannot be presumed that they know categorically what these needs are. The service provider may be best placed, because of specialist training, to anticipate these needs or may be able to provide information, which is outside the expertise of the parent. Ultimately though, it is the parent who wants (or does not want) this expertise. The findings from the 47 providers perspective are mapped out in a matrix gird in the qualitative report in the South Eastern Health Board by Conway (2003).

Following the brief but interesting engagement with providers it can be argued that there is a vast range of providers of child health and related support service information within the statutory, voluntary sectors and associated media. The information they share is distributed within a variety of communication methods and assortment of channels. A recurrent theme from the providers is the need for systematic dating and updating of the information imparted, especially in print form. The Health Promotion Unit of the Department of Health and Children has established a National Health Promotion Information Project, which will strive towards addressing this issue. Objectives of that project include establishing a database of health promotion literature available nationally and reviewing existing Health Promotion Unit literature and updating it. Also, the project addresses raising awareness of the need for continuous updating of literature by partner agencies such as Health Boards and Voluntary Agencies. While the project focused is on written health promotion material only, it does strive towards addressing some of the issues brought up by providers as well as participants in this study.

Another comment by the providers related to the importance of training and updating of skills in order to keep abreast with current issues. It is important to link standardised training and updates on clinical issues for the providers with communication training issues, as the participants identified this. The content and delivery of information were just two of the observations from the engagement with the providers.

While contact with the providers was not detailed in terms of identifying their needs and views, the initial contact did set the scene for further opportunities to help to develop the resulting information package. The engagement process with providers provided an overview of aspects of the child health information and related support service providing role of caregivers, their views on the information and its provision, their value judgments and recommendations.

(b) Engagement with Parents/Carers

Qualitative Approach

A pre-supposition was that parents might not actively recognise, or be willing to admit the difficulties they had in accessing or understanding information. A qualitative research approach enables the parent a more detailed opportunity to express and clarify issues they may have. It also affords an opportunity to understand the concepts, reasoning and pathways followed by parents when looking for and acting on information.

Ethical considerations

The study was presented to The Waterford Regional Hospital Ethics Committee for ethical approval, which was granted.

Sample

Purposive sampling was used and the participants were accessed via link service providers, co-ordinators and community-based workers. The inclusion criteria for the sample was a woman or her partner in the antenatal period or the parent/carer to a pre school child. The ten groups identified as essential for inclusion by the CHISP Steering Committee were: ante natal women and their partners; parents of babies; toddlers; pre school children; lone parents; teenage (young) parents; fathers; parents of special needs children or chronically ill children; traveller parents; and parents who are asylum seekers / refugees. Parents from different urban / rural backgrounds as well as socio-economic groups and diverse cultures were included within this wide access.

Pilot Study

A pilot study enabled the researcher to gain trustworthiness and credibility in the data, its collection and analysis method, and tested the appropriateness of the chosen data collection method.

Data Collection – Focus Groups

Conducting ten focus groups, with between 3-11 participants in each group, provided multiple perspectives on the issues linked to information seeking and needed and this maintained objectivity. Table 1 illustrates the list of the focus groups and the number of participants who attended.

Table I

Number of focus groups interviews conducted and the participants	
Focus Group	Number of Participants
a. Fathers	3 Fathers.
b. Lone Parents.	10 Mothers.
c. Parents of babies (0-12 months old).	8 Mothers & 2 Carers.
d. Parents of toddlers (1-3 years old).	8 Mothers.
e. Parents of children with chronic illness /special needs.	7 Mothers, 2 Fathers, & 1 Carer.
f. Asylum Seekers/Refugees.	7 Mothers.
g. Antenatal Women and their Partners.	4 Women & 2 Men.
h. Travelling Community.	9 Mothers & 2 Carers.
i. Parents of pre-school children (3-5 yrs).	4 Mothers (1 also had dual role of carer.)
j. Young Parents (Teenage)	5 Mothers.
Total: 74 participants	

Two researchers, acting as co-facilitators/ scribe attended six of the focus groups and the remaining four were conducted by one person who acted as both facilitator and scribe. In the focus groups, the researcher used a series of question or themes that were related to the aims of the project or taken from the literature review and correlated with identified gaps in the empirical research. Also, specific issues that emerged in a focus group were incorporated into subsequent focus group sessions in order to identify if the findings truly reflected the lived experience.

Data Analysis
Verbatim transcriptions of the 10 taped focus groups were conducted. At the primary stages of the data analysis, the researcher and two colleagues coded copies of the same transcript separately. Significant themes were identified through a combination of the emergent ideas raised by the participants and the research aims. These were then analysed in accordance with established qualitative research techniques. To ensure trustworthiness of the study, the data was simplified and reduced and themes established to describe the experience under study as credibly as is possible.

Findings
The themes and the categories that emanated from this study illustrate clearly

the information needs as identified by the parents and carers and their perceptions of the providers of this information. On analysis, the views expressed by the antenatal women, parents and carers of young children were divided into 5 emergent categories and are subsequently illustrated with participant narrative:

(a) People as information seekers.
(b) Social context for making decisions.
(c) What information parents want and the issues affecting this.
(d) Participants perceptions of information providers.
(e) Suggestions offered by the participants.

a) People as information seekers

Actively seeking information and issues around the sources accessed was established as a backdrop to understanding the adult's experience of information seeking and attainment pathways "But until I actually knew I was pregnant there, I didn't start (seeking)".

The decision of where to seek information may stem from an initial lack of parenting experience with reduced self-confidence thus, there is a sense of doing as you are instructed, without the ability to balance the information with previous experiences.

> "When it's your first time, no matter what age you are, you don't know like everything, and you have to learn like, if they say you can use this, or you have to do this, because you don't know why, you have to do this then".

As a parent builds confidence, they appreciate if the information giver values the experience and capacity of the parent to make the best decision for the child (given that for some information needed, there is no absolute right or wrong way to do something, and all that may be needed is moral support and affirmation).

> "I was afraid and after three weeks, she (Public Health Nurse) said to me you're fine, there's no need for me to call back and I felt

great like … you feel great when someone would say something like that to you, do you know what I mean".

(b) Social context for making decisions

While the wider social context is relevant in understanding where people are coming from in the decision making process, it is the specific examples of this, which are embedded in the life history, tradition, role-modelling and patterns of experiences from family of origin, that appear to have an impact on the way parents are informed and the way they act. "That's normal like, when we grew up that's what (we saw), it's the same again as well". This gave expression to where people were socially and traditionally coming from, and the parenting role they observed their parents engaging in.

Interesting evidence of where history and tradition has assisted the smoothness of birth and parenting was found within the travelling community. This may be because the basic role model doesn't appear to have changed from generation to generation. "My mother had seven children at the time and I found out all about them, I knew how to make bottles, everything then, and (this induction) helped myself like, that and I had do everything myself that time".

(c) What information parents want and the issues affecting this

In short, parents want a brief overview of information to recognise the normal development is what parents' want and some advice on the day-to-day parenting role:

"Parenting tips mainly" and to "see what, what milestone they should be hitting, you know and, you know say if you have a problem, who to contact, you know if your child is not say, you know speech-wise". If problems were detected parents wanted to know the referral pathway to local services or access to deeper repositories of specific information (Conway, 2003).

People and local services that provide information within the formal sector are identified, and a rationale for a positive rating is offered:

> "The public health nurse was brilliant" and "she listens anyway",
> or, "I find the chemist very good, you know, they're nice and
> more understanding, I think".

The informal providers that parents-to-be and parents access include family and other parents:

> "Most of the (antenatal) information you do get from friends or family and most people have had babies themselves" or "I find that you (family & friends) can reassure each other, you know if they're at the same stage".

Parents identified the various mediums of seeing and attaining information that suits them, such as "I think one-to-one is very good," or "hands-on, you know, or then listening".

In terms or printed matter: "A leaflet is usually a good way. You're used to leaflets and they work." " But not in bulk, like"!

In relation to the right time to attain the child rearing information, parents said they want to be informed just leading up to a milestone stage, such as approaching the 'terrible twos'! "Three months before they start to give us a war!".

Ranges of barriers to information seeking and attainment are established, "explain it to us in English like that we'd understand, not in doctors terms." Attitudinal and personal emotions and feelings experienced by users were also ascertained. For example, if the parent felt the communication process with a professional was not a good experience for her," She made me feel stupid."

(d) Participants perceptions of information providers
A positive or negative evaluation of the individual person or profession was realised, as was evidence of conflicting and inaccurate information being furnished "one nurse gave out to me for leaving him sleep on his back, the other one gave out to me for letting him sleep on his stomach!"

Evidence of a sense of a 'dual' remit was experienced by a few participants about some providers, "I thought she was going to report me to some people, I don't know. People say tome the child will be taken." This may be as a result of aspects of the provider's statutory remit and child health / welfare role being misunderstood by the parent or perhaps a poor communication process on the day.

An emerging communication process between the giver and seeker was then mapped out "attitudes, communication, and listening are coming up as the key issue."

(e) Suggestions offered by the participants

The participants, in relation to presentation and delivery of materials and improving the information and services, offered suggestions such as "Keeping it [information] simple and straight forward."

Conclusion

This research presented the views, issues, perceptions, and concerns, from the perspective of the service user. A critical element for the parents and carers was that health information needs to be given in a timely and appropriate fashion. For the information to be useful, it needs to be based on individual perceptions of need and this can only be gained through careful assessment. From the data, it would appear that parents want information that addresses their concerns at a given time. Professional attitudes and listening skills were also identified by the service users as areas of interpersonal communication requiring attention. Raising the profile of some service providers was another area identified by the participants as requiring attention in order to improve the relationship between the giver and receiver. Issues in relation to current service provision, from the users perspective, included having an appreciation that there are a diversity of groups and ethnic considerations to bear in mind when giving information.

A central conclusion was that quality information and effective communication empower the parent and are linked with improved health. Furthermore, quality information provision is not just a bi-product of the service provision but requires active management in its own right.

Recommendations

The recommendations were summarised from the main findings and conclusions and set out in the context of the terms of reference / aims. The principles underlying the recommendations include that the parent and child are at the centre of the service and building on existing service and good practice is supported. It must be appreciated that while many recommendations are possible, not all the proposals will be achieved within the scope of the CHISP project. However, mapping out the overall suggestions under key headings provides a platform for focus, reflection, and action by ranges of service planners and providers.

(1) Recognising that there are a diversity of groups and ethnic considerations when dealing with parents/carers and not one generic group requiring information. Therefore, there is an overriding need for appropriate and timely quality information in a variety of consumer friendly media, that best suit individual needs at a given time.

(2) This involves sourcing or developing suitable materials to fill the identified gaps.

(3) Appropriate training and timely updates for providers, which would include training on communication and interpersonal issues.

(4) As the value of various community groups in the delivery of some health information was heightened in the study, it is important to forge stronger links with these groups.

Bibliography

Best Health For Children, (2002). *Investing in Parenthood to achieve Best Health for Children.* Dublin: Best Health for Children.

Brazey, J. E. Anderson, B. M. H., Becker, P. T., and Becker, M. (2001). How parents of premature infants gather information and obtain support. *Journal of Neonatal Nursing.* Vol. 20(2). P4108.

Clavero, S. (2001). *Parent Support: An International Overview.* Dublin: Best Health For Children.

Commission on the Family, (1998). *Strengthening Families for Life.* Dublin: Stationery Office.

Conway, E. (2003). I*dentifying the Child Health Support Service Information Needs of Parents/Carers from the Ante natal to Pre school Years.* Kilkenny: South Eastern Health Board (Unpublished).

Cortis, J. D., and Lacey, A. E. (1996). Measuring the quality and quantity of information giving to in-patients. *Journal of Advanced Nursing.* Vol. 24 (4). P 674-681.

Cullen, W., Leahy, M. and Bury, G. (2002). Patients' views of the good doctor.

British Medical Journal, Vol. 325 P697-70.

Denyer, S., Thornton, L., and Pelly, H. (1999). *Best Health for Children: Developing a Partnership with Families*. Dublin: National Conjoint Child Health Committee.

Dempsey, M. (2001). *The Experience of Teenage Pregnancy in the South East of Ireland*. Kilkenny: South Eastern health Board.

Department of Health and Children, (2001). *Quality and Fairness: A Health System for You*. Dublin: Stationery Office.

Department of Health and Children, (2000). *National Health Promoting Strategy: 2000 –2005*. Dublin: Stationery Office.

Fanning, B., Veale, A., and O'Connor, D. (2001). *Beyond the Pale: Asylum-seeking children and Social Exclusion in Ireland*. Dublin: Irish Refugee Council.

FitzGerald, T. (2001). *Review of Community Child Health Services provided by South Eastern Health Board*. Kilkenny: South Eastern Health Board

Fisher, H. (2001). The needs of parents with chronically sick children: a literature review. *Journal of Advanced Nursing*. Vol. 36 (4). P600-607.

Friel, S., Gabhainn, N.S. and Kelleher, C., (1999). *The National Health and Lifestyle Surveys*. Dublin: Department of Health and Children.

Garavan, R., Winder, R., and McGee, H. (2001). *Health and Social Services for Older People (HeSSOP)*. Dublin: National Council on Ageing and Older People.

Hall, D.M.B. (1996). *Health for all Children*. (3rd edition). Oxford: Oxford University Press.

Henderson A.D. & Brouse A.J. (1991). The experience of new fathers during the first 3 weeks of life. *Journal for Advanced Nursing*, Vol. (16). Page 293-298

International Year of the Family Committee (1994). *An information revolution for families: using no magic answers*. Wellington: International Year of the Family Committee.

Kennedy, P. and Murphy-Lawless, J. (2001) *The Maternity Care Needs of Refugee and Asylum-seeking Women*. Dublin: University College Dublin.

Lyons, S., Collins, C. and Staines, A. (2001). *Are Universally Available Supports for Families Effective and Efficient?* Dublin: National University of Ireland.

McKeown, K., Ferguson, H., and Rooney, D. (1998). *Changing Fathers? Fatherhood and Family Life in Modern Ireland*. Cork: Collins Press.

McKeown, K. (2000). *A Guide to What Works: Family Support Services for*

Vulnerable Families. Dublin: Department of Health and Children.

Mid Western Health Board, (2001). *Professional Guidance on use of the Personal Health Record – My Personal Health Record.* Limerick: Mid Western Health Board.

National Adult Literacy Agency, (2002). *Health Literacy: Policy and Strategy Report.* Dublin: National Adult Literacy Agency.

North Western Health Board, (2000). *Review of Antenatal Education in Sligo/Leitrim.* Manorhamilton: North Western Health Board.

Riordan, S. (2001). *Supporting Parenting: A Study of Parents Support Needs.* Dublin: Dublin Institute of Technology.

Roche, M. (2000). *Towards a Parenting Strategy: A Draft Position Paper.* Sligo: North Western Health Board. [Unpublished]

Ruddle, H. Prizeman, G. Haslett, D. Mulvihill, R. and Kelly, E. (2002). *Meeting the Health, Social Care and Welfare Services Information Needs of Older People in Ireland.* Dublin: National Council on Ageing and Older People.

Rylands, J. (1995). *A study of Parenting Programmes in Ireland: Exploration of Needs and Current Provision.* Dublin: Department of Health and Bernardo's.

Saunders, M.R. (1999). Triple P–Positive Parenting Program: Towards an Empirically Validated Multilevel Parenting and Family Support Strategy for the prevention of Behaviour and Emotional Problems in Children. *Clinical Child and Family Psychology Review,* Vol. 2 (2). P71-89.

Smith, L., and Daughtrey, H. (2000). Weaving the seamless web of care: and analysis of parents" perceptions of their needs following discharge of their child from hospital. *Journal of Advanced Nursing.* Vol. 31 (4). P 812-820.

South Eastern Health Board (1999). *Women's Health in the South East: 2000 and Beyond.* Kilkenny: South Eastern Health Board.

Sweetland, J. (2000). Users' perceptions of the impact of information provided by a Consumer Health Information Service: an in-depth study of six users. *Health libraries Review.* Vol. 17. P 77-82.

Young, K.T., Davis, K., Scholes, C., and Parker, S. (1998). Listening to Parents: A National Survey of Parents with Young Children. Archives of Paediatric and Adolescent Medicine. Vol. 152. P 255-262.

Wagner, T .H., and Greenlick, M. R. (2001) When parents are given greater access to health information, does it affect paediatric utilisation? *Med Care.* Vol. 39 (8) P848-55.

www.cidb.ie, (2001). *Setting up an Information Service: Maintaining a Quality Service.*

www.parentlineplus.org.uk. (2003). *Help and information for Parents ... because children come without instructions.*

Section Three

Disadvantage and Special Needs

On Target?
Presentation of rationale, findings and recommendations from an Audit of Services Targeting Disadvantage and Special Needs among children aged birth to six in Ireland

Jacqueline Fallon

Introduction

The Centre for Early Childhood Development and Education (CECDE) was established in 2002 by the Minister for Education and Science under the joint management of St. Patrick's College and the Dublin Institute of Technology (DIT). The main focus of the work of the CECDE is the development of a National Framework of Quality standards applicable to all early childhood care and education (ECCE) settings in Ireland. The other main functions of the CECDE are developing and implementing innovative research projects in the areas of disadvantage and special needs, and laying the groundwork for the establishment of the Early Childhood Education Agency (ECEA) as envisaged in the White Paper on Early Childhood Education, Ready to Learn (DES, 1999). The CECDE remit covers all settings for children between the ages of birth and six years in Ireland, with a particular interest in the needs of children experiencing disadvantage and of children with special needs arising, for example, from a disability.

Within this context, one of the first actions determined by the CECDE Programme of Work (CECDE, 2001) was an audit of existing services targeting disadvantage and special needs among children in the birth to six year old age range. This project culminated in the publication of 'On Target? An Audit of Provision of Services Targeting Disadvantage and Special Needs among Children from birth to six years in Ireland' (CECDE, 2004). This paper presents two aspects of 'On Target?'; the rationale, which relates to the need for reliable data on which to base policy and provision, and the major findings which were used to generate recommendations for policy in ECCE in Ireland.

Rationale

While data on provision is not available in a planned or systematic way, the CECDE has assembled a database of approximately 1,400 services. In gathering entries for the project database, a crucial question arose – how to determine whether a service was targeted or not? There is a debate about universal provision versus targeted initiatives (McGough, 2001; Hayes, 2002), but in this instance the brief was clear, namely to determine the level of targeted provision. Within the terms of this project, criteria for determining whether a service could be included or not were devised. If a service was associated with an agency, initiative, non-governmental organisation (NGO) or Government Department with a specific brief to target disadvantage, social exclusion or special needs, and if this connection could be clearly established by documentary evidence, then it was included. This methodology provided a clear solution to what emerged as the key and primary finding[1]. Accurate information on the range and nature of ECCE services targeting disadvantage is extremely difficult to access. The situation regarding information on services targeting special needs is even more marked. This finding led to a consideration of issues which centred on the place of empirical data in development and co-ordination work across a broad range of spheres which could be loosely described as relating to social inclusion.

Irish context

The audit took place at a time when there was growing awareness nationally of the necessity for developments in service provision across many sectors to be evidence based, sustainable and supported by reliable information (Barry, 2000; Corrigan *et al.*, 2002; Department of Social and Family Affairs (DFSA) 2003; Health Research Board, 2003). In *An Audit of Research on Early Childhood Care and Education in Ireland 1990-2003* (CECDE, 2003a:144) the CECDE states that "... research to date and all future research must be instrumental in shaping policy and practice in the Irish context." The CECDE Research Strategy (2003b: 3) further states that "(i)n terms of providing policy advice to the Department of Education and Science on issues related to early childhood development and education, research evidence will be used to inform recommendations made."

Sanderson (2002:4) has noted that "(a) key driver of modernization is evidence-based policy making and service delivery ...", modernisation in this context referring to development and progression. At this juncture in the development of ECCE in Ireland, when considerable developments are taking shape and progression towards a cohesive pattern of provision is becoming apparent, it is crucial that all the elements of successful development be considered. The two aspects referred to above – policy making and service delivery – are of equal importance in the work of the CECDE. Our brief includes developing policy advice and also working with service providers in the development of quality standards, using research to support both (CECDE, 2003b.). In terms of 'On Target?', as the Equality Authority has pointed out "(d)ata is required to establish baseline positions." (Barry, 2000:Foreword). It is certainly germane to this rationale to add that "(a)ddressing data gaps is an essential strategy for better policy formulation and for understanding how we live." (Cantillon *et al.*, 2001:xxxii)

Current emphasis on evidence-informed policy.

The current emphasis on evidence based, or perhaps more accurately 'evidence-informed' policy (Sebba, 1999) can be traced to the field of medical research, and the empirical basis for medical practice (Coe, Fitz-Gibbon and Tymms, 2000). Currently there is considerable debate on the nature of evidence, its relationship to the development of policy, and how to maximise the role of research evidence in both policy and practice. Considerable literature emanates from Great Britain on foot of "... the strongly emerging philosophy, as postulated by the United Kingdom government Research and Development strategy, that policy and practice have to be based on evidence deriving from research ..."(Iwaniec and Pinkerton, 1998: xi). While there is a high level of research activity in Ireland, there is very little specific attention given to the role of research evidence in informing policy in the public sector, specifically education policy.

> There has been little by way of study of the relationship between policy making and research in this country and, although there have been a number of analyses and discussions of the research-social-policy relationship, education has received little attention in these analyses. (Kellaghan, 1989:193)

There is no evidence available by way of literature to indicate that the situation has changed in the fifteen years since Kellaghan made these remarks.

Empirical data

However, while this may be the case, there has been a growing awareness here of the need for reliable empirical data to underpin development in a wide range of spheres. As far back as 1986 "… the Review Group on Mental Handicap Services, established by the Department of Health and Children, found that one major stumbling block which lay in the path of systematic planning was the absence of reliable data on the extent of the needs of people with intellectual disability in Ireland.'" (Health Research Board, 2003:1.1) Certainly the same could be said at the moment about the need for reliable data on current provision for children experiencing disadvantage and children with special needs.

The ultimate result of the findings of the aforementioned Review Group is the National Intellectual Disability Database (NIDD), which is supported by a sophisticated, well-resourced data collection, management and storage system under the auspices of the Health Research Board. A National Physical and Sensory Disability Database (NPSDD), which will identify people with physical or sensory disabilities who are currently availing of, or require, specialised health and personal social services is in the process of being implemented throughout the country since January 2002. Data collection is at various stages of completion in each Health Board area. A challenge for the future may well be to find a way to incorporate data from the NIDD and NSPDD relating to children in the birth to six age group into a database of provision for all children in that age group.

Compatibility of data, and data collection time frames, will have an impact on any such efforts. Compatibility of data depends on the format in which information is stored across all agencies, whether the formats are similar and therefore easily compiled, and whether the items and range of information collected are similar and easily matched across agencies. Agencies generally collect their data at specific times on a regular basis, generally year-on-year, but if different agencies collect information at different times, then one agency's data is out-of-date while another agency's is still current, thus militating against the compilation of a single, comprehensive current database.

Returning to the NIDD, such a structured system is not the norm in Ireland, and much closer to the experience of 'On Target?' is the comment from the Equality Authority that "(g)enerally data is highly uneven and variable, dispersed across a variety of different organisations and structures, reflecting a lack of co-ordination and integration in the approach to data and data collection systems in this country." (Barry, 2000:5). It was this experience which prompted the Equality Authority to develop its data strategy, 'Building the Picture: The Role of Data in Achieving Equality' (Barry, 2000).

On the wider issue of social inclusion, an issue very germane to provision of early education services to children experiencing disadvantage and children with special needs, there is no equivocation about the importance of data among the Social Partners. Corrigan *et al.* (2002:vii) point out that both "(t)he Programme for Prosperity and Fairness (PPF) and National Anti-Poverty Strategy (NAPS) Building an Inclusive Society, emphasise the collection of data for the comprehensive monitoring of poverty trends". Monitoring poverty trends and monitoring the provision of services for children with multiple needs are different exercises. The basis for both is, however, the same – the need for data on which to base such a monitoring system.

The Department of Social and Family Affairs (DSFA) is also engaged in developing a data strategy. "The revision of the National Anti-Poverty Strategy underlined the need for timely, accurate and relevant statistical data to support policy development." (DFSA, 2003:49) To this end, a Technical Advisory Group has been formed, and is engaged with the development process. While the DFSA plans for a data strategy have grown out of the specific need to monitor progress in relation to anti-poverty targets, "... all (Government) Departments are to produce formal data strategies." (DFSA, 2003:49) Within the DES, the development of the Primary Pupil Database indicates "... the possibility of creating links with databases of other Government agencies ..." (Educational Disadvantage Committee, 2003:3). Evidence presented by the Educational Disadvantage Committee establishes a medium to long term time frame for such links to evolve, but such moves indicate the importance now accorded to the maintenance of dependable data.

It is clear that important national agencies have identified solid, comprehensive empirical data as the bedrock for addressing pressing national problems such as poverty, disadvantage and inequality. On Target? cuts across all three of these areas, and it was in this context that such an audit was identified as one of the first actions of the CECDE. "There is now little challenge to the idea that good policy requires good information, and that good information can and has influenced and informed policy and provision." (Corrigan *et al.*, 2002:4) Kellaghan (2002:25) is less positive in his assessment of the situation here in Ireland in relation to interventions in educational disadvantage; "The important role that research findings and reflection on the experience of interventions have to play does not always seem to be fully recognised when a rationale for action or the nature of interventions is being determined." This situation raises questions about the availability of structures within which connections can be made between research evidence, policy making and practice here in Ireland.

Forms of evidence

The constituent elements of evidence are wide, varied and subject to much debate (Davies and Nutley, 2002). Equally, there are many conflicting demands in the policy making process (Leeuw, 1991). While the CECDE is clear on its commitment to evidence-based policy development, evidence must be tempered by other considerations, including, for example, individual rights and values and cultural considerations.

It would be disingenuous not to recognise that policy makers derive evidence from many sources (Sanderson. 2002:5). The complexity of the social systems served by policy makers is inevitably mirrored by the complexity of proposed solutions; "... (W)e should perceive the interaction of various interest groups, who have access to policy makers as a necessary process in rapidly changing, turbulent environments." (Wilson, 1999:9) Certainly, as 'On Target?' has shown in its profile of provision, the ECCE sector in Ireland – a social system – is heterogeneous , has a complex history of development, and consequently a broad range of stakeholders. The interaction of all stakeholders is viewed as crucial by the CECDE, and for this reason the CECDE engaged in a consultation process with the ECCE sector to further the development of the National Framework for Quality (NFQ) (CECDE, 2004a). The other sources of evidence supporting the development of the NFQ are a review of international and national quality standards, and of the implications for quality of how the child learns and develops.

Research evidence

Research evidence is of critical importance to the policy development process, a position for which there is support in the literature. There is certainly evidence that "(r)esearch on children and families has the potential to contribute to the policy process at every step of the way – through theory building, agenda setting, and informing policymaking, as well as policy and program development, implementation and evaluation." (Susman-Stillman *et al.*, 1996:2) This would seem to be corroborated by Weiss (1999:195) who notes that;

> ... in-house research within the Education Department of Tasmania concluded that what research did was to:
> a) Develop shared understanding among policy-makers as a foundation for policy-work;
> b) Refine policy-makers' working knowledge of the issues; and
> c) create a climate of expectation for policy development or implementation.

If we take the example of *Ready to Learn*, the White Paper on Early Childhood Education (DES, 1999), the influence of research evidence on the policy position outlined there is clear. Research evidence is cited on, for example, enhancing dispositions and readiness to learn (DES, 1999:8), returns to the individual on investment in early education (DES, 1999:9) and the importance of early childhood interventions being of high quality (DES, 1999:11). The literature cites many other examples of the effectiveness of research evidence in effecting policy change (Bullock et al, 1998; Wilson, 1999; Coe, Fitz-Gibbons and Tymms, 2000), but none of these examples relates to the Irish context.

While "(r)esearch can influence policy, ... it is not an easy or a direct line from study results to policy use." (Kirst, 2000:389) There are documented examples of instances when research evidence did not make any discernible impact on relevant policy developments (Leeuw, 1991; Sanderson, 2002), and, indeed, research evidence is not always welcome to those envisaged as end users (Bullock *et al.*, 1998; Kirst, 2000; Helmsely-Brown and Sharp, 2002;). A knowledge of the conditions pertaining to the Irish context in which research evidence both did and did not have an impact would be helpful in understanding the dynamics of policy development here.

Relevance and dissemination

The CECDE is fully cognisant of the complicated, "... dynamic and unpredictable nature of policy influence" (International Development Research Centre (IDRC), 2002:v), but this does not mitigate our view of the critical importance of research evidence. One of the functions of the CECDE is providing policy advice to the Minister for Education and Science. Ensuring the relevance of research to that function has been a key concern in the development of the CECDE Research Strategy (CECDE, 2003b). Davies and Nutley (2002:3) have identified "(f)our requirements for improving evidence use in policy and practice." The second of those requirements is "(a) strategic approach to the creation of evidence, together with the development of a cumulative knowledge base." (Davies and Nutley, 2002:3) This strategic approach is characteristic of the CECDE Research Strategy (2003b:1) which refers to the "... the integral role that research plays in the realisation of this purpose."

If relevance of research activity is fundamental to its function as a basis for policy development, "... the key questions for research development continue to be about the effectiveness of dissemination strategies." (Bullock *et al.*, 1998:8) The complexities of the dissemination discussion are well worth airing, but such a consideration is outside the parameters of this paper. Briefly, though, there appears to be some consensus in the literature around 'policy diffusion' (Davies and Nutley, 2002). Pinkerton (1998:31) has described a model which "... demonstrates impact as depending on the forging and sustaining of social alliances within the context of a dynamic system." Davies and Nutley (2002:9) have commented that "... multiple channels of communication – horizontal as well as vertical; networks as well as hierarchies – may need to be developed ...". Sanderson (2002:8) refers to "(n)etworking (or 'relational interaction)" , and Kirst (2000:385) notes that " ... the primacy of personal contact emerges as a major aspect of successful research dissemination." The CECDE is well placed in this model of research diffusion, as the Programme of Work (CECDE, 2001:2) states that " ... consultation and/or networking are seen as a prominent part of almost all of the Centre's work." The inaugural CECDE International Conference – Questions of Quality; Defining, Assessing, and Supporting Quality in Early Childhood Care and Education – demonstrates the commitment of the CECDE to the dissemination and promotion of research evidence as a support to the development of the ECCE sector in Ireland.

Provision, practice and partnership
On the evidence of 'On Target?', ECCE provision in Ireland is very diverse,

encompassing many types of provision for young children. In particular educational provision for children with special needs is even more diverse. While this diversity is a great strength, it poses great difficulties for those charged with co-ordinating service provision and developing common quality standards. Sanderson (2002) has commented on the importance of all key stakeholders involved in development work improving their understanding of the issue at hand, and of the possible policy options available. 'On Target?' provides an evidential basis for common understandings between the CECDE, policy makers and service providers in the key areas of disadvantage and special needs.

All work undertaken by the CECDE supports the development of the NFQ which will be held in common by all involved in provision of ECCE services. Quality provision is of special significance to children experiencing or at risk of disadvantage and children with special needs. "The benefits of (quality early childhood education) may accrue to all children, but as in the case of children with special needs, research shows that they are particularly significant for disadvantaged children." (DES, 1999:97) 'On Target?' was, therefore, not an isolated exercise but one of the initial steps towards a cohesive process of development and co-ordination of ECCE in Ireland.

All developments must be based on the principle of partnership. "It is through open partnerships that span the creation, validation and incorporation of research evidence that we are likely to see more effective use of such evidence for the betterment of public services." (Davies and Nutley, 2002:12) 'On Target?' is not viewed as a project independent of service providers, but one which draws its data from the sector itself, and which will in turn support partnership between the CECDE and stakeholders. Nor is the commitment to partnership based only on the principles of mutual respect and recognition of expertise, but on the belief that partnership provides the most effective way to ensure successful outcomes. "...(E)xamples of successful development of policy from suggestive evidence, policy that is then seen through to practice change and beneficial outcomes, often display an unusual degree of partnership working." (Davies and Nutley, 2002:7)

Findings and recommendations

'On Target?' represented the first attempt to assemble information on targeted interventions in Ireland, and brings together information on the Infant classes in schools in the same context as all other out-of-home settings. This was an important aspect of the project, as such information spans one of the most important transitions of a child's life – that from the pre-school setting, be it at home or out-of-home, to the primary school. This also represents a shift in viewpoint away from defining early years in terms of pre-school and in-school, to an identification of early years as birth to six years, whatever the setting. 'On Target?' did not attempt to map childminder provision as it did not prove possible to identify childminders who target children experiencing disadvantage or with special needs.

Main finding

In order to gather the data from that broad range of providers, possible sources of information were conceptualised on a continuum;

▸ national structures or bodies with a national profile of involvement;
▸ intermediary structures, or those with regional involvement;
▸ local structures or groups;
▸ individual providers.

Agencies and groups which fitted this profile were contacted with requests for information on services. Following the final date for return of information requested by the CECDE, the level of response from each county was assessed. As well as the criteria developed for the inclusion of each individual service[2], criteria were also developed to determine the point at which adequate information had been received for each individual county. Information came in a variety of forms, and in many cases, such information was only available as a result of individual effort.

▸ The primary and key finding of 'On Target?' is that accurate information on the range and nature of early childhood care and education services targeting disadvantage is extremely difficult to access. The situation regarding information on services targeting special needs is even more marked. A major contributing factor is that data on targeted services is not generally disaggregated within universal datasets.

The valuable baseline data collected during this audit, while not comprehensive enough to yield a definitive picture of targeted service provision in Ireland, is a first step in developing a model for a national information bank for the ECCE sector.

Therefore, a number of general observations can be made regarding service provision:

▶ Sessional services dominate.
▶ Services targeting children in the birth to 2 age cohort (*e.g.* full day care and parent and toddler groups) are very limited.
▶ Similarly services targeting children in the 4-6 age cohort outside school hours are very limited.
▶ Services are more concentrated in urban centres.

These observations correspond with the findings of previous research (DJELR, 1998; 1999; Area Development Management (ADM), 2003) that has been conducted on general provision of early childhood services. This indicates that these issues continue to be challenges for the development, co-ordination and enhancement of targeted services for children aged birth to six years.

Criteria for interventions

On the evidence of this audit there is no nationally understood protocol or set of criteria in the context of targeted services for children. Criteria are developed anew for each initiative and relate to eligibility for funding rather than to the children. Criteria for targeted interventions should include a rationale for intervention. Also included should be a clear objective in terms of child outcomes. The criteria should incorporate the principles of the UN Convention on the Rights of the Child (UN, 1989) and of the National Children's Strategy (Department of Health and Children (DHC), 2000) in order to ensure that interventions involving children uphold their rights, rather than using children's lives as sites of intervention for the benefit of others.

▶ The CECDE recommends co-operation between the relevant Government Departments to develop a national protocol for targeted interventions, incorporating agreed indicators, criteria and child-centred objectives. This protocol will be suitable for use in all contexts in which targeted interventions with children take place, and will lead to effective co-ordination of initiatives originating in the Government Departments involved.

Data strategy

The process of information gathering for 'On Target?' demonstrated a broad range of capacity within the sector to deliver information. Up to this point, lack of baseline data has been an inhibitor in terms of policy development and co-ordination of services, both at national and regional level. Additionally, such information as has been gathered for various administrative purposes has reinforced the dichotomy between care and education reflecting the structural divisions which exist in this regard. There is now an awareness nationally of the importance of relevant, comprehensive information to progress in any area, and of the significance of a carefully considered, widely applicable data strategy to support the collection of such material. Data collection, as modelled in this audit, can further support efforts to move away from what is now recognised as the artificial divide between care and education.

▸ The CECDE recommends that the relevant Government Departments, in consultation with key stakeholders, develop a national data strategy for the ECCE sector. The goals of any such strategy must be clearly articulated. The strategy will support a national data collection system, which will provide reliable information on existing provision to facilitate planning, policy development, and the optimal allocation of resources.

Special needs

Identification of services for children with special needs proved especially difficult. It would appear that there is considerable regional variation in service provision. Currently, negotiating the system is difficult and challenging for parents who encounter it for the first time seeking to access services for their children. Both parents and children are dependent on local capacity in terms of service provision. Pressure on services is acute, and it is unlikely that there is further capacity available at service level to engage in the planning and integration that future development will require.

▸ The CECDE recommends a national strategy to afford equity of access to,
▸ Information;
▸ Identification;
▸ Service provision;
▸ Ongoing support;
   for all children with special needs. Such a strategy will require the co-ordinated

efforts of all Government Departments, Health Boards, Voluntary Agencies, parent groups and the National Council for Special Education.

Provision between birth and three years

'On Target?' has revealed that within the context of targeted services, there is also a big discrepancy between the number of full day and sessional services. In addition, the distribution of these services is concentrated in urban locations. Sessional services tend to accept children from two and a half to three years of age onwards, which, combined with minimal numbers of parent and toddler groups and home visitation schemes, suggests that children aged birth to three are poorly served by targeted interventions. This finding is of concern given the body of research that exists in support of the critical importance of early intervention in the first three years of life in tackling disadvantage and social exclusion. (Hart and Risley, 1995; Shonkoff and Phillips, 2000). It is the view of the CECDE that focused attention must be given to deepening our understanding of the role of targeted interventions with children aged birth to three years in Ireland.

▸ The CECDE recommends that research be undertaken and disseminated by the Early Childhood Education Agency[3] on the following issues affecting provision for children in the birth to three age group at risk of disadvantage:

▸ Suitable indicators for identifying disadvantage among this age group;

▸ Criteria for interventions;

▸ Models of intervention.

Transition

It has been recognised for some time that the ECCE sector in Ireland would benefit from co-ordination and development, hence the CECDE's brief to " "develop and co-ordinate early childhood education ... and to advise the Department of Education and Science ... on policy issues in this area"" (CECDE, 2001:2) One aspect of that co-ordination in terms of targeted interventions is continuity of services at key transition points in a child's life, notably from pre-school settings (in-home or out-of-home) to school.

> Discrepancies between the most important contexts of development and learning, and early frequent interruptions may render the developmental and learning processes less effective. (Leseman, 2002:40)

The lack of communication between school-based providers and, in particular, community providers means that many children in disadvantaged areas, or other situations of disadvantage, are making the transition into school from community or other playgroups with no communication between the school and the provider. Given the lessons outlined by Leseman (2002), we can assume that these discontinuities are not conducive to effective interventions. It is particularly important that intervention conditions be continuous, as the experience of Rutland St. has shown (Kellaghan, 1977), to ensure that early gains are not lost on entry to the Primary school.

▸ The CECDE recommends that research be undertaken to identify, evaluate and disseminate effective models supporting co-ordiation and continuity of provision for children experiencing disadvantage and with special needs. Such models must protect and enhance any gains from early intervention.

Inter-face of disadvantage and special needs

'On Target?' dealt with special needs and disadvantage separately to ensure clarity. However, it would not be accurate to give the impression that as categories they are mutually exclusive. Reference is made, for example, to evidence of a higher incidence of Mild General Learning Disability (MGLD) among children experiencing disadvantage. There is also concern for children with MGLD for whom environmental factors, arising from social disadvantage, are contributing factors to the disability. Neither is there any reason that a child with any other type of disability cannot also be experiencing disadvantage. What is of concern is not that such an intersection exists, but how children in such circumstances are served by the system of intervention.

▸ The CECDE recommends that flexible inter-departmental and inter-agency structures be developed to meet the needs of those children who experience both disadvantage and special needs.

Conclusion

'On Target?' sought to place its main finding in the wider context of the relationship between evidence, policy and practice. However, there is no evidence here in Ireland of a debate on the inter-connected relationship between these three elements which interact to drive and underpin development. There does not appear to be an ongoing discussion here on how, or even if, research evidence impacts on policy and practice, particularly in relation to education. The audit of research conducted by the CECDE (CECDE, 2003a) demonstrated the amount of work which has been carried out here on ECCE. Yet the community of interest made up of researchers, policy makers and practitioners have no context within which to debate how, for example, research is made available to policy makers; how policy can draw upon the wealth of research evidence available; or indeed, how practice relates to what research tells us about what works for specific children in specific circumstances. Such questions are being addressed in the international context, but these debates are of limited value here. ECCE in Ireland has its own particular history and, more importantly, its own particular future, and needs its own particular debate.

While the connection between provision and policy make seem tenuous and remote at times, especially in Ireland where provision of services for young children has developed in the absence of national policy, we should not lose sight of the importance of good policy in supporting best practice. For good policy, we need good information, and for that we need good data. 'On Target?' has identified areas of ECCE about which we know little, a position which makes it difficult to determine how to proceed. It has also, however, identified the kind of information which is necessary, and how it might be collected.

1   The key findings will be addressed in more detail in the section entitled "Findings and Recommendations"
2   The criteria developed for the inclusion of each service is outlined in the section entitled "Rationale"
3   The CECDE was established to prepare the groundwork for the Early Childhood Education Agency (ECEA). The functions of the ECEA are described in Ready to Learn, the White paper on Early Childhood Education (DES, 1999;133)

Bibliography

Area Development Management (ADM) (2003). *National Childcare Census Baseline Data 1999 – 2000.* Dublin: Area Development Management.

Barry, U. (2000). *Building the Picture: The Role of Data in Achieving Equality.* Dublin: Equality Authority.

Bullock, R., Gooch, D., Little, M., & Mount, K. (1998) *Research in Practice;*

Experiments in Development and Information Design. Aldershot: Dartington Social Research Unit/Ashgate.

Cantillon, S., Corrigan, C., Kirby, P., and O'Flynn, J. (Eds.) (2001). *Rich and Poor; Perspectives on Tackling Inequality in Ireland*. Dublin: Oak Tree Press/Combat Poverty Agency.

Centre for Early Childhood Development and Education (2001). *Programme of Work*. Dublin: Centre for Early Childhood Development and Education.

Centre for Early Childhood Development and Education (2003a). *Audit of Research on Early Childhood Care and Education in Ireland 1990-2003*. Dublin: Centre for Early Childhood Development and Education.

Centre for Early Childhood Development and Education (2003b). *Research Strategy; A work in Progress*. Dublin: Centre for Early Childhood Development and Education.

Centre for Early Childhood Development and Education (2004a). *On Target? An Audit of Provision of Services Targeting Disadvantage and Special Needs among Children from birth to six years in Ireland*. Dublin: Centre for Early Childhood Development and Education.

Centre for Early Childhood Development and Education (2004b). *Talking About Quality: Report of a Consultation Process on Quality in Early Childhood Care and Education*. Executive Summary. Dublin: Centre for Early Childhood Development and Education.

Coe, R., Fitz-Gibbon, C., and Tymms, P. (2000). *Promoting Evidence-based Education; The Role of Practitioners*. Paper presented at the British Educational Research Association Conference, Cardiff University, September 2000. Published on the web at: http://www.cem.dur.ac.uk./ebeuk (Accessed August 2003)

Corrigan, C. (Ed.), Fitzgerald, E., Bates, J. and Matthews, A. (2002). *Data Sources on Poverty*. Dublin: Institute of Public Administration/ Combat Poverty Agency.

Davies H. and Nutley S. (2002). *Evidence-based Policy and Practice: Moving from Rhetoric to Reality*, Discussion Paper 2, Research Unit for Research Utilisation, University of St Andrews. Published on the web at: http://www.st-andrews.ac.uk/~ruru/publications.htm (Accessed September 2003)

Department of Education and Science (1999). *Ready to Learn – A White Paper on Early Childhood Education*. Dublin: The Stationery Office.

Department of Health and Children (2000). *The National Children's Strategy. Our Children-Their Lives*. Dublin: The Stationery Office.

Department of Justice, Equality and Law Reform (1998). *Study of the Economics of Childcare in Ireland.* Dublin: The Stationery Office.

Department of Justice, Equality and Law Reform (1999). *National Childcare Strategy, Report of the Partnership 2000 Expert Working Group on Childcare.* Dublin: The Stationery Office.

Department of Social and Family Affairs. (2003) *National Action Plan against Poverty and Social Exclusion.* Dublin: The Stationery Office.

Educational Disadvantage Committee (2003). *Identifying Disadvantage for the Purpose of Targeting Resources and Other Supports.* Submission to the Minister for Education and Science. Published on the web at: http://www.education.ie/servlet/blobservlet/edf_archer.doc (Accessed July 2003)

Hart, B. and Risely, T.. (1995). *Meaningful Differences in the Everyday Experience of Young American Children.* Baltimore: Paul H. Brookes Publishing Co.

Hayes, N. (2002). *Children's Rights – Whose Right? A Review of Child Policy Development in Ireland. Studies in Public Policy 9.* Dublin: The Policy Institute at Trinity College Dublin.

Health Research Board. (2003). *National Intellectual Disability Database Information Manual.* Dublin: Health Research Board.

Helmsley-Brown, J. and Sharp, C. (2002). T*he Utilisation of Research by Practitioners in Education; Has Medicine got it Cracked?* Paper presented at the Annual Conference of the British Educational Research Association, University of Exeter, September 2002. Published at: http://www.nfer.ac.uk/research/papers/BERA02JHB.doc (Accessed July 2003)

International Development Research Centre (IDRC) (2002) *Strategic Evaluation of Policy Influence: What Evaluation Reports tell us about Public Policy Influence by IDRC-Supported Research.* Abra Adamo; IDRC. Published on the web at http://web.idrc.ca/uploads/user-S/10359910880strategic.pdf (Accessed July 2003)

Iwaniec, D.and Pinkerton, J. (Eds.) (1998). *Making Research Work; Promoting Child Care Policy and Practice.* Chichester: John Wiley & Sons.

Kellaghan, T. (1977). *The Evaluation of an Intervention Programme for Disadvantaged Children.* Windsor: NFER.

Kellaghan, T. (1989) The Interface of Research, Evaluation, and Policy in Irish Education (in) Mulcahy, D. and O'Sullivan, D. (Eds). *Irish Educational*

Policy; Process and Substance. Dublin: Institute of Public Administration, pp. 191-218.

Kellaghan, T. (2002). Approaches to Problems of Educational Disadvantage, (in) Zappone, K. and Haran, N. (Eds.) (2002). *Primary Education: Ending Disadvantage.* Proceedings and Action Plan of National Forum. Dublin: Education Disadvantage Centre, pp. 17-30.

Kirst, M. (2000). Bridging Education Research and Education Policymaking. *Oxford Review of Education,* Volume 26, Nos. 3&4, pp. 379-391.

Leeuw, F. (1991). Policy Theories, Knowledge Utilization and Evaluation. Knowledge and Policy: *The International Journal of Knowledge Transfer.* Fall 1991, Volume 4, No.3, pp 73-91.

Leseman, P. (2002). *Early Childhood Education and Care for Children from Low-Income or Minority Backgrounds.* Paris: OECD.

McGough, A. (2001). Educational Provision for Preschool Children: A Response to the White Paper. *Reach,* Volume 15, pp. 2-13.

Pinkerton, J. (1998). The Impact of Research on Policy and Practice: A Systemic Perspective (in) Iwaniec, D. and Pinkerton, J. (Eds.) (1998). *Making Research Work; Promoting Child Care Policy and Practice.* Chichester: John Wiley & Sons, pp. 25 – 45.

Sanderson, I. (2002). *Evaluation, Policy Learning and Evidence-based Policy Making. Public Administration,* Volume 80, No. 1, pp. 1-22.

Sebba, J. (1999) *Developing Evidence-informed Policy and Practice in Education.* Paper presented at the British Educational Research Association Conference, University of Sussex, September, 1999. Published on the web at: http://www.leeds.ac.uk/educol/documents/000001097.doc (Accessed July 2003)

Shonkoff, J. and Phillips, D. (Eds.) (2000). *From Neurons to Neighbourhoods; The Science of Early Childhood Development.* Washington, D.C.: National Academy Press.

Susman-Stillman, A., Brown, J., Adam, E., Blair, C., Gaines, R., Gordon, R., White, A. and Wyn, S. (1996). Building Research and Policy Connections: Training and Career Options for Developmental Scientists. *Social Policy Report,* Volume X, No. 4, pp. 1-19.

United Nations (1989). *United Nations Convention on the Rights of the Child, Adopted by the United Nations General Assembly, 20th November 1989.* (Ratified by Ireland, September 1992) Geneva: United Nations.

Weiss, C. (1999). Research-Policy Linkages: How much Influence does Social

Science Research have? (in) Kazancigil, A. and Makinson, D. (Eds.) (1999). *World Social Science Report.* Paris. UNESCO/Elsevier, pp. 194-199.

Wilson, V. (1999). *Linking Research to Policy: The Pre-School Agenda.* Paper presented at the Scottish Educational Research Association Annual Conference, University of Dundee, September 1999. Published on the web at: http://www.leeds.ac.uk/educol/documents/00001231.doc (Accessed July 2003).

They don't Speak English:
Young Children Learning English as an Additional Language in Early Years Settings

Máire Mhic Mhathúna

Introduction

This paper sets out to examine the needs of young newcomer children learning English as an additional language in Early Years settings in Ireland. The particular needs of these children can be categorised as being both social and linguistic and are in addition to the broader needs of all pre-school children. The main countries of origin will be given, according to available information, and the different language backgrounds that the children may bring with them will be described. The role of the Early educator in supporting children and their parents through the process of second language acquisition will be discussed and the value of the European Language Portfolio will be critically examined.

Who are the newcomer children who don't speak English?

It is assumed that the children who do not speak English are, in the main, recent arrivals in Ireland or that their parents are recent arrivals. Figures for children coming into Ireland are not compiled as a distinct category, and one must extrapolate from figures for adults to gain some indication of the trend in countries of origin. Newcomer adults include Work Permit Holders, Refugees and Asylum Seekers and recent arrivals from other countries who have established residency in Ireland on other grounds. The countries of origin for work permit holders and asylum seekers are given below.

Work Permits issued in 2003	
New Permits:	21,965
Renewals:	25,039
Group:	547
Total:	47,551

Main countries of origin 2003	
Poland:	4,808
Lithuania:	4,551
Latvia:	4,160
Philippines:	4,042
Ukraine:	2,866

It can be seen from these figures (www.entemp.ie) that the main countries of origin in 2003, the latest available figures, were Eastern European countries and the Philippines.

Applications from Asylum Seekers	
2001:	10,325
2002:	11,634
2003:	7,900

Positive recommendations	
2001:	458
2002:	893
2003:	345
(not all processing completed)	

Main Countries of Origin of Asylum Seekers in 2003			
Nigeria:	3,110 (39.4%)	Moldova:	243 (3.1%)
Romania:	777 (9.8%)	Czech Rep.	186 (2.4%)
DR Congo:	256 (3.2%)	Other:	3,328 (42.1%)

Positive recommendations for residency were made in a relatively small number of cases in each of the above years (www.orac.ie) and Nigeria was by far the largest country of origin, with Romania in second place. In spite of the impression given in the media, the numbers of asylum seekers and especially of those granted asylum, is small in comparison to the number of work permit holders. It is impossible to say how many of the newcomer adults have children attending pre-school services, but anecdotal accounts suggest that increasing numbers of children from Eastern Europe and from Nigeria are attending services around the country. With the entry of the ten new accession countries into the enlarged European Union on May 1, 2004, (Cyprus, Czech Republic, Estonia, Hungary, Latvia, Lithuania, Malta, Poland Slovenia and Slovakia), it can be expected that children from these countries may also come to Ireland.

The Needs of Newcomer Children
In addition to the broader needs of all pre-school children, particular social and linguistic needs of newcomer children can be identified. In the first instance, the newcomer children must be regarded as individuals and not as part of a homogeneous group of "foreigners" or "Africans." There are, for example, wide differences in language and culture among the various

groups in Nigeria and individual and ethnic differences must be respected. (Baker & Jones, 1998: 364,365).

Social Needs
The emphasis on respecting children as individuals is related to their need to build an identity which helps them integrate with the host community but which resists assimilation or eradication of their cultural and linguistic richness vis à vis the dominant culture (Handscombe 1994:336). Cultural messages about an individual's value to society can facilitate the development of either a positive or negative self-concept. The literature on racism and indeed recent Irish experience shows that children are never too young to learn negative attitudes and behaviours (Giddens, 2001:251, Murray & Doherty 2001:17). Fortunately, they are never too young to develop positive attitudes and behaviours as well, either based on first hand experience or connections made by understanding adults (Derman-Sparks, 1989:4,5). Some children may have witnessed traumatic events or experienced hardship and need ongoing support in dealing with these matters (Rutter & Hyder 1998:10).

Newcomer children come to early years services in Ireland with distinctive identities and ways of interpreting the social world that have been shaped in important ways by their particular linguistic and cultural experiences (Pease-Alvarez and Vasquez 1994:83). These identities are essential to their sense of well-being and have a profound effect on the way they negotiate new social situations, such as the task of interacting verbally and non-verbally with both adults and other children. This desire to make contact with other children and to interact and play with them will be a large part of their motivation to learn English as an additional language.

Language Needs
As adults we tend to think of language skills as vocabulary, grammar and syntax but a child would probably prioritize language skills in a much more pragmatic way, *i.e.* how to stop other children taking their toys, how to become included in games, how to complain to an adult if they are victimized. In summary, they need to learn how to express and assert themselves in a second language with adults and children. Indeed many early educators report that the first English words that many newcomer children speak are "No, Stop and Gimme." Tabors (1997: 63) gives examples of the same process in the study she carried out of

young children learning English as an additional language in the U.S. The need for self-protection and self-promotion has to be taken into consideration when planning a language programme in a formal or informal way. The child's linguistic background must also to be taken into consideration.

The children may speak or have some understanding of

▸ Home language only, *e.g.* Polish.
▸ Home language plus one or two other languages, *e.g.* Russian.
▸ Home language plus English. This may be a dialect of World English with which we are not familiar, *e.g.* Anglo-Nigerian (Mann 1996).
▸ English only.

What is important is to realise that a child who does not speak English, will usually have developed age-appropriate competency in their home language and is therefore learning English as an additional language. They know how to communicate through their first language, they know the structure and vocabulary of the home language and the communication strategies of their own cultural community. What they need to learn is the fact that others may not understand their first language and that they need to acquire the vocabulary, grammar and ways of communicating of the host community, *i.e.* appropriate ways of communicating with other children and with adults. Language learning will be easier if the child deals with familiar or concrete concepts at first, but soon they will be required to learn new concepts through their second language, a much more challenging task.

Home Language

What is also of great importance is the language(s) that their parents speak or are sufficiently proficient in to express their deepest feelings, thoughts and emotions. The American and British experience has been that children generally lose their competence in their native tongue if it is not actively maintained and developed. It is particularly tragic if the children turn to English, when their parents only develop basic competency in this language. According to Wong-Fillmore (1991:343)

What is lost is no less than the means by which parents socialize their children. When parents are unable to talk to their children, they cannot easily convey to them their values, beliefs, understandings or wisdom about how to cope with their experiences... Families lose the intimacy that comes form shared beliefs and understandings.

What is also lost is the ability for children to talk to their grandparents and other members of their family who have remained in the home country. The implications for family cohesion and family ties are serious, as well as the individual's sense of family and group identity.

Some well-meaning professionals advise parents to stop speaking their native language to their children and to turn to English only, in the mistaken belief that the human mind can cope with only one language at a time. Extensive research since the 1960s has shown that this is not the case and that indeed bilingualism, rather than monolingualism, is the world norm, (McCluskey 2001:9) Research has also shown that children can benefit from opportunities for complex thought in their first language while their second language develops and that they can continue with both languages, without damaging their cognitive or linguistic competencies (Baker 2000: 14).

The Role of the Early Educator

Attitude of adults working with children

The attitude of adults working with newcomer children is all important as it will affect their interaction with the newcomer and established children in all aspects of their work. They must genuinely welcome the diversity offered by the newcomer children. The emphasis should be placed on communicating with the children and on trying to meet their needs. Multilingual and intercultural approaches show the value of diversity in fostering positive relationships and in providing a rich variety of learning experiences for all children. The intercultural approach recognises the totality of people's lives and does not reduce it to the visible dimensions of dress, food and holidays (Derman-Sparks, 1989:7). Anti-bias approaches such as the Éist project (Murray & O'Doherty 2001) extends this respect for the culture and rights of others to finding ways of combating incipient racism or any feeling of superiority because of skin colour. Partial or incomplete presentation of the diversity of culture within the host country is misleading and excludes newcomer children from full participation in the culture of their peers.

Background information on child

In order to work best with the child and the family staff need to find out background information about the child and his abilities, needs and practical details. A very good example is given in Galway City and Country ChildCare Committee's multilingual and bilingual information pack: *Caring Together* (2004). This pack is available in 8 languages, Arabic, French, Igbo, Lingala, Romanian, Russian, Spanish and Yoruba as well as Irish and English. The pack contains information on the types of services available in Galway, a contact list of family agencies and a sample bilingual registration form. This means that many newcomer families now have material that they can read in their own language, they can make more informed choices and can contribute more information about their child to the service.

Adult's Use of Language

Early educators need a knowledge of the process of Second Language Acquisition (Ellis 1994: 251, Siraj-Blatchford, 2000:62) and how to modify their own language by using

- ▸ Gestures, objects and the immediate context
- ▸ Short, simple sentences.
- ▸ Repetition and paraphrase
- ▸ Establishing routines in Early Years setting to help the child predict action and talk
- ▸ Expanding and extending the child's talk.
- ▸ Giving the child the opportunity to talk.
- ▸ Having high but realistic expectations.
- ▸ Progressively providing more complex language opportunities

Activities

Opportunities for language acquisition can best be facilitated in small group activities, such as playdough, water play and board games. The other English-speaking children should also be involved. The adult should explain to them that the newcomer child speaks another language at home and is now learning English as well. She/he should ask them to include the new child in their games and to speak to them slightly more slowly and simply than they do to their other friends. Multicultural and multilingual stories and songs should be included in the repertoire for all children and have particular advantages for a minority language child. All the parents, *i.e.* the parents of the new and established children, could be invited to contribute their favourite children's songs. This would facilitate the contribution and integration of the parents as a group, while at the same time avoiding singling out the newcomer parent as an exotic exhibit or on the other hand, ignoring the majority culture. As singing is a group activity, it has the added advantage of putting less pressure on the child as he/she can be involved as he/she wishes. Through songs, children build up a store of knowledge about language, even if it is not immediately used productively. Other routines such as Lunch-time offer language-rich opportunities for extended conversation in a more relaxed and informal way, about food, a subject that is of great interest to the children. The materials and resources in the room, *e.g.* posters, jigsaws, games, toys and books, should reflect the culture and background of all the children and lists of suitable books and other resources are provided by Murray and O'Doherty 2001 and Coghlan *et al.* 2002. In this way, the uniqueness of each individual child and their family is recognized, without highlighting the differences between them.

European Language Portfolio

Another extremely useful tool for guiding early years professional in their language development work is the European Language Portfolio. This is based on the Common European Framework or benchmarks for assessment in second language proficiency (Council of Europe 2000) and consists of a series of global descriptors for six levels of proficiency in understanding, speaking, reading and writing a second language. The primary version for Ireland then links these with the revised Primary Curriculum. It is available from Integrate Ireland Language and Training.(IILT, 2001) (www.iilt.ie) The Pre-primary version is currently being piloted and should be available from the same website in 2005.

The European Language Portfolio for primary children includes:

▸ A Language Passport: a record of proficiency in the languages known
▸ A Language Biography: a record of progress in language learning
▸ A Dossier: portfolio of samples of work carried out.

This allows the child to gain credit for the totality of his/her language skills, to see how progress is being made and what needs to be done in the future. The descriptors show the level of detail that can be expected at each stage and map out the way forward. It also means that a child can take the portfolio with him/her if they change teacher or school.

The framework covers a range of language functions for all ages and as such, needs to be extensively adapted for younger children to meet their needs and to be culturally appropriate. The primary version for Ireland covers the formal curriculum in a very clear and logical way, but does not appear to take the interactive nature of child-child language into account. It handles the domain of adult-child language well but the less formal but equally important domain of child-child language is not featured in the type of descriptors documented. One hopes that the functions of self-protection and negotiation will be included in the pre-primary version and that it will offer clear links to the type of concrete experiences and context-embedded language that young children experience in pre-schools as reported by early educators in Ireland and as documented by Tabors in the American context (1997:102). It is to be hoped that the pre-primary version will be activity and interaction based and will link in with the language aims of the proposed Framework for Early Learning from the National Council for Curriculum and Assessment (NCCA) 2004.

Contact with parents
Parents too are individuals. There may well be differences between those from the same country, and their values and beliefs must be respected. Some parents may already know English; some may be learning it for the first time and may find it difficult to understand exactly what is being said. Some parents may be familiar with other scripts, *e.g.* Cyrillic or Arabic scripts. Following the example from Galway, it may be possible to provide some written information in the family's language, that they can read at ease.

Current linguistic research strongly advocates maintaining the home language, as it will be the more developed language that the child knows in the early stages of second language acquisition. This will allow for greater cognitive complexity and development in that language as well as being the language of the family, of the parent-child relationship and of contact with other family members, such as grandparents in the home country. However, we must respect the parents' decision in relation to their language choice. Families from other cultures and countries, *e.g.* Eastern Europe, may have different experiences and expectations about Early Years services. It is essential to try to establish what their expectations are and to explain what the Irish approach is. It is important to plan how newcomer children and their families will be welcomed into the Early Years setting and how contact with the family will be maintained.

Conclusion

Based on the figures for Work Permit holders and Asylum Seekers, it would appear that in the short and medium term, most newcomer children will probably come from Eastern European countries such as Poland, Lithuania and Latvia, the Philippines and Nigeria and perhaps from the new accession countries in the European Union.

The particular social and linguistic needs of these children include the need to form a positive identity in terms of their country of origin, to integrate, but not to become totally assimilated into their host country and to learn how to interact verbally and non-verbally with their peers and adults.

Early educators need to realise that English may be an additional language for these children and to actively include and take account of their proficiency in their mother tongue, as well as helping the children develop competency in English. We are slowly building up a repertoire of experience in this field. We can also gain help from developments such as the Éist project, the European Language Portfolio and the multilingual material published by Galway City and County Childcare Committee. The experience of the naíonra movement in working for the most part, through Irish as a second language, also offers guidance and a bank of experience to draw on, allowing for the similarities and differences in the respective contexts.

We are now at the beginning of normalizing the needs of newcomer children by including modules on their needs in some training courses for early educators, such as the Éist project and the module on Bilingual Children in DIT. This is only the beginning of a process that should be informed by the views of practitioners, the views of the parents and children involved and the gathering and distillation of Irish data on the experience of young children learning English as a second language in Early Years settings.

Bibliography

Baker, C. (2000) *The Care and Education of Young Bilinguals: An Introduction for Professionals.* Clevedon, Avon. Multilingual Matters.

Baker, C. & Jones, S.P. (1998) *The Encyclopedia of Bilingualism and Bilingual Education.* Clevedon, Avon. Multilingual Matters.

Coghlan, Susanna *et al.* (2001) *Changing Faces: a guide to multicultural books for children.* Dublin, IBBY Ireland.

Council of Europe (2000) *Common European Framework of Reference for Languages.* Strasbourg: Council of Europe.

Derman-Sparks, Louise, (1989) *Anti-bias Curriculum Tools for Empowering Young Children.* Washington: National Association for the Education of Young Children.

Ellis, R. (1994) *The Study of Second Language Acquisition.* Oxford: Oxford University Press.

Galway City and County Childcare Committee. (2004) *Caring Together. Multilingual Information* Pack about Childcare Services in Galway. Galway: Galway City and County Childcare Committee.

Giddens, A. (2001) *Sociology.* 4th.ed. Cambridge: Polity Press.

Handscombe, J. (1994) *Putting it all together. In Genesee, Fred, ed. Educating Second Language Children.* Cambridge, Mass., Cambridge University Press, pp331-356.

Hoffman, C. (1991) *An Introduction to Bilingualism.* London: Longmans.

Hyder, T. Rutter, J. (1998) *Refugee Children in the Early Years.* London: Save the Children.

McCluskey, J. (2001) *Voices Silenced. Has Irish a Future?/ Guthanna in Éag. An mairfidh an GhaeilgeBeo?* Dublin: Cois Life.

Mann, C. (1996) Anglo-Nigerian Pidgin in Nigerian Education. In Hickey, T. & Williams, J. (eds.) *Language, Education and Society.* Clevedon, Avon.: Multilingual Matters.

Murray, C. & O'Doherty, A. (2001) *Éist: Respecting diversity in early childhood care, education and training.* Dublin: Pavee Point.

National Council for Curriculum and Assessment (2004) *Towards a Framework for Early Learning.* Dublin: National Council for Curriculum and Assessment.

Pease-Alvarez, C. &Vasquez, O. (1994) Language Socialisation in Ethnic Minority Communities. In Genesee, Fred, ed. *Educating Second Language Children.* Cambridge, Mass., Cambridge University Press, pp82-102.

Rutter, J. & Hyder, T. Refugee *Children in the Early Years: Issues for Policy-Makers and Providers.* London: Save the Children.

Siraj-Blatchford, I. & Clarke, P. (2000) *Supporting Identity, Diversity and Language in the Early Years.* Bucks: Open University.

Tabors, Patton O. (1997) *One Child, Two Languages.* Baltimore, USA, Paul Brookes.

Wong-Fillmore, L. (1991) When Learning a Second Language means Losing the First. *Early Childhood Research* Quarterly. Vol.6, 323-346.

www.entemp.ie. Department of Enterprise and Employment. Accessed 01.04.04.

www.orac.ie. Office of the Refugee Applications Commissioners. Accessed 01.04.04.

A Study of Pre-school Children with Visual Impairments in Ireland: Findings and Recommendations

Rosaleen Dempsey

This decade has seen a period of rapid change with regard to the education of children with visual impairments. Never before have so many young children with visual disabilities been taking part in mainstream education, whether at pre-school, primary or post primary level. Because of this many assessment and support services have been called upon to meet the needs of these young children.

In the early chapters of my study I discussed the definitions (medical and educational) of visual impairment. It is very difficult to define what is meant by "normal" vision. In everyday usage people tend to consider their eyesight as adequate if they can cope with everyday tasks such as reading a newspaper or driving "The clinical measurement of visual acuity using the Snellen chart has an arbitrary standard of normal vision that permits us to carry out mundane activities" (Webster and Rose 1998, pg. 22).

However there are many people who carry out such tasks with less than average vision. Therefore in the educational sense it is functional vision rather than visual acuity that is examined. Functional vision relates to the specific demands of real situations.

The Snellen Eye Chart

An individual's visual impairment is usually assessed on the basis of visual acuity although it represents only one aspect of vision and not necessarily the most salient aspect. The Snellen Eye Chart is the standard Chart used to measure visual acuity. This chart has rows of different sized letters arranged in decreasing size, which can be read by the "Normal eye" at different distances (Webster and Rowe, 1998, page 23). The largest letter is 60 millimetres high; it has a viewing distance of 6 metres. The smaller letters have viewing distances of 48, 36, 24, 12, 9, 6 and 5 metres. A normal eye reads the 6 metre letters at a distance of 6 metres. Visual acuity is measured separately by asking the person to read the letters at a distance of 6 metres with one eye covered.

Visual acuity is expressed for each eye as 6 over the smallest line of letters that can be read. In the United Kingdom and Ireland, normal vision is expressed as 6/6, in the United States of America it is 20/20 and 1.0 in some European countries. A visual acuity of 6/12 indicates that the smallest line of letters that the person can see is 12 at a distance of 6 metres. The person can therefore see at 6 metres what a person with average eyesight can see at 12 metres.

For some people with low vision, visual acuity can be measured at a distance of 3 metres. Their visual acuity can be expressed as 3/60 for example. This would mean that the smallest line of letters that the person could see would be 60 millimetres at a distance of 3 metres. The World Health Organisation Chart in 1980 describes near total blindness as less than 1/60. For children or people with learning disabilities it can be difficult for examiners to interpret an individual's responses to the test or to know whether or not instructions have been understood. There are several new tests, which have been developed for children. One such test, which can be used for young children who cannot yet read, is to give them a cut out letter E and ask them to identify it on a chart at different orientations.

I also set about answering questions posed by Mason and McCall (1997) and Webster and Rowe (1998). These questions include: Do children with visual impairments have special characteristics? What impact does visual impairment have on a child's language development?; Does visual impairment affect a child's problem solving skills?; How can we promote mobility, play, exploration and social skills? It would seem that children with visual impairment can become 'stuck' in certain developmental stages. This is likely to happen if the professional help and advice, that facilitates the child's progression, is not available for parents. The more severe the visual loss, the more the likely the child will experience lack of progress across the developmental stages.

> Children with disabilities may have even more dependence on their social and physical environment during their early years than other children, with their development being particularly susceptible to the integrity and coherence of their relationship with the world. (Coolahan, 1999, p. 93)

He cites that, for example, the relationships between young children and their caregivers are vulnerable to disruption and breakdown in attainment.

It is vital, therefore, that early intervention by appropriate specialists is the normal experience of children who have visual impairment. In the course of my interview with a Community Resource Worker for the National Council for the Blind of Ireland I asked her to describe some of the support she provided to children and families. She said that her main remit in this area was to listen to the fears of parents and to establish what their particular needs were. She would then help to alleviate their fears and suggest ways in which their needs could be met. Providing advice to parents was a large part of the service she offered. The period after a child has been diagnosed with a visual difficulty can be a difficult one for parents and support services must take cognisance of this and act quickly to support where necessary. Peer support; where parents under similar situations can meet and discuss ways to promote the child's development, or even how they feel after the diagnoses was made, could mean the difference between a positive or negative attitude towards the child's visual difficulty. Facilitating the setting up of peer groups is a valuable aspect of the support services offered by the Community Resource Worker for the National Council for the Blind in Ireland.

My research was also concerned with the changes in attitude towards, and structure of, education for children with visual disabilities in Europe as a whole, in Britain and Ireland in the seventeenth century, and in Ireland from 1907 to date. Education for children with visual difficulties moved from being a social issue, *i.e.* relieving the burden on the 'poor rate', to being an educational issue in its own right. We moved gradually through the 1980s and 1990s towards integration in education. However we have now reached a certain point in the history of the education for children with visual impairments. As the special school for girls, in Dublin, is likely to close, parents must choose either to send their daughters to Belfast for special education or to local mainstream schools. At this time the plan to set up a National Centre for Children with a Visual Impairment became more important then ever before.

Following the publication of the Special Educational Review Committee (SERC) report in 1993 and the subsequent White Paper in 1995, the matter of reconstructing the present facilities to provide adequately for the educational needs of girls, as well as boys, became a matter of urgent concern. (Unpublished Report of the Planning Group for a National Centre for Children with a Visual Impairment, 2000, p.5)

It was a shock to many, therefore, that plans for the new National Centre were shelved; following the Department of Education's refusal to sanction funding in April of this year. It is my view that the Department of Education should re-consider its stance and communicate with the various agencies involved with the provision of support for children with visual difficulties. A decision, that puts the needs of the children first, could then be made. If the complete centre cannot be set up at once, then perhaps services could be 'phased in' as and when funding becomes available.

Parents should be free to choose as to whether their child attends mainstream or special school. The decision should depend purely on the particular needs of the child and gender should not be a disadvantage. By this I mean that provision must be made for girls to remain within special education in this state if that is what is desired. Since the conclusion of my study, girls with visual disabilities have been included in St Joseph's School for the Visually Impaired, which was originally a school for boys. This is a very positive development, which illustrates the rapid change in provision for children with visual disabilities in Ireland.

In my 'Findings and Analyses' chapter I discussed the results of my interviews with professionals and my case study observations. I divided the professionals into three categories, those who screen or assess children for visual disability *i.e.* the Maternity Hospital, the Public Health Nurse and the Ophthalmologist, those who assess children once visual impairment has bee diagnosed such as the Visually Impaired Children's Assessment Team (VICAT) for the National Council for the Blind of Ireland, which included an Educational Psychologist, a Physiotherapist, a Speech and Language Therapist and an Occupational Therapist. Lastly I described the roles of professionals who support children with visual difficulties and their families and the ways in which they thought the services (a) were positive and (b) could be improved. Such professionals included, the Visiting Teacher for the Visually Impaired, the Orientation and Mobility Officer for the Visually Impaired in Munster, The Rehabilitation Worker for the National Council for the Blind of Ireland and Community Resource Worker for the National Council for the Blind of Ireland. I then carried out three case studies in the company of certain support professionals. The children who took part in these studies were Jane, Sam and Mary. At the beginning of the study Jane was 2 years 2 months old, Sam was 6 years 1 month old and Mary was 4 years 8 months old (All children's names were changed for the purposes of confidentiality). I observed the children and asked them their views, where appropriate. I also interviewed their parents to discover their feelings about the support they received. From all of these research techniques I have drawn several conclusions.

Firstly, in regard to the ophthalmic services, it seems that a gap exists in assessment and provision between the medical and support professionals. Ophthalmologists tend to refer children who have been diagnosed with visual impairment to other relevant professionals only. This results in parents having to find information on their own. I recommend that ophthalmologists should provide information, in the form of leaflets, for example. These could detail the various support services available to children with visual impairments, such as the pre-school group Féach at the National Council for the Blind in Ireland. Armed with such information parents would be empowered to seek advice and support as regards the future of their young child.

The Visually Impaired Children's Assessment Team (VICAT) has had many referrals from the various support services for children with visual disabilities. The highest referral rate has been to the Community Resource Worker for the NCBI, with the visiting teachers service referring a large number of children as well. The assessment of a child this multi-disciplinary team can be a vital tool for parents and professionals with regard to service provision. However it has been suggested, that in order to minimise the disadvantage of geographic location, that a more multi-regional assessment team should be available for young children with visual impairments. Some would argue that the number of children with visual impairment in the country as a whole means that this would not be feasible. However if such a team were available once a month, or once every two months, in the main city in each region it would be of great benefit to parents and would not necessarily put a great strain on funding. It may also help to alleviate waiting lists for assessment services in the health boards, as illustrated in my third case study.

In the case study section I described the pre-school run at St. Joseph's School for the Visually Impaired. The added support of specialist pre-schools can be of great value to those in main-stream pre-schools who wish to enrol a child with a visual impairment but who are unsure what support it would entail. The National Council for the Blind of Ireland has set up and early-learning centre in Clondalkin, South Dublin. The school is due to be opened this September. While having a pre-school in both the north and south of Dublin City will be advantageous to parents and children in these areas it is unlikely to benefit children from other regions to any great extent. I would recommend that a specialist pre-school be set up in Cork City on a part-time basis, or even that a pre-school advisory team, consisting of professionals who specialise in pre-school education for children with visual impairment be created in each region. Such a team could be available to mainstream pre-school services throughout the country and they could advise on any aspect of visual impairment and the young child.

I interviewed two men and two women who had attended special, mainstream or both types of educational settings in the 1980s. My final question was concerned with changes that will be made to improve the quality of education for young children with visual disabilities in Ireland. All of them stated that planned integration was the only desirable option in the case of mainstream education. This view is reflected in my case study findings, and exactly ten years ago the Irish National Teachers Association made this comment.

During the course of my study I noted that the support services available to children with visual impairments in Munster operated on an individual client-based level. This is one of the most valuable aspects of the services. They could be further improved, therefore, by increased communication between professionals who work with each child and family as several of them pointed out. Of all those I interviewed within the support service framework, only the Orientation and Mobility Officer stated that she would make contact with any other professionals who were involved with the child and family. I would suggest that meetings between professionals working with the same client be arranged. This would enable them to discuss their roles in consultation with parents and would prevent any duplication of service provision.

The Visiting Teacher for the Visually Impaired believes that improvements with regard to numbers of personnel should be made in the services for children with visual difficulties. The government must make funding available in the Department of Education and Science and of Health and Children to decrease waiting lists for vital services. There is still a relatively small number of visiting teachers covering large areas of the country as a whole. An increased level of provision in this area would mean that children's progress in mainstream education would be monitored more closely.

After useful levels of communication are established between the various support professionals and agencies that work with children with visual disabilities, collaboration between them is necessary. For example the National Council for the Blind in Ireland and St Joseph's School for the Visually Impaired could work together on issues such as training for personnel. This would give each person a broader perspective with the expertise of St Joseph's staff with regard to education and the knowledge and the NCBI about the home life of the child and the community in which he lives.

Increased funding for Braille and for mobility training is necessary to ensure the complete integration of children with visual impairments in mainstream schools and society as a whole. The Braille Production Unit carries out very valuable work but services are overstretched. This is also the case for the mobility services. Paul (see interview in appendix 2) suggested that this problem could be alleviated by adopting the policies of the United Kingdom whereby mobility for children is the responsibility of the Local Education Authority rather than that of voluntary organisations, which tend to be under funded with heavy demands on their resources.

In order to ensure that the integration of children with visual disabilities is successful the needs of the teacher and the other children in the class or pre-school must be considered. Teacher training and childcare courses for pre-school practitioners should contain a module on Special Needs. This module should cover each area of disability in a positive manner and suggest ways in which a child with such a disability could be enabled to participate fully in the class. "A module on the teaching of children with disabilities should be included in the pre-service education of all primary teachers in future" (INTO, 1993, p.68).

To my knowledge this has not yet happened. I would recommend that any such training should include a discussion on language and disability. This would enable trainee teachers to examine their attitudes towards children with disabilities since language derives from attitudes. The language with regard to disability is transient. Michael Oliver commented that

> What is acceptable can change over time, even between writing something and the text appearing in published form. For instance, when I wrote *The Politics of Disablement* there was a debate going on about the terms learning difficulty and mental handicap. By the time the book came out the debate had been resolved and I had chosen wrongly. (Oliver, 1996, P. 5)

Teachers and pre-school staff must be informed about the current terms and definitions around disability. The young children in their care can mirror their attitudes, as children tend to imitate adult behaviour at this age.

In the first year of my study I accompanied the Orientation and Mobility Officer for Munster to a small rural school in North Country Cork. We were there to undertake an awareness afternoon with a class of nine-year-olds which included a child who was blind. The Orientation and Mobility officer began by asking the children a list of questions such as "Can a child who is blind (a) feed themselves, (b) dress themselves, (c) go out and play, etc?" At first the predominant answer was no. She then showed the children a video of a child in England who was blind and fully included in her mainstream school. When she asked the children the list of questions again they had all changed their minds. This illustrates very powerfully that children are not inhibited by the same prejudices or fears of adults towards any form of difference. If we can instil a positive attitude towards visual impairment in children we will break down the many barriers faced by people with visual difficulties in Ireland today.

Bibliography

Coolahan, J. (1998) *Report on the National Forum on Early Childhood Education* National Forum Secretariat.

Ellis, K. (1974), *The Development of Education of the Blind in Ireland*, Irish association for the Blind.

Mason, H. and McCall, S. (1997) *Visual Impairment: Access to Education for Children and Young People* David Fulton Publishing Ltd.

Oliver, M. (1996) *Understanding Disability: From Theory To Practice* Macmillin Publishers Ltd.

Unpublished, (2000), *Report of the Planning Group for a National Centre for Children With Visual Impairment* Unpublished

Webster, A. and Rowe, J. (1998) *Children with Visual Impairments: Social Development, Language and Learning* Routledge.

Section Four
Play

Pedagogical Practices in the Civics Institute of Ireland Playgrounds, 1933 to 1976

Margaret Kernan

Introduction

Prompted by a concern regarding the large numbers of unsupervised children playing on the streets of Dublin in the 1920s and '30s, the *Civics Institute of Ireland* [1] established ten playgrounds where children between four and fourteen years of age could play after school hours and during school holidays, throughout the whole year, and under the guidance of play leaders. The overall aim of the playgrounds was to train the children attending in civic behaviour. This paper [2] analyses the circumstances which led to the establishment of the playgrounds and describes the pedagogical practices of the playgrounds from when they were first established in the 1930s until they were handed over to the control of Dublin Corporation in the mid 1970s. For the purposes of this paper, pedagogical practices are understood to encompass the design of the physical environment, the availability and use of materials and the role of the playleaders.

The research considered the practices and experiences in the playgrounds from multiple perspectives. These included 'the voice of officialdom' as represented in the various papers and documents of the Civics Institute *i.e.* annual reports, minute books, correspondence, newspaper clippings and accounts of ex-Civics Institute Committee members. Ex-playleaders and assistant playleaders who were able to provide first-hand accounts of the day-to-day pedagogical practice in the playgrounds were also interviewed in the course of conducting the research. The researcher also had the opportunity of capturing the voice of 'the child player', albeit through the memoried childhood of a small number of ex-playground attendees [3].

A critical component of the documentary evidence collected and analysed that served to support and verify the recollections of informants, were the photographs taken by Marie Falksten in Hill Street Playground in 1971. These provide a vivid representation of the play experience in a Civics Institute playground at a particular time, and a selection is used to illustrate this paper [4]. Emerging from these first-hand accounts are the multiple 'affordances' [5] of the playground environments (Heft, 1988), which were not always made explicit in the official accounts.

The Civics Institute of Ireland

In order to understand the Civics Institutes' motives for involvement in such an initiative, it is important to briefly review the socio-political developments in the city at the time when the Civics Institute was established in 1914. Dublin in 1913 was a city of much turmoil, labour discontent, strikes, and street riots. The Labour Movement, which was developing in Britain between 1900 and 1910 into a strong and powerful pressure group, was slow to gain footing in Ireland. Because there was little heavy industry in Dublin, there were few trade unions. However, the establishment of the Irish Transport and General Workers Union (ITGWU) under the leadership of Jim Larkin led to a bitter dispute between employees and employers leading to the famous 1913 Dublin 'Lock-out' (Yeates, 2000). The consequence of the industrial dispute was severe hardship for the striker's families. It also resulted in a greater visibility of the poverty of the majority of the city's population. At the beginning of the twentieth century, the problem of working class poverty had not aroused the same interest and commitment in Dublin that was found in certain sections of British society at the time (Daly, 1984). However, in the aftermath of the 'Lock-out' there was an increased awareness amongst the middle and upper classes of the need to improve the living conditions in Dublin (Daly, 1997).

It was in this context that a small group of people who shared a common interest in the development of civic spirit and improvement of amenities in Ireland's cities and towns came together in April 1914. The outcome of this first meeting was the formation of the Civics Institute of Ireland. Led by J.E. Canavan, a Jesuit priest, the membership principally comprised professional and businessmen and some women who gave of their time and services on a voluntary capacity. Unlike many groups and organisations operating on a voluntary or philanthropic basis in Ireland, the Civics Institute was strictly non-sectarian maintaining a neutral position with regard to the religious traditions of the country (J. Walmsley, personal communication, November 2003). Although originally developed to serve the whole of Ireland, urban and rural, most of its activities appear to have been centred on the city of Dublin. The very first activity of the Institute was the promotion of a town planning competition which was part of the Civics Exhibition held in the Linenhall Buildings in the summer of 1914. The outbreak of World War I in 1914 drew attention from the Exhibition, however, in the following years the *Civics Institute* grew and expanded its range of activities, although its prime focus up to the 1930s was in the area of town planning[6].

In the summer of 1930, the *Women's National Health Association* organised a play conference the purpose of which was to consider what could be done to provide playgrounds for children in Dublin[7]. Arising from the conference, a Joint Playgrounds Committee was appointed which included members of the Civics Institute. One of the first activities of the Committee was to write to the City Manager of Dublin's municipal authority, Dublin Corporation, for a list of possible sites in the city that could be used as playgrounds. In a letter to The Irish Times on 6th October 1930, the Committee made its first public appeal for money for supervised play centres. The appeal was made on the following three grounds:

(1) Public health, because children must have suitable recreation under sanitary conditions
(2) Public morals, because children who are happily playing under supervision will not ultimately become juvenile delinquents.
(3) Public safety, because children playing in the streets are a contributory cause of accidents and a danger to themselves and others (Papers of Civics Institute of Ireland, Dublin City Archives, B12/7/1).

In this appeal we are given an early insight into the beliefs about children and children's play outdoors which underpinned the rationale for the playgrounds. These beliefs positioned children in danger themselves, vulnerable and, at the same time, a source of danger, a threat to others and society at large. Interestingly, these beliefs still resonate in the contemporary discourse on the position of children outdoors albeit the dangers are perceived somewhat differently (see for example: Jenks, 1996; Strandell, 2000; Prout, 2003; Valentine & Mc Kendrick, 1997).

The first Civics Institute Playground opens at Broadstone, 1933
On 12th September 1933, the first playground was opened at Broadstone with one supervisor attending and voluntary helpers[8]. The 1933 Annual Report of

the Civics Institute recorded the event as follows:

> In September 1933, the Dublin Corporation handed over to the Institute the newly equipped playground at Broadstone for supervision. Some 800 children attended every day except during November and December when the numbers dropped to an average of 400. The large area to be covered and the number of children attending made it impossible to continue with one supervisor, and an assistant was appointed. The Playground was equipped in consultation with the Institute and the Corporation gives a grant to meet the supervision (Civics Institute of Ireland, Annual Report, 1933).

The agreed arrangement between Civics Institute and Dublin Corporation was that the Corporation would provide the sites, and supply and install fixed playground apparatus and undertake the maintenance of the playgrounds. The Civics Institute would be responsible for the management and supervise the day-to-day running of the playgrounds through the employment of trained play leaders who would supervise the large numbers of children attending and organise a range of games and activities.

Between 1933 and 1939, the number of playgrounds opened and managed by the Civics Institute gradually increased to ten. With the exception of the Cabra playgrounds, all were located in the north and south inner city. Hill Street Playground was the second playground to open on 1st April 1935. Three playgrounds were opened in Cabra on 2nd March 1936 one for very young children in Ventry Park, West Cabra, and separate playgrounds for boys and girls on Faussaugh Ave. The South Dock Street playground opened on 1st September 1937, followed by Mountjoy Square on 15th May 1938. Two more playgrounds were opened in 1939, one at Pearse House on 1st April 1939 followed on 1st June 1939 by the St. Joseph's Mansions, Killarney Street playground. Although the original intention was to establish many more playgrounds around the city within a short time, lack of funds and difficulty accessing equipment due to war shortages prevented this happening (Annual Report 1940-41). Just one further playground at Pearse Square was opened after the war[9].

In 1938, Dublin Corporation formally requested the Civics Institute to draw up and submit a programme for the leisure time activity of boys and girls which should provide for enclosed playgrounds for children under the age of 14 years under fully qualified Play Leaders[10]. The Civics Institute created the position of Director of Recreation and Welfare to undertake this work and to be responsible for the day-to-day management of the playgrounds. A Playground Subcommittee, comprising selected members of the Civics Institute was also established to oversee and support the development of the playgrounds.

The Playgrounds were open throughout the year and when schools were closed: 3 or 4 pm to 6 pm in winter months and 3 pm to 8 pm during the summer school holidays. During school holidays and at weekends they were open all day. Children between the ages of 4 years and 14 years could attend. In practice however, many children outside this age range used the playgrounds. Frequently, children brought along younger siblings, many of whom were babies in prams. An early plan was that the playgrounds could be opened during the morning as nursery playgrounds, where it was felt working mothers could leave their pre-school aged children under trained supervision (Annual Report, 1935). However, a year later it was recognised that the use of the playground for morning use as a day nursery required a more specialised and costly training than that of the play leader (Annual Report, 1936). This most likely refers to the training for nursery school teachers provided by the *Nursery School Association of Great Britain and Ireland,* which was available in Belfast or London. Although it would be four more years before the Civics Institute opened separate provision for pre-school aged children in the form of nurseries centres[11], the playgrounds continued to provide for the needs of younger children[12] (see section on pedagogical practices).

Two adults generally staffed the playgrounds at a time: a play leader and an assistant play leader. In the early years of operation, the numbers of children attending on any given day could have been as many as 500 children, depending on the time of year. According to figures cited in the 1938 Annual Report, approximately 2,000 children were accommodated in the existing five playgrounds which had at that time been established at that time.

Pedagogical practice in the playgrounds

Design of the physical environment

The facilities in the playgrounds could be considered basic by contemporary standards. The particular activities provided and the affordances of the environment varied from playground to playground depending on the space and resources available and the particular interests and skills of the play leaders, visiting specialists and children. In general, the playgrounds consisted of a flat outdoor area with an asphalt surface and an indoor shelter that was essentially like a basic sport's pavilion. This was often referred to as "the hut" and it provided protection from the elements during very inclement weather. According to one ex-playground attendee the hut was "a place where you could get a welcome hot cup of tea on a cold day". It was also where children could take part in Arts and Crafts activities.

Individual playgrounds had particular physical features. The Hill Street playground, which was located on the site of a Church of Ireland graveyard, retained the gravestones and these became part of the play landscape and offered opportunities for climbing. Some of the lower gravestones functioned as occasional table for sitting on or for putting board games on.

©Marie Falksten.
The pleasure of climbing. Part of the play landscape in Hill Street Playground

Four of the playgrounds: Broadstone, Cabra, Mountjoy Square, and Hill Street had sections equipped for children of pre-school age. St. Joseph's Mansions playground', which comprised a smaller space than the other playgrounds, was for younger children only[13]. In addition to the regular playground opening hours, Infant playgrounds were open for two hours every morning except for Sundays. Babies and toddlers slept in prams and older siblings fed them bottles of milk when required. Infant sections also contained a sand garden, which was an essentially a sunken pit in the ground filled with sand and equipped with buckets and spades and other loose play props[14].

© Marie Falksten. The sand 'garden' (sandpit) was a source of interest and involvement. One of the wooden rockers, supplied by Dublin Corporation is visible in the background. Hill Street Playground, 1971

The Cabra playgrounds had gardens divided into individual allotments which the children attended to. In the 1945-46 Annual Report, there is reference to 24 garden plots. Seeds were supplied free by Messrs. Drummond & Co. and children were encouraged to grow a variety of vegetables which they could take home. Each summer there was a competition for the best plot, which was judged by a horticulturist[15]. There are a few references to unspecified difficulties with this particular activity. However, it seems that the benefits of the experience in terms of developing interests and skills for the future encouraged the Civics Institute to persevere.

> The interest taken by the children in cultivating their little
> gardens holds promise that they will readily avail themselves of

any opportunity they may have later on to cultivate gardens or allotments (Annual Report 1945-46:11).

Whilst there is no reference to any contact between the *Civics Institute* and the *School Garden Association of America*, there are some similarities regarding the perceived benefits of the gardening evident in the Civics Institute Annual Reports and written documentation of the *School Garden Association of America*[16]. This association, formed in 1910, was founded on the belief that young children should be brought into direct contact with nature in order to be thoroughly educated and that a child "can only come into his own by working more upon his own initiative in the open" (Van Evrie Kilpatrick, 1914: 20). In this aspect there are many similarities between the philosophy of the *School Garden Association* and Froebelian pedagogy. Froebel's first kindergarten, located in the rural idyll of Bad Blankenburg, in the Thuringia Forest, Germany was designed to include both individual and communal garden plots to provide children with an educational introduction to nature through naming plants, identifying their uses, and encouraging observation of and care for nature (Hoof, 1977; Liebschner, 1992). *The School Garden Association of America* aimed to provide training and the foundations for self-support, taking responsibility and teaching elementary agriculture. In these respects it mirrored the pragmatic motives of the Civics Institute. The older children in the other Civics Institute playgrounds were also brought into closer contact with nature through organised trips and hikes to the Dublin and Wicklow Mountains and to the beaches north and south of Dublin City.

Availability and use of materials

Overall, the playgrounds were characterised by the wide range of activities available to the children, the emphasis being on fresh air and outdoor activities throughout the year. The fixed playground equipment supplied by Dublin Corporation included swings, see-saws, jungle-gyms and "ocean-wave". Playgrounds with infant sections had small swings, see-saws, wooden rockers and an external tap for water. However, perhaps of more significance for the children were the seasonal street games: hop-scotch or "beds"; marbles, tops, "Snatch the Bacon", "Rats and Rabbits", organised team games such as "Round towers" (rounders), Padder tennis, basketball and football and imaginative and creative play. All of these activities required the provision of loose materials and props, such as balls, ropes, bats, sand, and buckets. The membership of the Civics Institute and the play leaders and volunteers were constantly seeking donations of such equipment. There is also evidence of much resourcefulness in gathering materials and play props. In many cases children made use of 'found materials' such as cardboard, old prams wheels and tyres. Play leaders interviewed recall the use of old hop sacks donated by Guinness Brewery which were sewn by the girls and transformed into nets for padder tennis. This fact is also referred to in a newspaper article written in 1971 by Nell Mc Cafferty about Hill Street Playground. Marie Falksten's photographs illustrated the article. The article noted that "the checker boards had been made by the boys of old wood, wheeled from the factory across the street. The pieces were bottle tops, painted during the art classes" (The Irish Times, 12th August 1971)[17].

The inter-playground tournaments in Padder tennis, handball, rounders, football, basketball and figure dancing which took place during the summer months and which culminated with 'The Finals', in Mountjoy Square playground generated great excitement throughout the whole playground service.

©Marie Falksten
Padder tennis in Hill Street Playground

© Marie Falksten
Focus and concentration – a younger player practises skills required for padder tennis

Role of play leaders

The only adults permitted into the playgrounds were the play leaders, or authorised visitors such as visiting specialists. There were both men and women play leaders and assistant or part-time play leaders although the majority seemed to have been women. The play leader was considered central to the success of the playgrounds. At the outset it was envisaged that he/she would be trained and would have studied children's development, social conditions and welfare and first aid. However, there was no standard accredited training for play leaders available in Ireland. By the 1950s, a short course in training in play leadership had been organised by the Civics Institute and certificates awarded to those play leaders who passed an exam and attained a standard of proficiency in play leadership. Part-time play leaders, who were mainly university students, received "hands-on training" which was facilitated by the permanent play leaders[18]. In general, play leaders and assistant or part-time play leaders were recruited because of their personal attributes and because they had specific skills or particular interests which they could share with the children in their care. Additionally, play leaders were required to be familiar with all the seasonal games the children played. Great emphasis was laid on their ability to organise children to take turns and engage in fair play. The Annual Reports provide some insight into the more personal, qualities deemed to be necessary when working with children in the playgrounds. In the earlier Annual Reports it seems the emphasis was clearly on the ability to discipline and manage large numbers of 'wild' children and win over their respect.

> She must prove herself capable of managing a large crowd of children of all ages up to 14, of maintaining discipline, and of

organising an otherwise unorganised mob by her own personality. A crowd of slum children in a few minutes turn down the candidate who has no gift for children, and, if once a Play Leader has shown herself so turned down, she may never win her way back to leadership in the city playground. (1938 Annual Report: 9)

In later reports unobtrusive play facilitation skills are highlighted as being central to the role of the play leader:

Her influence is evident in the general air of pleasant, purposeful activity, in the sense of order without regimentation, of competition without loss of co-operation. (Annual Report 1952-53: 8).

The memoried account of an ex-playground attendee recalls the play leader as being strict but fair – "like a second mother, we called her Miss Millea, for to us she was like a lady".

Visiting specialists were volunteers who gave 'lessons' in music, singing, Irish dancing, Irish language, art, handicrafts, sewing or needlework. They generally visited the playgrounds on a rotational basis.

© Marie Falksten
The visiting specialist for Céilí dancing, Miss N. Fitzgerald in Hill Street playground in 1971.

Dublin Corporation assumes total responsibility for playgrounds

By the 1960s and '70s attendances at the playgrounds had dropped off fairly dramatically from their peak in the 1930s and 1940s. There were a number of factors accounting for this. Due to the rehousing policies of Dublin Corporation from the 1950s which relocated families from city centre flats and tenements out to new housing projects in areas such as Ballyfermot, Crumlin, Drimnagh and Donnycarney, the child population in the city was much reduced compared to the 1930s. The advent of television was a further significant factor. By the 1970s, television was beginning to offer an alternative indoor form of leisure to children.

As the Civics Institute of Ireland began to wind down its activities, Dublin Corporation began to assume greater responsibility for the out-of-school play and leisure time of school aged children in the city. In 1971, the Civics Institute handed over the overall management of the playgrounds to the Park's Section of Dublin Corporation, although their day-to-day administration remained the responsibility of the Director of Recreation and Welfare. In 1976, in response to the reduced usage of the playgrounds, Dublin Corporation decided to undertake a critical reappraisal of the playgrounds which was to include recommendations for its future development (Egan, 1976). At this point, overall responsibility for the playgrounds had been delegated to the Community Development Officer attached to the Community Environment Department within Dublin Corporation (Egan, 1976)[19]. In the internal report produced in 1976, it was suggested that the low usage of the playgrounds was due to the dull, drab and general unattractive appearance of the centre, the absence of facilities to play with water, lack of imaginative games and hide-away spaces and green areas. In rationalising a future approach for managing the playgrounds, which would offer a "good practical possibility rather than a perfect solution", the author of the report stated that there was no such thing as the ideal playground and therefore no such thing as an ideal playground philosophy (Egan, 1976). Dublin Corporation committed (at least provisionally) to keeping the existing playgrounds open, although viewed the summer only play schemes as a more economic way of meeting Dublin Corporation's objective of providing facilities for children's play in the city.

Thus, in the mid-1970s in an era of depressed employment and general economic hardship, the concept of developing citizenship through supervised and organised play gave way to pragmatic and imperfect solutions that had the effect of changing the experience of the city playgrounds. New risks and dangers for children emerged in the now unsupervised playgrounds. Drug pushers, drugs, dirty needles and other hazardous waste were a constant threat. The indoor and outdoor environments of the playgrounds were transformed from settings of play and active involvement of adults in that play, to empty and hazardous wastelands. Hill Street playground is illustrative of the process of degeneration which occurred throughout the 1980s. Although the playground remained open and continued to be equipped with the standard metal fixed playground equipment, children rarely played there as parents became increasingly anxious about the dangers outdoors. The sand-garden was filled in with concrete. "The hut" which had once been the setting for arts and crafts activities and for playground captains' elections, became derelict and was eventually locked up by Dublin Corporation.

Conclusion

In his seminal work *The Child in the City* (1978) geographer Colin Ward speculates about the ways in which the link between the city and child can be made more fruitful and enjoyable for both the child and the city. Commenting in a later article that every city was once rich in both incidental and intentional resources for children, Ward (1994) observed that the three R's of children's use of their environment are resourcefulness, responsibility and reciprocity. It was these features in addition to the intensity and vitality of the children's play in Hill Street Playground, that first caught Marie Falksten's attention and which are clearly apparent in her photographs[20].

Analyses of the photographic evidence in addition to interviews with ex-play-leaders and former child 'players', revealed additional functions and benefits of the Civics Institute playground experience which were above and beyond the 'official' aims such as the removal of children from the city streets. One such function was to provide a vital social support to mothers by giving them a break from their child rearing duties made more arduous in cramped living conditions. Additionally, the multiple 'affordances' of the environment in the playgrounds during the period when they were managed and supervised by the Civics Institute reveal a further benefit and provide an insight to what it was like to be a player in the playgrounds. Key aspects of the Civics Institute Playgrounds were that the outdoor and indoor physical environments contained loose parts, and transformable materials in addition to fixed equipment. These facilitated resourcefulness as well as involvement and creativity. Relationships with adults and children were key. Contact with adult playleaders, who valued play and encouraged co-operation and responsibility, supported the players' development of positive relationships with adults as well as with children. Players were also encouraged to be responsible for their environment. Playing alongside other children, boys and girls of varying ages supported children in their developing social relationships and being responsible for others as well as for their own behaviour. These were the means by which the Civics Institute educated Dublin children into citizenship – they were also the means by which thousands of Dublin children were provided with an intentional resource in the city, that facilitated and supported their play.

Postscript

Hill Street Playground in 2004

At a time of greater prosperity in the 1990s, the Government of the day established the Integrated Services Initiative, which was piloted in the North East Inner City area of Dublin. Its remit centred on the co-operation of agencies towards resolving issues which occur in socially deprived areas. Arising out of this initiative, support and capital funding became available to re-establish a play service for the residents of the area surrounding Hill Street. In 2000, the indoor "hut" underwent a major renovation and the *Hill Street Family Resource Centre* was opened offering a very valuable social support to families with young children. A large proportion of the families served are Dublin's newest citizens: newly arrived immigrants seeking a better life for themselves and for their children. The focus of the service is primarily on supporting parents to play with their own children during the pre-school years. Parent and Child groups take place indoors in an equipped indoor play room. The outdoors is still perceived as hazardous. Although it has been recently equipped with shiny new fixed playground equipment, according to staff in the Resource Centre, it is hardly used by children because of parents and staff fears regarding what the children might find on the ground. In 2002, Dublin City Council (formerly Dublin Corporation) appointed a Play Development Officer. The responsibilities of the role included raising awareness of the developmental value of play to children, developing a play policy and providing a resource for communities who are trying to improve their children's play opportunities. A stated aim of Dublin City Council is to create a child friendly city for the future (Play Development Team, Dublin City Council).

1   The Civics Institute of Ireland is referred to as the Civics Institute throughout.
2   This research is part of a larger project titled "Children's Experiences of Outdoor Play in Early Childhood Education Settings in Urban Areas". The research is being funded by a National Children's Strategy Doctoral Research Scholarship, National Children's Office, Ireland.
3   The author is very grateful for all informants' contributions. In some cases this involved reading earlier drafts of the paper and providing additional insights.
4   The author would like to acknowledge with gratitude Marie Falksten's permission to include her photographs in this paper.
5   Defined by perception psychologist James Gibson (1979) as the possibility for action on the part of an actor in an environment. Using Gibson's concept of affordances, Heft (1988) illustrated the significance of the functionality of children's outdoor environment.
6   The Civics Institute provided advice, information and encouragement in areas such as: town planning, housing, juvenile delinquency and the formation of Friendly Societies. It was also instrumental in the establishment of training courses in Social Science both in Trinity College, Dublin and University College Dublin in 1930s. For many years, the Civics Institute organised the practical element of these courses. Between 1942 and 1956, the Civics Institute of Ireland organised several series of external lectures in Public Administration, which later developed into the foundation of the Institute of Public Administration (I.P.A.). In 1969, it played a key role in the formation of The Irish Pre-Schools Playgroups Association, a detailed account of which is provided in Douglas (1994).
7   The Women's National Health Association (WNHA) had been founded in 1905 by Ishbel, Countness of Aberdeen and wife of the British Viceroy in Ireland. Most well-known for its work in raising public awareness about hygiene and the prevention of disease, particularly tuberculosis, the WNHA had established a garden playground in St. Augustine Street in 1912 for pre-school aged children (Irish Times, April 3rd, 1912). In 1930, when the play conference was held, WNHA were also managing a supervised playground in Constitution Hill.
8   From evidence gathered in the course of this research, it appears that it was the Civics Institute alone in agreement with Dublin Corporation, which assumed control of the playgrounds. There is no mention of further involvement of the Women's National Health Association or Committee Members from other organisations after the early 1930s.
9   Precise date of opening of Pearse Square playground unknown.
10 At the same time, the Civics Institute was asked by Dublin Corporation to submit a programme for "separate provision for playgrounds for young adults of both sexes under proper leadership provided and directed by the Civics Institute". There is no evidence to suggest that such a programme was ever pursued.
11 The Civics Institute established two nursery centres in Dublin. The first of these was St. Brigid's, Mountjoy Square, which opened in 1940. A second nursery centre, St. Joseph's Nursery Centre opened 15 years later in Morningstar Road, the Coombe in 1955. Both centres continue to operate in 2004.
12 Early on in her appointment as Play leader in Hill Street, B. Heran recalls being sent to London where she undertook "An Emergency Course of Instruction for the Care of Children under 5 Years" . This course which took place between 30th September and 18th

October 1946 in the Froebel College, Roehampton, Surrey.

13 The playground in St. Joseph's Mansions, seems to be one of the few playgrounds where parents were present as onlookers on a regular basis. This seems to be due to the fact that it was surrounded on all sides by the flats where children attending lived. However, The Irish Times on 20th September 1943 refers to an initiative to encourage parental interest in the playgrounds. This was Parents Week at the playgrounds during which "children have been asked to bring their parents along so that they may meet the playleaders and see how the children are taught to occupy their leisure time" (The Irish Times, 20th September 1943)

14 In 1942, the expertise of Civics Institute regarding sand gardens for children's play was called upon in advising the keepers of St. Stephen's Green regarding a proposed sand garden for the Green (correspondence to B.J.Coote, 23rd September 1942, Civics Institute of Ireland Records, National Archives).

15 The Evening Herald Newspaper 5th August 1953 carried a photograph of two girls aged 9 and 10 years tidying up their vegetable plot before the adjudication in the competition at the Cabra Play Centre. A. Bracken, playground assistant between 1954 and 1958 in Cabra who had particular responsibility for helping the children with their garden plots, recalls the feverish preparation in the days before the adjudication, which at that time was undertaken by a Professor Williams.

16 School Garden Association of America was just one of a host of schemes and projects which positioned children at as a point of intervention and investment in the future and which proliferated at the end of the nineteenth century and beginning of the 20thcentury. It could also be assessed as being part of the Fresh Air Movement (see Bryder, 1992)

17 The gendered aspect of the activities in the playgrounds is evident in this quotation. It is also evident in some of the photographs included in the paper. The space limitation in the present paper prevents further analysis of this aspect of the playgrounds.

18 Holiday work in the playgrounds was much sought after by university students during the 1950s when summer jobs were scarce (E. Mc Caul, personal communication September 2003).

19 Note at this time Dublin Corporation also took over responsibility for the six Catholic Youth Council Playgrounds which were: Ballyfermot, Russell Road, Neagh Road, Church Street, Sheriff Street Boys and Sheriff St Sheriff Street Girls

20 Marie Falksten came across the players in Hill Street Playgrounds by chance on her wanderings around Dublin City in 1971 as a visiting student photographer from Göteberg, Sweden in search of a subject for an assignment.

Acknowledgements

The author acknowledges with gratitude the feedback of Prof. Kevin Brehony, Froebel College, Roehampton University of Surrey, Dr. Hans de Frankrijker, University of Leiden, the Netherlands and Anne Fitzpatrick, Dublin Institute of Technology to earlier drafts of this paper. This paper was prepared whilst the author was a guest researcher at the University of Leiden, the Netherlands.

Bibliography

Published books and articles

Bryder, L. (1992) 'Wonderlands of Buttercup, Clover and Daisies": Tuberculosis and the Open-Air School Movement in Britain, 1907 – 39. In R. Cooter (Ed.), *In the Name of the Child: Health and Welfare 1880 – 1940*. London: Routledge.

Coote, B.J. (1942) *Playgrounds for Children*, Dublin: The Civics Institute of Ireland.

Daly, M.E. (1984). *Dublin, The Deposed Capital: A Social and Economic History 1860 – 1914*. Cork: Cork University Press.

Daly, M.E. (1997). *The Spirit of Earnest Inquiry: The Statistical and Social Inquiry Society of Ireland 1847 – 1997*. Dublin: Statistical and Social Inquiry Society of Ireland.

Douglas, F. (1994) *The History of the Irish Pre-School Playgrounds Association 1969 – 1994*. Dublin.

Gibson, J. (1979) *The Ecological Approach to Visual Perception*. Boston: Houghton-Mifflin.

Heft, H. (1988). Affordances of Children's Environments: A Functional Approach. *Children's Environments Quarterly*, 5, 3, 29-37.

Hoof, D. (1977). *Handbuch der Spieltheorie Fröbel's Untersuchungen und Materialien zum Vorschulischen Lernen*. Braunschweig: Westermann.

Jenks, C. (1996). *Childhood*. London: Routledge.

Liebschner, J. (1992). A Child's Work: Freedom and play in Froebel's *Educational Theory and Practice*. Cambridge: Lutterworth Press.

Prout, A. (2003). *Children, Representation and Social Change*. Keynote Address, ECCERA Conference, University of Strathclyde, Glasgow, September 2003.

Strandell, H. (2000). What is the use of children's play: preparation or social participation? In H.Penn (Ed.), E*arly Childhood Services: Theory, Policy and Practice*. Buckingham: Open University Press.

Valentine, G. & Mc Kendrick, J. (1997). *Children's outdoor play: Exploring parental concerns about children's safety and the changing nature of childhood*. Geoforum, 28, 2, 219 – 235.

Van Evrie Kilpatrick (1914). The School Garden Association of America, *The Child*, 4, 20-22.

Ward, C. (1978). *The Child in the City*. Penguin.

Ward, C. (1994). Opportunities in Childhood in Late Twentieth Century

Britain. In B. Mayall (Ed.), *Children's Childhoods: Observed and Experienced.* London: Falmer Press.

Yeates, P. (2000) *Lockout: Dublin 1913.* Dublin: Gill & Macmillan.

Newspaper Reports

Garden Playground, *The Irish Times,* 3rd April 1912.

Parents Week, *The Irish Times,* 20th September 1943.

Mc Cafferty, N. & Falksten, M. Dancing on the Grave, *The Irish Times,* 12th August 1971.

Unpublished Reports

Egan, G. (1976) Internal Report on the Dublin Corporation Play Service, Community and Environment Department, Dublin Corporation, 26th November 1976.

Manuscripts, unpublished documents

Records of the Civic Institute of Ireland, 1911 – 1969, National Archives, Bishop Street, Dublin Accession No.: 1198

Records of the Civics Institute of Ireland, Dublin City Archives, Pearse Street, Dublin. Accession No.: B12

Annual Reports of Civics Institute of Ireland

The Civics Institute of Ireland Ltd Annual Reports:
1932; 1935; 1936; 1938; 1941-42; 1945-46; 1946-47; 1949-50; 1952-53; 1953-54; 1966-67-68.

Children of the Global Village:
Playing the Way into Communities of Practice
Part One

Carmel Brennan

Children around the globe play. It is common to the young of the species and even across species. Yet play themes and scripts are local, situated in and part of a cultural community. So in many ways, one might say that play connects the village to the global world and the global world to the village. In the early years, Gussin Paley (1997) tells us 'an intuitive programme called play, works so well that the children learn the language, mannerisms and meaning of all the people with whom they live. They know what every look means, every tone of voice, who their family is, where they come from, what makes them happy or sad, what place they occupy in the world'. They learn these very complex concepts through playful, pleasurable participation in complex social activity. Children play their way into community scenarios that allow them to engage with real life learning. Surely such a powerful learning tool warrants further study and more widespread usage.

This paper is based on the ethnographic research involved in the IPPA Quality Improvement Programme in Irish preschool services. It involves observation of play episodes (supported with video, photographs and field / portfolio notes), the review and analysis of these episodes and relating practice to theory, particularly post-modern theory. This research demonstrates the multi-functional role of play in children's learning and explores our understanding of children's play and its role in helping children to adapt, to make sense of the world, to come to terms with emotions and relationships. The IPPA publication (2004) 'Power of Play' documents many of these observations. This paper draws on observations of children in play to demonstrate the concept of learning in 'communities of practice' (Lave and Wenger 1991) and its particular appropriateness to help adults understand and support children's learning.

Through this research, we have engaged with the concept of learning as situated in social activity and 'distributed' in the community (Lave and Wenger 1991). In analysing our observations and in particular through our shared analysis of video clips of play scenes, we made the shift from the image of the 'needy' child to the image of the 'competent' child. We began to discover all that these very young children could already do and we were prompted to ask: 'Where did they learn these things?', 'Who taught them?', 'How do they know?'

As we watched a group of boys build a goal post and enact a game of soccer, we were astounded at the detail they applied, from kicking or diving for the ball to the team-building huddle. We realised that these children were not merely playing football, they were playing at being footballers. This involves taking on the persona of the professional footballer, including the language, the shapes and gestures, the routines and rituals. These children had not specified or agreed these behaviours before the play. They seemed to emerge because this is knowledge that is distributed in the community. It is negotiated in the transaction between individuals and society. It is appropriated (Rogoff 1990) by those who participate in the related social activities. This concept is based on the Vygotskian socio-cultural theory and proposes that we should study children's learning, not in terms of universal stages of development but in terms of how they make meaning in their own complex cultural worlds.

Pretend Play as Situated Learning

Why is play such a powerful tool for learning in early childhood? In order to investigate this question, we need to explore the concept of learning. The task of childhood is to begin the process of meaning making, of making sense of the world and his or her place within it. It is a big, lifelong task and we know that in early childhood children make major leaps in this area. They learn how to communicate through both language and gesture, how to use a range of available cultural artefacts from eating utensils to computers, who they are and how they are related to others, even what other people may be thinking or feeling and how they might empathise or influence that thinking to achieve their own goals and all of this in the first thousand days of life. According to Bruner (1996 p162) 'meaning making involves situating encounters with the world in their appropriate cultural contexts in order to know what they are about'. Meaning may be in the mind but it is derived from the meaning that is socially created. Because meaning is socially created through shared experiences, we can negotiate it and communicate about it. Because our culture provides us with symbols, such as language, we have a shared mechanism for communication. Without common experiences and a common symbol code, we cannot communicate and negotiate meaning. Because we are different and experience and interpret interactions differently as well as bringing different experiences to each interaction, meaning must be negotiated. Reality is constructed through shared negotiation. Again Bruner (1996 p161) tells us that 'it is not just words that make this (negotiation) possible but our capacity to grasp the role of the settings in which words, acts and gestures occur. We are the inter-subjective species par excellence'. When we de-contextualise the elements of the lesson, we lose the intricacy of the transaction.

For this reason, Bruner promotes the concept of the community of learners, based on mutuality and collaboration rather than the traditional one-way transmission system view of learning. As he talks about this 'mutual' community of learners, he could equally be describing the community of players. "The point is for those in the group to help each other, get 'the lay of the land' and the 'hang of the job'," he says. Again he proposes that 'finding a place in the world, for all that it implicates the immediacy of home, mate, job and friends, is ultimately an act of the imagination' (p162) and with this lens to observe play, we can see children imaginatively create a world based on their previous and combined experiences, which they can control and to which they can belong. In the 'Power of Play' (IPPA 2004) all the stories demonstrates how children negotiate meaning and scaffold each other in imaginative and creative ways as they experiment with possible selves in dramatic pretend play. These experiments bring them into a range of communities, each of which has specific goals, specific valued behaviours, rules and routines.

Agentive players

Bruner (1996 p172) identifies agency and self esteem as the two elements of selfhood that are universal and prioritises them as learning objectives. 'What characterises human selfhood is the construction of a conceptual system that organises, as it were, a 'record' of agentive encounters with the world'. He suggests that school and school learning are among the earliest of these records but I propose that play is the place where children are truly involved in agentive encounters. In her comparative study of peer and adult-child interactions, Rogoff (1990 p186) proposes that 'it may be the absence of external controls, the freedom to play with the rules themselves and to recast the goals of an activity from moment to moment that is unique and invaluable in peer interactions. Play exploration among young children may be especially important for developing new solutions to problems'. This is what agency is about and it is a valued skill in the community of players. In our observations, children enjoyed playing with others who initiated ideas and became involved. In 'The Bold Girls' (IPPA 2004), we see many of the characteristics of the community of players. Children demonstrate the skill of stepping into the pretend frame of play (Batteson 1956) and out of it again to agree a new course of action. In 'The Fire Brigade' the role of the players changed numerous times, from housekeepers and parents to emergency workers and dogs. The children welcomed initiative.

Apprenticeship and Guided Participation (Rogoff 1990)

Like Bruner, Rogoff (1996) was also influenced by Vygotsky. Following from her cross-cultural research, she describes learning as guided participation in joint activity. The term 'guided participation' as in Vygotsky's 'zone of proximal development' implies the need for a more capable partner who guides the learning. In our research we often saw children play this role. In the 'Building Togetherness' (IPPA 2004) story, based on a construction play scenario, Seán shows Keith how to join in the cone construction by explaining the activity, offering him an initiative and befriending him. In the same play scene, he models a way of interacting co-operatively with Derek with obvious effect on the collaborative and inclusive ethos of the group. He does this to far greater effect than any adult could. Within any group of children, there is inevitably someone who is more advanced on the spectrum of capabilities in particular skills. Indeed we see in this episode that the newcomer posing the naïve question also offers opportunity for learning and perfecting skills. As in Bruner's (1996, p162) 'mutual' community, this play community 'models ways of doing or knowing, provides opportunity for emulation, offers running commentary, provides scaffolding for novices and even provides a good context for teaching deliberately'. Rogoff (1990 p39) draws parallels between the roles of young children and the roles of novices in apprenticeship. They both actively try to make sense of new situations and put themselves in a position to learn. The apprenticeship model often involves a group of novices who are a resource to one another in developing skill and understanding. They differ in levels of expertise and act, within the group, both as teachers and learners. Again, she could be describing playgroups when she says (p39) 'the model provided by apprenticeship is one of active learners in a community of people who support, challenge and guide novices as they increasingly participate in skilled, valued socio-cultural activity'.

Communities of Practice

Lave and Wenger (1991 p85) engage with Rogoff's 'apprenticeship' view of learning. To embrace both the 'apprenticeship' model and their view that 'learning is an integral and inseparable aspect of social practice', they describe all learning as 'legitimate peripheral participation in communities of practice'. Newcomers to any community of practice must learn the ways and skills of that community. The term 'implies emphasis on comprehensive understanding involving the whole person rather than receiving a body of knowledge about the world'. Learning is about changing identity in a community of practice. As participate, we begin to form an identity related to that community. We may identify with a place or a trade or sport. We may come to see ourselves as literate, as caring, as scientists. Viewing children's play with this lens, it is clear that children are not merely in the business of learning skills or concepts but are embracing the whole identity of members of each community of practice that they enter in their play. As in the story 'Engineers at Work' (IPPA 2004), the children investigate the flow of water but as they do, their demeanour, voices, commentary, etc. indicate that they have entered the role of workmen in its totality. Inevitably foremen and masters appear to lead the activity. As children become more familiar with one another, we know that the play scenes are repeated and the play becomes more complex. Lave and Wenger (1991) describe expertise as moving towards full participation in that community. With practice, children are quicker to move into role and more knowledgeable and skilled in meeting the demands of the role. If planning is part of that community of practice, then children practice planning. If literacy is important then children engage with literacy. If counting is important, they learn to count. And of course, if creativity or co-operation is valued in that community, children learn these skills. The children become more expert in the community of practice depending on their level of participation Communities of practice are not isolated entities, they have overlap and connections with many other communities as do the players in each community. Following this thinking, I would like to propose and demonstrate from observations of children's play, a number of communities of practice which children experiment with and enter in play.

With this 'community of practice' lens we can integrate the theories of Bruner, Rogoff, Lave and Wenger and Gussin Paley and the new Irish 'Framework for Early Learning' (NCCA 2004). This framework is based on the New Zealand curriculum for early childhood, Te Whariki (1996). It proposes a curriculum for children from birth to six years in Ireland based on four themes: (1) well being (2) belonging and identity (3) communication and (4) exploration and thinking. In a shift from a subject-based curriculum, the Framework proposes that these four areas of learning are the work of early childhood, in particular. The IPPA publication 'Power of Play' documents through learning stories (Carr 2001) how children through play develop these areas of learning. Through the use of video clips, readers are invited to observe children as they practice agentive participation in a range of communities of practice. These include the communities of peers, players, pioneers, professionals and phantasmagorical characters.

Communities of Peers

In this community, the priorities may be about developing friendship, generating activity and involvement and developing a sense of belonging. Vivian Gussin Paley (1986), in her book 'Molly is Three' describes Molly's attempts to come to an understanding of friendship. Is friendship something to do with age? Are people friends because their favourite play characters, such as Batman and Robin, are friends? Finding one's place in the group demands complex negotiation and understanding. Corsaro (1985 p171) saw a pattern in the communal sharing of social activities among peers that was influenced by 'a set of activities or routines, artifacts, values, concerns and attitudes'.

Here we see two boys as they pretend to drink tea together. This is a culturally friendly event. The photograph captures the intimacy of the occasion. The boys have found a cosy spot for two and we can see that they are in the process of being friends. The comfort of the location, the activity of making and drinking tea, the conversation, the two-someness, all contribute to recreate a familiar cultural scenario. One might say that the boys are demonstrating tea making skills, fine motor skills, communication skills but that would be to disintegrate the experience. Ultimately, this is a complex story that can only be understood within its entire context.

This is the 'cone construction' story ' Building Togetherness' referred to earlier. The photograph shows Keith, the newcomer (to the right of the tower), thanks to Seán's interventions now fully integrated and helping to build. In the meantime, Seán is making eye-to-eye contact with Derek who moves on to co-operate in the construction. As we watch, we see children develop co-operation and collaboration in a joint project. Different children become the more expert peer and guide the participation of others. Ultimately, they want to create a very tall structure that they can enjoy demolishing and in their eagerness to involve others in the play, they are motivated towards negotiation and collaboration.

The little girl/telephonist in this photograph is familiar with office routines and the work and mannerisms of an office telephonist. In this domain, she is the more skilled peer. Other children can learn these routines from her and develop scripts for dealing with people in that sector. Indeed, this may be as helpful as real life experience of office routines. Learning the scripts for

cultural social activities such as going to school, eating in a restaurant, going to the supermarket or the doctor, gives us a sense of mastery and competence and allows us to feel comfortable in the community. It contributes to our self-confidence, our well-being and sense of belonging.

Community of Players

This is a skilled community in which children learn through participate. Reynolds and Jones (1997) use the term 'master players' to describe children who are particularly skilful in this community, implying that children move from apprentices or novices to master status. From this video clip, I have selected two photos. The first shows children in pretend play. Kira is the Mother and her waving finger and direct eye contact combined with the assertive stance of Katie indicate that this is a scenario about reprimand and defiance. We can surmise this from the details of gesture. These girls are in role.

In the second photo, the stances and gestures are more relaxed. The girls have stepped outside the play to agree the direction of the next scene. Kira suggests that she will be the babysitter and the Mother will go out for the evening. Now the play can continue.

These players know the rules of pretend play. It demands that they suspend reality and apply imagination. They know how to initiate an idea, pick up cues, seek clarification, opt in and opt out of the play. Pretend play, like any community of practice is stylised. Children can communicate within the frame about the roles they are playing and move outside the play frame to communicate about the play. This meta-communication (Bateson 1956) is necessary to both establish inter-subjectivity (Trevarthen 1999) and to allow the players to stay in role in the play. Play is at its most continuous and complex when there is inter-subjectivity within and without the frame. With familiarity and practice, children become more expert, become fuller participants. Play scripts grow longer and more complex. Children learn to negotiate, to compromise, to develop a theory of mind (Leslie 1987), to direct and choreograph within the complexity of the social activity. These are skills that cannot be learned without engaging with the complexity of living situations.

Community of Pioneers and Explorers

We call him Ali, the Scientist because for thirty minutes, we have watched him on video as he experiments with the flow of water. He compares and contrasts, estimates and measures, seeks pattern. Ali needs this first hand experience of water so that he develops an intuitive sense of its properties. As he pursues his interest, Ali demonstrates an extremely high level of involvement as described by Laevers (1994). We know that the feeling of flow (Czickzenmihali 1979), the sense of mastery that Ali experiences, contribute hugely to his well-being and help him to develop such lifelong learning dispositions as the ability to pursue an interest, to persevere and to concentrate.

Likewise, in the story "You be the Fireman', the children discover siphoning and combustion and when they have mastered the concepts and the skills, they

then integrate them into a play scenario. Like all science, sometimes trial and testing is repetitive and painstaking, sometimes discoveries are made by chance. This exploratory play is described by Hutt (1979) as 'epistemic' play. It is significant in this story that typically, the children move from exploratory to pretend play when they are confident that they have mastered the skills. Role-play can only happen when children have a shared concept of the behaviours and skills required in that community.

Community of Professionals

In a society where children have little access to the working lives of adults, pretend play becomes all the more important. It allows children to enter and experience many communities of practice that in real life they can only observe from a distance or on a television screen. In other societies, children, through a process of guided participation (Rogoff 1990), are initiated into the trades and survival skills of adults from a very young age. We know that in Western industrialised societies children play more and adults encourage them and engage in play (Goncu 1999). Perhaps this is the culture's way of compensating for children's exclusion from real life learning/apprenticeship opportunities.

Maggie, the hairdresser in this photograph 'has a friend whose aunt is a hairdresser' (IPPA, 2004 p17). She has her own hair styled. Her visits to the hairdresser have been action-research focused. This is not the learning of a passive observer. This is the learning of the apprentice who has acquired may of the peripheral skills '... before moving on to fine art of hair design' Lave and Wenger might describe this as legitimate peripheral participation in the community of practice of hairdressers. Without this expression of interest, sufficient knowledge to give her a feel for the work and the sense of competence she gets from the work, Maggie is unlikely to move towards fuller participation and become more expert in this community.

These road-builders are not just building roads, they have entered the community of practice of road-builders. Concepts of slope and distance and angles are important in this community and they pre-occupy these children. The expert road-builders take on the persona of road engineers and the long planks of wood allow them to engage with the gestures, commentary and sensation of carrying heavy weights. New comers to the practice are more reticent, less able, slower, less skilful and less tuned in to others thinking.

Each community has a cultural way of being and meeting their goals and its practices must be understood in terms of the history, the economic and social influences and the way logic and meaning are constructed in that community. For these children, this is the action research of the practitioner. It is learning negotiated within the complexity of activity. This play is doubly complex in that it requires that children are skilled in the community of players as well as the community of builders. Children seem to put themselves in the way of this kind of learning (Rogoff 1990). In play, they often engage in communities of hospital staff, shop keepers, parents, repair workers, post- men and women, librarians, bin collectors, police officers, the list is endless.

Community of Phantasmagorical Characters (Sutton Smith 1997)

Sutton Smith (1997) refers to play involving superhuman characters and extraordinary events as 'phantasmagoria' and suggests that in societies that are comfortably adapted to their environment, this type of play allows opportunities to engage with danger, to safely experience the extremes of emotion, and to generate flexible thinking and creative solutions. In Western societies, much play is characterised by superhuman characters and extraordinary events.

Gussin Paley (IPPA Conference 2004) tells us that children's playscripts and story-telling, like theatre and novels, often follow such universal themes as 'someone is lost and finds a friend, is unloved and finds love, confronts life and death, is weak and then strong'. Sutton Smith (1997) that play lifts us out of the routine and humdrum to create a sense that life is worth living. Play is the antidote to the rigidity of successful ecological adaptation. It keeps us alert and open to change. 'Play's engineered predicaments model the struggle for survival ... Play actualises what are otherwise only potential brain and behaviour connections' Sutton Smith (1997, p229). So, not only does play allow children to engage with existing communities of practice but they are invited to engage with the imaginary, the possible and even the impossible.

Communities of Practice – Why is This an Important Concept?

The concept of learning in communities of practice is important because it emphasises situated learning in the community as opposed to the de-contextualised learning associated with schooling. School is a particular community of practice with its own values and goals. I propose that in order to engage with the abstracted learning of school, children first need time to make sense of the complex, concrete learning that can only happen within its related cultural context. 'Knowledge only carries meaning when it is located in a specific context. That is why stories are so powerful in conveying ideas, often more so than an articulation of the idea itself' (Lave and Wenger 1991 p86). Play scripts are stories that embrace the complexity of human activity. There is a sense of: this is how things are done in this community: concepts and skills have a 'past, present and possibilities' (Bruner 1996): being part of the community is a transaction between self, activity and society.

As a lens with which to view play, it allows us to see the experiences children bring to play and to recognise the cultural communities that have already impacted on their learning and identity. In recognising the situated nature of learning, we recognise that children learn what is in the environment to be learned. Learning is cultural and cultural concepts survive because they serve a cultural goal, *e.g.* we plan for the future because we are confident of the future: we become literate because the society demands and values the written word: we value individuality because we live in a competitive world that rewards individual entrepreneurship. It prompts us to question what we value as learning and indicates that any redirection in that learning must be negotiated with the important communities in the child's life.

As the expert in a pretend community of practice, the adult has an opportunity to introduce valued practices and skills and to promote their development. The teacher in an early childhood service needs expertise in the communities of practice that engage the children in her/his group. She/he needs to know the rituals, routines and skills involved in being a home maker, a builder, a nurse or a Super Cat in order to guide children's participation. In a society that values such things as planning, numeracy, literacy and reflection, a community of builders might be encouraged to plan and design the construction, a community of housekeepers might be prompted to count the place settings at a table or make a shopping list, a community of scientists might engage in reflecting on what worked and didn't work. A society that values relationships and co-operation might identify and affirm such supportive interactions as they happen.

This concept of situated or socio-cultural learning has its protagonists and antagonists. While I recognise that there is a body of knowledge in each discipline that is important and that must be passed on from generation to generation and that there is individual variation in ability to progress useful knowledge and that some knowledge in our society is more useful in achieving worthwhile societal goals, I also recognise the complexity of human activity and knowing. I feel fortunate to work in the area of early childhood where it is easier to reach a consensus that young children need first and foremost to adapt to their environment and to make sense of the world and their place within it. The child needs to establish a sense of self, primarily as someone who is loved and can love, who is competent and agentive and belonging in the community. Depending on what is valued in that community, they will choose to be literacy or visually or auditory dependent, to become independent or interdependent, to be compliant or creative or to strike a balance anywhere along a myriad of spectra. The goal is to achieve a healthy feeling of well-being, a sense of belonging, an ability to communicate and the enthusiasm and skills to explore (NCCA, 2004). This is a journey of changing and growing identity through participation in social activity and can only be achieved by engaging in cultural communities of practice.

Conclusion

In summary, this paper proposes, in particular, that play is about communities of learners (Bruner 1996), learning through 'guided participation' (Rogoff 1996) in a range of complex contexts, and about the changing identity of the players in communities of practice (Lave and Wenger 1999). In play, the child enters a 'community of practice' (Lave and Wenger 1991) and becomes an apprentice (Rogoff 1990) in that community, becoming more skilled as they engage more fully with the practices of that community through participation. In early childhood settings, the child participates in the communities of pretenders and learns the behaviours, skills and attitudes that are part of that community. Within that frame of pretence, children enter a range of communities of practice *e.g.* pioneers, professionals and 'phantasmagoricals', and engage with the complexity of life and valued skills within each community. Children will learn about co-operation or competition if it is part of or relevant to that community. Children will be creative if the activity demands it. Children will learn about literacy if it is practised in that community. To support the child in, for example, becoming literate, the adult, rather than de-contextualising literacy, integrates it into the rituals and values of the community. To guide children's participation in any community of practice, the adult must be more expert and/or co-learner. This view of learning has major implications for childcare practice and the 'communities of practice' lens suggests ways of understanding and assessing children's learning within the context of family and community and of guiding their participation in the larger community.

Bibliography

Bateson, G. (1956) The Message 'This is Play" in *Group Processes* B. Schaffner (Ed), New York: Josiah Masey

Bruner, J. (1996) *The Culture of Education,* Harvard University Press

Carr, M. (2001) *Assessment in Early Childhood Settings,* Paul Chapman Publishing

Corsaro, W. (1985) *Friendship and Peer Culture in the Early Years,* Norwood NJ: Ablex

Czickzentmihayli, M. (1979) The Concept of Flow, in B. Sutton Smith, *Play and Learning,* New York, Gardner

Goncu, A. (Ed), (1999) *Children's Engagement in the World,* New York, Cambridge University Press

Gussin Paley, V. (1986) *Molly is Three,* Cambridge M.A. London: Harvard University Press

Gussin Paley, V. (1997) *Story and Play: The Original Learning Tools,*

Conference, Walferdange, Luxembourg, 10th March 1997

Gussin Paley, V. (2004) '*Young Children as Story-tellers and Story-players*', IPPA Conference, Limerick, Ireland, 8th May 2004

IPPA (2004) Brennan, C. (Ed.) '*Power of Play: A Play Curriculum in Action Play*', IPPA, Dublin

Laevers, F. (Ed) (1994) *The Leuven Involvement Scale for Young Children* LIS-YC, Manual and Videotape, Experiential Education Series no. 1, Centre for Experiential Education, Leuven, Belgium, Leuven University Press

Lave J., Wenger E. (1991) *Situated Learning: Legitimate Peripheral Participation* Cambridge University Press

Lave J., Wenger E. (1999) Learning and Pedagogy in Communities of Practice in Jenny Leach and Bob Moon (Eds.) *Learners and Pedagogy* (1999) London, Paul Chapman Publications Ltd

Leslie, A. (1987) Pretense and Representation: The Origins of 'Theory of Mind' in *Psychological Review* 1987 Vol. 94, No. 4, 412-426

National Council for Curriculum Awards (2004) *Towards a Framework for Early Learning: A Consultative Document*, NCCA Government Publication, Dublin

Reynolds, G., Jones E. (1997) *Master Players: Learning from Children at Play*, New York, Teachers College Press

Rogoff, B. (1990) *Apprenticeship in thinking: Cognitive Development in Social Context* Oxford University Press

Sutton-Smith, B. (1997) *The Ambiquity of Play*, Cambridge Universtiy Press. USA

Vygotsky, L. (1978) *Mind in Society*, Harvard University Press, Cambridge Mass

Whiting, B. B. (1980), Culture and Social Behaviour: A Model for Development of Social Behaviours, Ethos, 8, p95-116 in Cole, M. (1998) 'Culture in Development' in Woodhead, M., Faulkner, D. and Littleton, K. (Eds) *Cultural Worlds of Early Childhood*, London, Routledge

Children of the Global Village:
Playing the Way into Communities of Practice
Part Two

Marlene McCormack

This small-scale study aims to investigate a framework for effective adult education in Childcare.

Background to Study – why is this study important?

Caring for young children outside of their home environment by someone other than mother, older sibling, aunt or granny, is a relatively new phenomena in Irish society. According to Kennedy (2001), mothers have always been the key figures in child care, sometimes on their own and sometimes supported by extended family. Not too long ago, 'a man never attended to small children. Should the wife be ill or die, another woman must come at once to take care of the children' (O Danachair, 1962, p. 188). Society was and to some extent is still conflicted about the care of young children outside their home, which undoubtedly has 'consequences for children' (Meluish 1993, p.21).

The need for quality childcare is a fact of life and the single largest influence on the quality of early childhood care and education for young children is, according to Athey (1990) the trained adult. The manner in which adults work with children demonstrates their values (Drummond, 1993) and those of the society in which they live. Practitioners need to understand themselves and to have developed personal and professional values and principles in working with young children (Pugh & De'Ath 1989). Much of this learning comes through training, experience and reflection.

There is overwhelming evidence (Blenkin & Yue, 1994) that once trained and qualified, practitioners are unlikely to pursue further qualifications or training of an award-bearing kind. If there is agreement that well trained adults have a direct bearing on the quality of every day experiences for young children and that in general these early educators only undertake one accredited programme, then it is incumbent on training providers to ensure quality training is delivered. But what constitutes 'quality training'? This small-scale study sets out to explore elements of quality training from the perspective of a range of adult learners.

Methodology – what we did and why?

In considering the concept of effective training and acknowledging that theory offers one perspective on the subject, this study attempts to integrate the experience as voiced by participants and in so doing address the 'optimal relationship between researchers and researched' (Rolfe and MacNaughton, 2001, p.9).

This small-scale study reflects through questionnaire/evaluations and interviews the preferences and effectiveness of IPPA training as perceived by three groups of participants. Each group undertook a different training programme but each programme was similar in the teaching methodologies used, levels of support to participants, underpinning philosophy and ethos of the tutors. These participants were engaged in:

IPPA/FETAC Level 2 certificate in Childcare	8 modules delivered over one academic year
IPPA/FETAC Level 3 certificate 'Supervision in Childcare'	4 mandatory modules plus 1 elective over one academic year
City & Guilds (7307) Certificate in 'Teaching Adult Learners'	Programme delivered over one academic year

Evaluations and interviews were undertaken with each group but for the purposes of this study a different emphasis is put on the findings from each programme. Questionnaire/evaluation data from Level 3 participants, gathered at the end of the course, focused on preferred/most effective methodologies and most useful aspects of the training. Information yielded from an exit interview with participants of a Level 2, conducted at the end of the training programme, explored the impact of the training on participants in a personal and professional capacity. As part of an evaluation, which drew on the Kirkpatrick module, a follow up interview was conducted with participants, who successfully completed a 'Training of Trainers' programme (7307). This evaluation explored participant's reactions to training, learning developed in addition to transfer and application of learning. The information pertinent to this study identified the level of further training undertaken by participants following completion of the 7307.

This study is confined to participants who have completed IPPA training on three specific programmes and is selective in the data it draws on. The data yielded indicates positive aspects of training as perceived by three groups who have engaged with learning delivered and underpinned by a common philosophy. However, knowledge arising out of the participant's responses is valid in its authenticity, that is, 'it is the true voice of the participants in the research' (Hughes, 2001, p.36). The approach used within this study 'seeks to understand individual's perceptions' (Bell, 1999, pl.7) and ultimately to gain insight rather than statistical analysis.

Findings – what does the data say?

At Level 3, 10 out of 15 questionnaire/evaluations were completed and returned (a return rate of 66%). While full returns are preferable, McCormick and James (1983) propose that there is no absolute guarantee that a number of data sources purporting to provide evidence concerning the same construct in fact do so. Of the 10 questionnaires returned 100% of participants found small group work as a methodology to be very effective. On participant reported 'I found the small group discussions most helpful as I found it easier to give my opinion and take on board the opinion of others'. 80% identified experiential workshops as useful/very useful and 80% also found large discussion groups to be effective. The one area where participants indicated uncertainty with methodologies used was that of 'rounds' (a explanation...) where 70% found the method useful/very useful while 10% found it not useful and 20% failed to reply. A 'round' is a method whereby participants have an opportunity to evaluate and feedback thoughts in a systematic way. It offers possibilities for each voice to be heard, which can be empowering or daunting for individuals. Overall participants liked the mix of methods used. According to one participant they (the variety of methods) 'allowed for greater understanding and exploration of topics'

The most useful/effective aspects of training as documented by the participants in narrative form at Level 3 included:

▸ tutors – that they were 'well learned and prepared' 'helpful and supportive', 'task and process orientated' 'adult centered' 'clear and consistent'.

- relevant subjects/content – 'training helped me start to think as a supervisor' 'I feel like a professional in my approach to children, staff and parents' 'modules enabled me gain understanding of what, how and why we do what we do in pre-school'
- support – comments related primarily to feedback and tutorials – 'Feedback came in written and verbal form and were both very valuable in helping me find the gaps I still needed to fill'. 'Feedback was very encouraging and supportive of work' 'Tutorials kept me focused'
- participants – comments identified the value of peer support – 'I felt support from all participants,' 'made friends within the group and had them to bounce ideas off'
- social aspect – the social aspect of stepping out of daily life for one day a week and 'doing something for myself' along with enjoying the 'social aspect of lunch and breaks' added to the learning experience.

Data compiled from exit interviews at Level 2 with a group of 13 practitioners, reflects three key areas where they have benefited from the training – the development of skills, the acquisition of further knowledge and an increased sense of professional status/confidence. According to one participant, 'I felt I had the knowledge and skills to organize and talk at a parent's night'. Another stated 'I now have the confidence to apply for a new job as manager' An increase in professional confidence/status was indicated by 9 of the practitioners. 'I have a terrific sense of worth in what I do' was echoed in a range of statements reflecting a heightened sense of professionalism. The experience at Level 2 enabled some participants to reflect on and improve their service 'I have made lots of changes in my workplace' and yet another 'I'm building a new premises and moving into full day care'. Another reported that 'I got a huge promotion in work, I'm now a Development Officer and my wages are increased three fold'.

Findings from the interviews of Trainer of Trainer participants indicate that 87% of the participants undertook further education/training, 100% remained in the sector which ensured the skills and knowledge filtered through to the areas of need and 100% have improved their employment situation.

Analysis – How do we interpret the data?
In examining this multiplicity of information from the perspective of the participants, some indicators of effective training become apparent, which echo

the findings of among others, Knowles (1980), Brookfield (1987), Katz (1977), Lave & Wenger (1991), Freire (1970) in the area of further and adult education.

Methodologies

Participants in this study clearly articulated the benefits and joy of learning through a range of methodologies 'loved the experientials' and 'small group work is more suited to me because I prefer to talk and interact with small numbers.' Elizabeth Jones (1986) believes that people who are going to become teachers of young children should be taught in the same way they will teach. This thinking is endorsed by Katz (1977). She names this the 'Principle of Congruity' – the ways in which adults work with adults should mirror the ways in which adults work with children. If we wish children to be actively involved in the construction of meaning and knowledge then we must work with adults in ways that 'emphasize experiential, participative and projective instructional methods, appropriate use of modeling and learning contracts' (Mezirow, 1983). Work undertaken by Kolb (1984) and Kolb and Fry (1975) indicate that all ages of learner tend to learn much more effectively if they are actively involved in the process. The tendency has therefore moved away from the traditional didactic or banking model (Freire, 1970) of education to a more student-centred, experiential approach. This approach supports the participant/learner engage, reflect, apply and evaluate learning experiences. Many of the methodologies enjoyed by the participants in what is taken as 'effective training' were based on the concept and practice of dialogue or storytelling, which is experiential and reflective in its approach. Dialogue ' is the moment where humans meet to reflect on their reality as they make it and remake it' (Shor and Freire, 1987: 98-99). . Dialogue and exploration of concepts/topics were ongoing features of each of the three courses. People like to tell stories and Eckhartsbert (1981) sees a direct connection between storytelling and the construction of knowledge, which is essentially a social process.

Content & Relevance

Knowles (1980) maintains that since adult's readiness to learn is frequently affected by their need to know or do something, they tend to have a life-, task- or problem-centered orientation to learning as opposed to a subject-matter orientation. Equally, Brookfield (1986, p.113)) agrees that 'the focus of activities (learning) is determined by adults' perceptions of relevance rather than being externally imposed' Learning for adults (indeed children) is never context-free. Adults are intrinsically motivated to learn within a social and cultural context. The issue of content or relevance in training highlights the role of the tutor/facilitator in assisting the participant define his/her learning needs, to support them in self-directed learning and to 'organise what is to be learned in relationship to his/her current personal problems, concerns and levels of understanding' (Suanmali, 1981, p.1-32). One of the participants, in responding to a question regarding course content, advised ' it (the content) made me start to think as a supervisor and the work that I do.'

Content relevance is one issue, but as Tennant (1988, p.140) reports on and attributes to Horton 'an unanalyzed experience is a kind of a happening'. A key skill that effective training should, (from the participant's perspective, and from IPPA's practice) promote is that of critical thinking which in turn supports reflective practice. Critical thinking/analysis is important because it involves 'examining the relevance of existing knowledge, challenging assumptions and imagining and exploring alternatives (Atkins & Murphy 1993, p.1190). While much has been written on 'reflection', it is as acknowledged by Moon (1999) frequently complex and difficult to apply. In supporting critical reflection, participants become empowered, thinking about their learning, thinking about their practice and engaging in an action research cycle, which positively impacts on practice.

Quality training therefore provides a goodness-of-fit between content to be covered and the needs/interests of the learner while actively modeling and facilitating reflection and critical thinking. As Shor, (1980) purports critically reflective teachers are likely to foster classrooms in which challenge and excitement are found.

Tutors

Participants in their varied responses attributed 'characteristics' or 'ways of being' to tutors which they found supportive, *e.g.*, ' positive and encouraging' 'well prepared' 'very approachable'. What do these attributes translate into when lifted into the arena of effective training with the tutor (and her/his role) under the microscope? It appears that tutor support; knowledge and attunement are essential to effective training.

Support takes many guises ranging from encouragement to critical questioning (Brookfield, 1987) to written feedback to tutorials to mentoring. These positive interventions by the tutor nurture self-directed learning, which is advocated by Knowles (1975) and Brookfield (1981). A supportive learning environment encourages learners in their efforts to change and take risks. Within this teaching and learning process, the tutor helps 'the learner to understand how to use learning resources – especially the experiences of other, including the educator and how to engage others in reciprocal learning relations' (Suanmali, 1981, p.31-32). Written feedback on work submitted in conjunction with regular one-to-one tutorials enables the participants to assume increasing responsibility for their own learning. People, according to Jones (1986) 'need both support and challenge to grow.' To do this effectively tutors must know their subjects intimately from theoretical thinking to the every day realities existing within the given sector, in this case childcare. Moving from the 'banking model' of education as critiqued by Freire (1970) to an 'emancipatory' model in which the focal point becomes not the world of the teacher but the world of the learner, the tutor must know and understand the working world or reality from which the participant comes.

Other players exist in the teaching and learning process, namely other participants. Learning is essentially social (Vygotsky 1978) and throughout this study participants have elaborated on the benefits of group support both emotionally and academically, 'I have felt supported and have made friends' 'I really enjoyed the social side of the course too. We still meet and its great to discuss our work with each other.' This highlights the need for tutors to ask what kinds of social engagements provide the proper contexts for learning take place (Wenger 1998). These groups of practitioners have, through the co-construction of knowledge and the deepening and sharing of experiences, become involved in a community of practice (Lave and Wenger, 1991), which adds social capital to the very fabric of our world. In facilitating social learning, tutors must set the conditions for learning, attend to the process as well as the task and take opportunities to establish points of connection within the group.

Conclusion

In analysing the data, it is clear that the tutor holds an enormous responsibility in delivering training, establishing the conditions for learning, involving participants in all aspects of the training, sharing control, valuing the experience of the participants and supporting learning, all of which become features of effective training. The outcomes of successful learning are evidenced through the numbers of participants who reviewed and made changes in practice, who engaged in further training, who felt confident and competent to progress in their careers within the sector and who achieved academically.

Perhaps a strong indicator of effective training is one which, in contrast to the earlier statement of Blenkin & Yue, (1994) – that once trained and qualified, practitioners are unlikely to pursue further qualifications or training of an award-bearing kind – enthuses and fires the learner onward in pursuance of life long learning. This tenet is espoused as a principle of education policy in the White Paper on Adult Education. (July 2000, p.24), which indicates 'a shift from a solely front-loading model of education provision to one in which lifelong learning becomes the overriding principle.'.

This study suggests that participants experience effective training as being supportive, social and empowering, as facilitating dialogue, promoting reflection, provoking critical thinking and developing pathways. A tall order for the providers of training!

Bibliography

Athey, C. (1990) *Extending Thought in Young Children.* London: Paul Chapman.

Atkins, S. & Murphy, K. (1993) Reflection: A review of the literature. *Journal of Advanced Nursing,* 18, 1188-1192. In McDrury, J. & Alterio, M. (2002) Learning through Storytelling in Higher Education. Using Reflection & Experience to Improve Learning. London: Kogan Page Ltd.

Bell, J. (1999) *Doing Your Research Project.* Third Edition. Buckingham: Open Uiversity Press.

Blenkin, G.M., & Yue, N.Y.L. (1994) Profiling Early Years Practitioners: Some First Impressions from a National Survey, 13-22. In: *Early Years.* Vol. 15. No. 1.

Brookfield, S.D. (1981) 'Independent Adult Learning. Studies in Adult Education. In Brookfield S.D., (1986) *Understanding and Facilitating Adult Learning.* Buckingham: Open University Press

Brookfield S.D., (1986) *Understanding and Facilitating Adult Learning.* Buckingham: Open University Press

Brookfield, S.D., (1987) *Developing Critical Thinkers.* Buckingham: Open

University Press.

Dept. of Education and Science (2000) *Learning for Life: White Paper on Adult Education.* Dublin: Stationery Office

Drummond, M.J. (1993) *Assessing Children's Learning.* London: David Fulton.

Eckhartsberg, R. (1981) Maps of the mind. In Vaille, R. & Von Eckhartsberg (Eds). The metaphors of consciousness. New York: Plenum. In McDrury, J. & Alterio, M. (2002) *Learning through Storytelling in Higher Education. Using Reflection & Experience to Improve Learning.* London: Kogan Page Ltd.

Freire, P. (1970) *Pedagogy of the Oppressed.* New York:Continuum

Jones, E., (1986) *Teaching Adults – An Active Learning Approach.* Washington: NAEYC.

Katz, L. G. (1977). *Talks with teachers: Reflections on early childhood education.* Washington, DC: National Association for the Education of Young Children. (ERIC Document No. ED144703)

Kennedy, F. (2001) *Cottage to Creche. Family Change in Ireland.* Dublin: Institute of Public Administration

Knowles, M.S. (1975) Self-Directed Learning: A Guide for Learners and Teachers. New York: Cambridge Books. In Brookfield S.D., (1986) *Understanding and Facilitating Adult Learning.* Buckingham: Open University Press

Knowles, M.S. (1980) *The Modern Practice of Adult Education: From Pedagogy to Andragogy.* (2nd Ed.) New York: Cambridge Books.

Kolb, D. (1984) *Experiential learning.* Englewood Cliffs, J.J.: Prentice-Hall. In Tennant, M. (1988) *Psychology and Adult Learning.* London: Routledge.

Kolb, D. & Fry, R. (1975). Towards an applied theory of experiential learning. In Cooper, C. (Ed.) (1975) *Theories of group processes.* London: Wiley. In Tennant, M. (1988) *Psychology and Adult Learning.* London: Routledge.

Lave, J. and Wenger, E. (1991) *Situated Learning.* Cambridge: Cambridge University Press.

McCormick, R. and James M. (1983) *Curriculum Evaluation in Schools.* Beckenham: Croom Helm. In. Cohen, L. & Manion, L. (1985) *Research Methods in Education.* Second Edition. Beckenham: Croom Helm.

Melhuish, E.C. (1993) Preschool care and education: Lessons from the 20th for the 21st Century. In: *International Journal of Early Years Education.* Vol. 1, No. 2, Autumn 1993.

Mezirow, J. (1983) A critical theory of adult learning and education. In Tight,

M. (Ed.) *Adult learning and education.* London: Croom Helm.

Moon, J. (1999) *Reflection learning and professional development.* London: Kogan Page Limited.

O'Danachair, C. (1962) 'The Family in Irish Tradition', Christus Rex, XVI, 3:185-196, July. In Kennedy, F. (2001) *Cottage to Creche. Family Change in Ireland.* Dublin: Institute of Public Administration

Pugh, G. & De'Ath, E. (1989) *Working towards partnership in the early years.* London: National Children's Bureau.

Rolfe, S.A., & MacNaughton, G. (2001) Research as a tool. In Mac Naughton, G., Rolfe, S.A. & Siraj-Blatchford, I. (Eds), *Doing Early Childhood Research.* Buckingham: Open University Press.

Shor, I. (1908) Critical Teaching and Everyday Life. Boston: South End Press. In Brookfield, S.D. (1987) *Developing Critical Thinkers.* London: Open University Press.

Shor, L. & Freire, P. (1987) A pedagogy for liberation: Dialogues on transforming education. Westport, CT: Bergen and Garvey/Greenwood Press. In McDrury, J. & Alterio, M. (2002) *Learning through Storytelling in Higher Education. Using Reflection & Experience to Improve Learning.* London: Kogan Page Ltd.

Smith, A. (1992) Quality and its measurement: socio-political issues, Paper given at Workshop on Defining and Assessing Quality, Seville, 9-12 September. In: Moss, P. and Pence, A. (Eds.) (1994) *Valuing Quality in Early Childhood Services.* London: Paul Chapman.

Suanmali, C. 'The Core Concepts of Andragogy.' Unpublished doctoral dissertation, Department of Higher and Adult Education, Teachers College, Columbia University, 1981. In Brookfield S.D., (1986) *Understanding and Facilitating Adult Learning.* Buckingham: Open University Press

Tennant, M. (1988) *Psychology and Adult Learning.* London: Routledge.

Vygotsky, L.S. (1978) Mind in Society: The development of higher mental processes. Cole, M., John-Steiner, V., Scribner, S. & Souberman, E. Cambridge, MA: Harvard University Press. In Berk, L. and Winsler, A. (1995) *Scaffolding Children's Learning:* Vygotsky and Early Childhood Education. Washington: NAEYC.

Wenger, E. (1998) 'Communities of Practice. Learning as a social system', Systems Thinker, http://www.co-I-l.com/coil/knowledge-garden/cop/lss.shtml.

Section Five

Spirituality

Spirituality and the Young Child

Mary Daly

Introduction

Developing spiritually is vital for the young child yet spiritual development is an area that is almost completely ignored in children. The heart of spirituality is to look inwards in search of meaning and purpose. It is to seek an understanding of what truly matters and why it matters. Spirituality can be described as those attitudes, beliefs, values and practices which emanate from a person's life. Being spiritually developed means having a proper balance between one's outer and inner world. Spirituality is a very vague and broad concept. The word spirit is derived from the Greek word for 'breath' *i.e.* that which gives life to our lives (Douglas 2003). However few words are as misunderstood in the English language today as is the word 'spirituality'. These tragic misunderstandings have led to the neglect of this vital aspect of human life. This article raises the subject of spirituality, spiritual development and one aspect of this – meditation in the hope that it will redress some of the present misconceptions in the area as well as highlighting the benefits of developing the child spiritually and in particular stressing the positive impact of meditation for young children.

Spirituality

Ancient societies, from prehistoric times, frequently showed evidence of a concern with spiritual matters and rituals and anthropological studies show evidence of spiritual beliefs and practices in all recorded societies. However, spirituality is to a large extent forgotten in the western world today, and yet developing spiritually meets certain basic needs of humans. People, modern and ancient, have sought a sense of meaning and purpose in their daily lives and personal choices. Over the millennia people have searched for answers to significant questions and people have always looked for and needed a focus for interaction and celebration. Rituals for important life events fulfil the need for a positive feeling of identity and help answer profound questions. Through time, this evolved into a belief in something outside the individual, something great, and for some led to a belief in God and for others, such as humanists, it led to more secular but no less spiritual beliefs (Lindon 1999). Fowler (1981 xiii) says spirituality is;

so 'fundamental' that none of us can live well for very long without it, so 'universal' that when we move beneath the symbols, rituals and ethical patterns that express it, faith is recognisably the same phenomenon in Christians, Marxists, Hindus and Dinka, yet it is so 'infinitely varied' that each person's faith is unique.

Gilmartin (1996) contends that spirituality is possessed by all people regardless of race, culture, education, intelligence or religion. It is not something acquired but is at the very core of a person's being.
Spirituality is something vital and non-negotiable which lies at the heart of every child's life. Fowler (1981) also contends that spirituality is a human universal. However, how each individual child develops this capacity, how it is activated and grows, depends greatly on how the child is welcomed into the world and what kinds of environment he/she grows up in. Spirituality is interactive and social, it needs language, rituals, nurturance, a community and its underlying principle and centre is, and must be, love. Spirituality is about being integrated as opposed to falling apart, it is about being in a community versus being lonely, about being in harmony with the earth versus being alienated from it. Regardless of whether or not we let ourselves be consciously shaped by any explicitly religious idea, we act in ways that leave us either unhealthy or healthy, bitter or loving, alienated or in community – what shapes us is our spirituality. However our present technological age has introduced the fragmentation of tasks, the shattering of community and the ascendancy of technological and materialistic values to the detriment of the spiritual. This has had drastic negative consequences for humans, particularly young children, and the experience of this spiritual vacuum gives rise to frustration, sadness, loneliness and to a sense of isolation and alienation. Pessimism is in the air as we begin the third millennium. All is not well with the world spiritually and as Aronson (1995 p.216) says: "Collectively as a society, we are starving for spirit; we whine from hunger pains; we are malnourished". Science, economics, technology and the consumer culture have so dominated and diminished the spiritual side of life that it has been repressed to almost non-existence. Thus the 21st century needs to reflect on a new level of spiritual wisdom and intuitive insight.

The importance of the early years for spiritual development
All people, including children, are driven by a specifically human longing to

find meaning and value in what they do and experience. Frankl (1985) claims that the search for meaning is one of the primary motivators in children's lives and he suggests that if this deep need for meaning goes unmet, then their lives come to feel shallow and empty. Children have a longing for something towards which they can aspire, for something that takes them beyond themselves and the present moment, for something that gives them and their actions a sense of worth. In other words, children need an overall context for their lives. Spiritual development is often neglected in young children and if it not developed it will be lost. It is easily damaged and needs sensitive nurturing, but if cared for properly it can be like 'watching a flower blossom'. Without spiritual growth children cannot develop to their full potential and will not fulfil their ambitions and dreams. If they are not helped to develop spiritually it can have a detrimental impact on their lives (Daly 2002).

Spiritual quotient

At the beginning of the 21st century there is a growing body of scientific data which shows that just as there is an intelligence quotient, there is also a spiritual quotient. Thus, the full picture of human existence can only be completed with a discussion on the spiritual quotient (S.Q.). S.Q. helps humans address and solve problems of meaning and value. It allows us to place our actions and our lives in a wider, richer, more meaning-giving context (Zohar and Marshall 2000). There are three main intelligences: – I.Q. (Intelligence Quotient), E.Q. (Emotional Quotient) and S.Q. (Spiritual Quotient). It is argued that, ideally, these three basic intelligences work together and support one another. Each on its own has separate areas of strength and can function separately but to develop optimally all three must work together. S.Q. is based on the brain's third neural system (the first and second being reason and emotion) and operates from the brain's neurological unifying functions, where synchronous neural oscillations unify data across the whole brain. S.Q. unifies, integrates and has the potential to transform material arising from the other two processes and facilitates a dialogue between emotion and reason, between body and mind and makes us the fully integrated creatures that we can be (Zohar and Marshall 2000). In recent neurobiological, psychological and anthropological studies of human intelligences and in studies of human thinking and linguistic processes, a great deal of scientific evidence for spiritual quotient (S.Q.) is beginning to emerge. To date, scientists have done much of the basic research revealing the neural foundations of S.Q. In 1997, neurologists Ramachandran and

Blakeshee discovered the existence of the 'God spot' or 'soul spot' in the human brain. This in-built spiritual centre is located among neural connections in the temporal lobes of the brain. On scans taken with Positron Emission Topography (P.E.T.) these neural areas light up whenever research subjects are exposed to discussions on spiritual and religious topics. These lighting-up experiences vary with culture and people respond to symbols meaningful to their own belief systems (Zohar and Marshall 2000). The 'God spot' or 'soul spot' does not prove the existence of God but does show that the brain has evolved to have a spiritual dimension and thus spiritual development must be a core area of development.

Spirituality and religion

> Our civilisation has suppressed truths about the human being's inner life, denied the importance of the non-material, and peddled a perverted spirituality, in the form of conventional religion, as a major weapon against the growth of the free, spiritually-connected, whole citizen (Randle 1989 p.61).

In the past, spirituality tended to be seen as being synonymous with religion and was the domain of the priest, rabbi and minister. However today, early years practitioners, psychologists, psychiatrists, social workers and counsellors are unable to avoid dealing with this issue; they acknowledge that it has relevance for all humans, especially young children. It is now taken for granted that spirituality is too important to be tied exclusively to religion, yet there is still a tendency to confuse the spiritual with the religious (Dowling 2000). Religions often neglect and ignore what is needed by children and adults to help them develop spiritually. Without losing sight of the significant contributions that religions have made to the world, they have also contributed to wars, human enslavement, gross injustices, victimisation and dehumanising practices. In fact, "too often religions have been destructive of human spirituality" (Gilmartin 1996 p.106). Gallagher (1998) says the passive and spiritually shallow approach to religion which has occurred to date is no longer acceptable and we have to create a different kind of religious community if religion is to be in any way beneficial to children's spiritual development. Part of the present-day unhappiness with religion, despite a simultaneous interest in spirituality, reflects religion's failure to give priority to assessing and caring for the spiritual needs of people, including children.

Spirituality, spiritual development and S.Q. are not the dogma of organised religion and have no necessary connection to religion. However, for some, spirituality may find a mode of expression through formal religion but being religious does not signify high S.Q. Many humanists and atheists have very high S.Q.s while many actively and vociferously religious people have very low S.Q.s (Zohar and Marshall 2000). Indeed, Allport's studies (1950) some fifty years ago showed that more people had spiritual experiences outside the confines of mainstream religious institutions than they did within them. Personal spiritual experiences are often disassociated from religion and are based instead on love or some profound commitment or insight. However, S.Q. can put us in touch with the meaning and essential spirit behind all great religions. A child high in S.Q. can practise any religion but without exclusiveness, bigotry or prejudice. Therefore, enhancing spiritual development is in no way anti-religious and in fact most of us need a religious framework as a guide for our lives, while at the same time having a deep and abiding respect for other traditions and other forms (Zohar and Marshall 2000).

Spiritual development

Young children are deeply spiritual, yet this aspect of child development is almost totally ignored. Dowling (2000 p.96) points out that "there has been almost no study of young children's spiritual development and little guidance on how it should be fostered." Rizzuto (1979) states that despite secularisation and religious fragmentation, spirituality is still widely present in our society. Virtually all children reaching school have constructed, with or without religious instruction, an image of God, or at least an image of something greater than themselves. In the past it was suggested that work with young children regarding spirituality was difficult because such children were considered too young to be spiritually aware. What work was done, tended to focus on older children. However, children at four and five are beginning to sort out their experiences of the world and have begun to ask questions about the things they do not understand.

Children are spiritual beings and have naturally what many adults spend years trying to reclaim. Children spend much of their childhoods wondering about nature, about the supernatural, about their friends and about thousands of other things. They start life with an innate sense of awe and wonder about their world, they are naturally open and intuitive and "where there is wonder, there is spirituality" (Doe and Walch 1998 p. xi). The way to maintain it is to recognise and honour children's innate spiritual connection and to ensure that they never lose it by making spiritual development a priority. We try to help children develop optimally and in particular we try to ensure that their cognitive development is optimised. Yet, we miss out on developing the very core of their being – the spiritual. Farrer (2000 p.167) claims that spiritual development;

> is a rock upon which character, behaviour, outlook, learning and happiness can be built. It is a means of reaching the inner world which has been so catastrophically neglected by the material lifestyle culture, and it is the route to real fulfillment and understanding.

Spiritual development is about liberating and nurturing the inner light which lives, however dormant, in every child. It is not just a state of mind but is a way of knowing, a way of being that utterly transforms our understanding and our lives. Helping children develop spiritually entails providing a humanly rich and rounded context of experience and needs to be encountered by the child in a self-evolving way (White 1996).

To develop spiritually, children must constantly revise and extend their understanding to include new knowledge of the larger world and cosmos, and there is no such thing as 'a good hand-me-down spirituality'. To be vital, to be the best of which one is capable, spirituality must be a wholly personal one, developed by questioning and doubting in the experience of one's own reality and experience. Spiritual development can be enhanced and indeed the further evolution of society depends upon it. We are at a very early stage of understanding human spirituality and spiritual development, as they are not aspects of human life and nature which have been studied in depth. Also, there is something vaguely incongruous about trying to measure spirituality. Trying to discern what is true in this area requires sensitivity and can only be done with the greatest of care and with reflective experience. Those who have experience and insight into the area of spiritual development warn against the view that spiritual growth is either automatic or subject to direct influence. Yet, through prioritising spiritual development, we can reconnect children with the deeper sources and meanings within and they can then use these reconnections to serve causes and processes much greater than themselves (Lindon 1999).

There are a number of generally accepted characteristics of mature human spirituality, and providing children with contexts which support the development of these can foster spiritual growth, insight and understanding. Zohar and Marshall (2000 p.15) set out the indicators of a highly developed spirituality as having:

- the capacity to be flexible;
- a high degree of self-awareness;
- a capacity to face and use suffering;
- an ability to face and transcend pain;
- the quality of being inspired by vision and values;
- a reluctance to cause unnecessary harm;
- a tendency to see the connection between diverse things (being holistic);
- a marked tendency to ask 'why', 'what if' questions and to seek fundamental answers;
- a facility to be what psychologists call 'field-independent', possessing an ability to go against convention when necessary.

Beck (1991) also provides a similar list of what he considers are key spiritual characteristics and contends that spiritual people are characterised by being aware, taking a holistic view, being integrative, expressing a sense of wonder, gratitude, hope, courage, detachment, acceptance, love, gentleness and energy. Evans (1993) also outlines the characteristics of a mature spiritual being as having basic trust, humility, self-acceptance, responsibility, self-commitment, concern and contemplation. Why would we not want these for our children?

Spiritual development entails taking in the goodness and wonder of the world. It is about people's thoughts and beliefs and is very important for the creativity of the child. It is developed by discovering that special, hidden part of the human and involves a feeling of 'cosmic connectedness'. Spiritual development is about having a belief in something that while not visible or explainable gives a person a sense of peace, well-being, purpose and 'joie de vivre'. It is about having a respect for the unknown and for that which cannot be explained and involves consciously tuning into and nourishing that part of us that acknowledges something mysterious, mystical and powerful beyond everyday things. It is a gradually increasing awareness of elements beyond our control, the ability to believe what we do not entirely understand and the realisation that we are part of the greater scheme of things. It involves the development of the whole person and is different for every child, but yet is a fundamental need of every child. Spiritual development involves a myriad of things including contemplation, reflection and meditation. Being able to detach oneself from the world and having time to reflect, develops a sense of optimism, hope and inner belief to sustain one throughout life.

Meditation

Being able to meditate is a very important part of the process of developing spiritually. Today children are uncomfortable with empty or silent times. They become bored and have to fill their time with constant activity or need to be entertained by television or computer games. Contemplating, meditating, quietening the mind, being able to detach one's self from the world and having the time and the ability to focus the mind is vital. Practising meditative skills involves a state of pure consciousness, during which the child is highly alert and aware but is not letting him/herself be taken over by past and future thoughts – he/she is living and being in the present moment, fully experiencing the world in a deep sense of calm. Many early years practitioners overlook a child's need to look inward and do not develop the ability to be still in children. Farrer (2000) claims that the practice of reflection and meditation is at least as rare in educational establishments as it is in the larger world. Not only will practising these help the child's physical and mental health, it will also help him to learn more effectively.

Meditation is a word that is applied to a variety of mental activities, some of which have little in common. In the past, the word had strong religious connotations but today there is substantial non-religious and scientific literature on meditation. Jessel-Kenyon and Shealy (1999) define meditation as the ability to reflect, to engage in contemplation, to consider deeply. They state that scientific evidence has come to light which proves that meditation is good for humans.

It is believed that meditation
- enhances perception;
- increases the ability to concentrate;
- can modify immunity and disease susceptibility;
- can help fight illness, both physical and mental, when it occurs;

- can help a person deal better with emotionally loaded and threatening stimuli;
- increases energy and alertness;
- helps children become more tolerant of themselves and others;
- helps children become more decisive;
- helps children become more creative;
- allows children to experience a greater sense of well-being;
- dramatically reduces anxiety. The reduction of anxiety seems to follow almost immediately on learning how to meditate. Not only does meditation reduce present anxiety but it also reduces the susceptibility to becoming anxious in the future (Carrington 1978).

In essence those who meditate are happier and more content with life. Thus there are strong reasons for adults to meditate themselves, as well as teaching children how to meditate. Meditation involves a turning from the outer to the inner world. It stills the mind's activity and involves a receptive rather than an assertive engagement with reality. The meditative state is characterised by relaxation of the body and an increase in alpha and theta brain waves (Griffith 1985). If children can successfully shut out external stimuli and shut down their thinking processes at the same time, they will experience a deeply spiritual state of inner peace. Stilling the mind is not easy. However, with regular and disciplined practice, pre-school aged children can learn to focus their minds steadily on where they want to go. Neville (1989) says that if meditation had no other function than this we would still have a strong argument for including it in the curriculum.

Western culture has a deep suspicion of meditation and this has its source in ignorance and superstition. This is irrational and is specific to western culture. To counter this, many writers on meditation would contend that the kinds of meditative activities which are practicable in the classroom or early years setting should not be called meditation at all. They would reserve the word to refer to the end-state, not the means of getting there and suggest instead calling it 'centring' or 'relaxing' techniques (Hendricks and Wills 1975). There is a variety of centring techniques that are easy for children to incorporate into their daily lives. Focusing on a mantra, resting on the floor in a state of deep quiet, without thoughts or images, listening to a piece of music, guided and spontaneous visualisation, Yoga, T'ai Chi (posture and breathing) are all options that young children could develop (See Appendix 1). Lindon (1999) says that children as young as four and five have been taught basic meditation techniques and that it has helped them relax and to feel positively calm. Peaceful times with a chance to reflect on and enjoy an experience without rational analysis are part of a rounded approach to education. Quiet times and centring techniques have been a valued exercise in the development of children in many cultures but so far have not been seen as valuable for children in the western world.

Conclusion

Robinson (1977) claims that a great deal is extinguished in the experience of children, because the adults they come in contact with are spiritually obtuse. The problems and limitations that many people experience come from a loss of connection to their souls and to humanity. Social problems impact heavily on the daily lives of children and emphasising spiritual development can help redress the balance. Spirituality has to do with living life to the full and is about discovering how to become more fully human. It is about self-discovery, discovery of others and of the world. It is not synonymous with religion nor is it opposed to it. It covers a wide range of human experience and can be experienced in awareness, in response and in ways of life and is vital to every child's development. It is important to create and incorporate spiritual habits into the lives of young children, particularly since: "An individual can no more flourish in a spiritually dead environment than could a tree in the midst of an ecological disaster" (Mott-Thornton 1996 p.80).

Being spiritually developed provides a life-time resource towards peace and tranquillity in an otherwise crazy materialistic world. Spiritual development is nurtured by helping children to love, respect and appreciate themselves and others in the world. It is about tapping into what is deepest within them and is a life-long process that gives meaning and depth to life. Taking time out, stopping and looking at things, being quiet and thinking, learning to appreciate and to meditate, all help in spiritual development (Daly 2002). Bradford (1978) proposed that children possess certain spiritual rights:

▸ the right to the best of the spiritual heritage of the culture into which he/she is born;
▸ the right to express his/her spiritual belief in private and/or public without discrimination;

- the right to deepen, doubt or alter the spiritual commitment into which he/she is being nurtured or educated;
- the right to schooling, family life and other institutional support complementary to his/her spiritual development;
- the right, especially in early life, to such protection from spiritual damage as is reasonable and appropriate.

These rights can be summarised as those of initiation, expression, choice, support and protection and should be available to all children. In a similar vein, Gallagher (1998) argues children have six basic spiritual needs:

- to believe that life has a meaning and purpose;
- to have a sense of community as a place for deepening relationships;
- to be appreciated and loved;
- to be listened to and heard;
- to experience spirituality as a journey and an adventure of growth;
- to have practical help in developing a mature spirituality.

Do children have these needs and rights fulfilled? Prioritising spiritual development could make such a difference in a child's life. Neglect of this vital area in the past has led to severe negative repercussions for children. There is no reason why it has to continue to be ignored. Therefore, it is vital that spiritual development is prioritised, as many children are not living life to the full today. Neglect of this vital area of child development has led to a "massive denial of spiritual energy, of intellectual enquiry, of aesthetic beauty and public virtue" (Abbs 1994 p.1). Irish medical consultant, Dr Michael Kearney (1996) calls lack of spiritual development 'soul pain'. He says it arises when a person becomes cut off or is at odds with the deepest part of himself. Just as connectedness with soul may bring wholeness and a sense of significance, soul pain results in an experience of fragmentation, alienation and meaninglessness. Kearney claims that lack of spiritual development is both at the root of and a cause of physical pain and illness. Myss and Shealy (1999) back this contention and state that the medical world is not yet ready to make official the relationship between emotional dysfunction/spiritual deprivation and their natural consequences to the physical body. However, they claim that western medicine is beginning to recognise that more factors have to be involved in the development of disease than just the physical ones.

Children can show a high degree of spirituality. They ask 'why' questions and seek the meaning of their own and others' actions. They struggle to get feelings and events in a larger meaning-giving context if afforded the opportunity (Zohar and Marshall 2000). Children who are encouraged to be spiritual beings experience things which give them deep feelings of well-being, of magic and mystery – experiences which give a glimmer of hope for the future. These children develop value systems of their own which incorporate emotions and feelings such as loyalty, love, integrity, joy, tenderness, kindness and empathy. They experience moments of intensity where beauty and understanding are prominent and many experience religion with all its powerful and mystic messages. Childhood has its moments of wonderment and as the child matures, experiences and value systems change, wither and/or grow (Kirkland 1996). Surely, it should be ensured that all children experience these moments?

If children are to reach their potential they must be allowed to make their spiritual journeys, as knowing and trusting that all life has a purpose and connection gives children meaning in a complex and confusing world. Also, discovering the sacred self allows them to transcend the physical world with all its inherent limitations and enables children to live in a world of everyday miracles (Doe and Walch 1998). Spiritual development is a vital area of child development and is about the formation of informed but personally chosen answers to questions about the nature and meaning of life. Its neglect in the past has led to severe negative repercussions for children and thus in future spiritual development must be a core area of development in all early years settings.

Appendix
Some ways to help children to relax, centre and meditate

▶ Show children how to be still and help create a place within and allow time for the mind to soar – dim the lights, rest heads on the table and ask children to pretend to be alseep or ask them to lie on the floor with eyes closed. Develop a calm atmosphere in the classroom and give children time for reflection, for daydreaming and for just looking. Silence provides an opportunity to support the thinking process, reflection and personal expression.

▶ Create 'mood settings' regularly, such as exposing children to soothing classical music, lighting a candle, burning some incense or using some essential oils and aromatherapy.

▶ Play lots of relaxing music – there is a variety of types available with the sound of running water, waves, dolphins, birds, calming melodies and so on.

▶ To commence relaxation/visualisation make sure hands and arms are lying loosely. Ask children if their forehead is smooth and invite them to put any worries or frustrations out of their mind and to enjoy this special bit of time for themselves. Children can experience a sense of community, togetherness and connectedness by engaging in such collaborative reflective, meditative exercises.

▶ Show children how to breath deeply and to keep spine erect to allow lungs to expand. With children lying on the floor get them to put one hand on their chest and one hand on the stomach. Encourage them to listen to their breathing and to breathe in through their noses and out through their mouths. Ask them to 'relax' and be 'calm'.

▶ Invite children to take a slow deep breath in through their nose, to hold it for the count of 3 –123 and breath out slowly through their mouths emptying their lungs. Do this three or four times. With every breathe tell them they are becoming more peaceful and calm. Ask them to continue to keep eyes closed and invite them to listen to a piece of music which will take them to a place of greater peace. When the music stops, ask the children to keep eyes closed and to focus on deep breathing again – in through the nose and out through the mouth (3 times). Slowly count back from 5 and ask them to open their eyes when they are ready.

▶ Guide the relaxation through visualisation. Adults do not need specialist training in relaxation techniques, there are a variety of books and tapes available, check local libraries or book shops. Examples of visualisation for young children include 'Go to a place where you feel safe, see your favourite toy/comforter there (teddy bear, blanket). Focus on the object, touching it and holding it or 'I want you to take your mind to (name part of the body in turn – toes, soles of the feet working up to the head). Before commencing ensure that there is a clear space for every child on the floor, make sure that every child can get into a warm comfortable position. Children need more guidance and help in the early stages, with practice it becomes much easier.

▸ Another approach is to focus on an object (a stone, shells, leaves, fir cone) and then to close eyes and to use the mental reconstruction of it to try and hold the mind in one place.

▸ Introduce children to yoga, yoga offers ideas on physical relaxation, breathing and meditation. Yoga helps combat stress and enables children to relax. Get the children to form a circle and to sit with legs crossed, ensure each child has enough space to stretch out on his/her own mat. Lower the lights or pull the curtains and light a small lamp or candle. Then with some quiet soothing music playing in the background children can do neck rolls, back stretches, balancing, breathing (in through nose and out through mouth). Use the video 'Yoga for Kids – Colin the Cobra's Forest of Secrets' Currie (2002) or the video 'Yogabugs', read *Yoga – An Illustrated Guide* Kent (2001) and see the article 'Yoga, Yoga, Yoga' in Volume One of *Project E.Y.E.* (Douglas, Horgan and O'Brien 2000).

▸ Children can also be introduced to T'ai Chi – a Chinese system of meditative exercises characterised by methodically slow circular and stretching movements.

Bibliography

Abbs, P. (1994). *The Educational Imperative*. London: The Falmer Press.

Allport, G. (1950). *The Individual and His Religion*. New York: Macmillan.

Aronson, L. (1995). *Big Spirits, Little Bodies*. Virginia Beach, V.A.: A.R.E. Press.

Beck, J. (1998). *Morality and Citizenship in Education*. London: Cassell.

Bradford, J. (1978). *The Spiritual Rights of the Child*. London: Church of England Children's Society.

Carrington, P. (1978). *Freedom in Meditation.* New York: Anchor.

Daly, M. (2002). *The Emotional, Social, Moral and Spiritual Development of the Young Child – Aiming towards Self-Actualisation* Unpublished Ph.D. Thesis Cork: University College Cork.

Doe, M. and Walch, M. (1998). *Principles for Spiritual Parenting.* New York: Harper Collins.

Douglas F., Horgan, M. O'Brien, C. (2000). *Project E.Y.E. (Early Years Education) An Irish Curriculum for the Three to Four Year Old Child, Volume One: Spiritual, Emotional and Moral Development,* Cork: The Early Years Unit, University College Cork.

Douglas F. (2003) 'The Breath of Life: The Young Child and Self-esteem' In N. Hayes and M. Kernan (Eds.). *Transformations – Theory and Practice in Early Education,* Cork, OMEP

Dowling, M. (2000). *Young Children's Personal, Social and Emotional Development.* London: Paul Chapman.

Evans, D. (1993). *Spirituality and Human Nature.* New York: SUNY.

Farrer, F. (2000). *A Quiet Revolution: Encouraging Positive Values in our Children,* London: Random House.

Fowler, J. (1981). *Stages of Faith.* New York: Harper Collins.

Frankl, V. (1985). *Man's Search for Meaning.* London: Pocket Books.

Gallagher, M.P. (1998). *Will Our Children Believe?* Dublin: Veritas.

Gilmartin, R. (1996). *Pursuing Wellness: Finding Spirituality.* CT: Twenty Third Publications.

Griffith, F. (1985). 'Meditation Research: Its Personal and Social Implications.' In J. White (Ed.), *Frontiers of Consciousness.* New York: Julian Press.

Hendricks, G. and Wills, R. (1975). *The Centring Book.* New York: Prentice Hall.

Jessel-Kenyon, J. and Shealy, C (1999). *The Illustrated Encyclopedia of Well Being.* Hants: Godsfield Press.

Kearney, M. (1996). *Mortally Wounded.* Dublin: Mercier Press.

Kent, H. (2001). *Yoga: An Illustrated Guide.* London: Element.

Kirkland, J.P. (1996). 'Helping to Restore Spiritual Values in Abused Children: A Role for Pastoral Carers in Education.' In, R. Best (Ed.), *Education, Spirituality and the Whole Child.* London: Cassell.

Lindon J. (1999). *Understanding World Religions in Early Years Practice.* London: Hodder and Stoughton.

Myss, C. and Shealy, C.N. (1999). *The Creation of Health.* London: Bantam Books.

Mott-Thornton, K. (1996). 'Experience, Critical Realism and the Schooling of Spirituality.' In R. Best (Ed.), *Education, Spirituality and the Whole Child.* London: Cassell.

Neville, B. (1989). Educating Psyche. Victoria, Australia: Harper Collins.

Ramachandran, V.S. and Blakeshee, S. (1998). *Phantoms in the Brain.* London: Fourth Estate.

Randle D. (1989) *Teaching Green: A Parent's Guide to Education for Life on Earth.* London: Green Print an imprint of Merlin Press.

Rizzuto, A.M. (1979). *The Birth of the Living God: A Psychoanalytic Study.* Chicago: University of Chicago Press.

Robinson, E. (1977). *The Original Vision.* Oxford: Religious Experience Research Unit.

White, J. (1996). 'Education, Spirituality and the Whole Child: A Humanist Perspective.' In R. Best (Ed.) *Education, Spirituality and the Whole Child.* London: Cassell.

Zohar, D. and Marshall, I. (2000). *Spiritual Intelligence: The Ultimate Intelligence.* London: Bloomsbury.

Gaia – Young Children and Their Relationship to the Outside World

Francis Douglas

> What man among you with a hundred sheep, losing one, would not leave the ninety-nine in the wilderness and go after the missing one till he found it? (Lk. 15:1-32)

Introduction

This paper argues that every child, every human being, is part of a much larger integrated system with a multitude of feedback loops. Every action, every thought, every desire has an impact, however small, on all the other things in our universe. Equally, everything in this universe impacts on us. In order to be happy, young children have to feel part of this 'wholeness' and feel that their actions are part of this greater universal process.

The Living Earth

Gaia, the Greek Goddess of Earth, was the name chosen by Lovelock (1979) for his brilliant hypothesis concerning the "living" world.

Lovelock knew that the heat of the sun has increased by 25% since life began on Earth and that, in spite of this increase, the Earth's surface temperature has remained constant at a level comfortable for life, during those four billion years. If the planet Earth were able to regulate its own temperature, the composition of its atmosphere, the salinity of its oceans, it would indeed be a living entity just like a living organism that is able to self regulate and keep its body temperature and other variables constant. His hypothesis was greatly strengthened by his collaboration with Margulis (1989).

Margulis, a microbiologist, had often asked the question "why does everybody agree that atmospheric oxygen ... comes from life, but no one speaks about the other atmospheric gases coming from life?"

The scientific backgrounds and areas of expertise of Lovelock and Margulis turned out to be a perfect match. Margulis had no problem answering

Lovelock's many questions about the biological origins of atmospheric gases while Lovelock contributed concepts from chemistry, thermo dynamics and cybernetics to the emerging Gaia theory. Thus the two scientists were able to identify a complex network of feedback loops which – so they hypothesised – bring about the self regulation of the planetary system.

The extraordinary feature of these feedback loops is that they link together living and non-living systems. We can no longer think of rocks, animals and plants as being separate. Gaia theory shows that there is a tight interlocking between the planet's living parts – plants, micro-organisms, animals and humans – and its nonliving parts – rocks, oceans and the atmosphere.

> Simply stated, the Gaia hypothesis says that the surface of the Earth, which we've always considered to be the environment of life, is really part of life. The blanket of air – the troposphere – should be considered a circulatory system, produced and sustained by life ... When scientists tell us that life adapts to an essentially passive environment of chemistry, physics, and rocks, they perpetuate a severely distorted view. Life actually makes and forms and changes the environment to which it adapts. Then that 'environment' feeds back on the life that is changing and acting and growing in it. There are constant cyclical interactions. (Margulis, 1989).

All human beings, including young children, are part of this constant cyclical interaction. We are all part of a living system. We cannot help but be strengthened by a sense of awe and wonder. Our spirits are part of the Earth and the Earth is part of us. Froebel's notion of "unity" has been given a concrete scientific foundation!

We must however remember that the concept of 'unity' and 'feedback loops' have been with us since the dawn of time. Anaxagorus of Clazomenae who was born about 500 BC wrote a book on natural philosophy which was the first such treatise, so we are told, to contain diagrams (Kenny, 1988).

Anaxagoras' account of the origin of the World is strikingly similar to a model that is popular today. At the beginning he said 'all things were together' in a unit infinitely complex and infinitely small which lacked all perceptible qualities. This piecemeal pebble began to rotate, expanding as it did so, and throwing off air and ether, and eventually the stars and the sun and the moon. In the course of the rotation what is dense separated off from what is rarefied and so did the hot from the cold, the bright from the dark, and the dry from the wet. Thus the articulated substances of our world were formed, with the dense and the wet and the cold and the dark congregating where our earth now is, and the rare and the hot and the dry and the bright moving to the outermost parts of the ether.

Anaxagoras maintained that in every single thing there is a portion of everything else; there is a little whiteness in what is black, and something lightweight in whatever is heavy. No better case can be made for the concept of unity. No better case fills our minds with such a sense of awe and wonder. Indeed, it would not be difficult to introduce young minds to a simplified version of Anaxagoras' work. A similar exercise could be undertaken with Lovelock's Gaia hypothesis making use of pictures, diagrams and models.

Social Systems as Part of Gaia

The relationship among the component parts of a living system give us its form. The structure of a living system will be a pattern of organisation which will provide the matter. And the life process of a living system will be the essence of its regeneration. ie: The component parts of a baby give us its 'Form'. The molecules, etc. in these component parts provide the 'Matter'. The replication of these cells is the 'Process'. Form, Matter and Process go hand in hand. You cannot have one without the other.

However, social life is predicated on a further fourth dimension. The ability to hold mental images of material objects and events allows people to choose among several alternatives, which is necessary in order to formulate values and social rules of behaviour. The power of mental imagery was spoken of by the Greeks and others in antiquity. Most of us hold our early experiences in the form of mental images and thus a wide variety of image creating situations are of vital importance in early childhood education. Further, conflicts of interest, based on different values, are at the origin of relationships of power. People's intentions, awareness of purposes, designs and strategies to reach identified goals all require the projection of mental images into the future. The ability to retain mental images thus gives *meaning* to our World.

To Form, Matter and Process must be added Meaning if we are fully to understand social phenomenon. For example, culture is created and sustained by a network (form) of communications (process), in which *meaning* is generated. The cultures' material embodiments (matter) include artefacts and written texts, through which *meaning* is passed from generation to generation. Thus a network of Early Childhood Practitioners, like the Irish Pre-school Playgroups Association, represents the 'Form'. The newsletter sent to each member would be one aspect of the 'Matter'. The 'Process' of communication would be through the postal system and the members reading their newsletter would extract the '*Meaning*'.

When we follow the development of the social sciences from the Nineteenth Century to the present, we can see that the major debates among different schools of thought seem to reflect the tensions between the four perspectives on social life – form, matter, process and meaning. Social thought in the Eighteen and Nineteenth Centuries was greatly influenced by positivism, a doctrine formulated by the social philosopher Comte. Its assertions include the insistence that the social sciences should search for general laws of human behaviour, an emphasis on quantification and the rejection of explanations in terms of subjective phenomena, such as intentions or purposes. (Baert, 1988).

In contrast to the above, the structuration theory of Giddens (See Baert, 1988, pp92ff) has been perhaps the most influential of the integrative theoretical frameworks.

Giddens employs two different but complementary methods of investigation. Institutional analysis is his method for studying social structures and institutions, while strategic analysis is used to study how people draw upon social structures in their pursuit of strategic goals. Giddens emphasises that people's strategic conduct is based largely on how they interpret their environment and more importantly, the interaction between social structures and human agency is cyclical just like Lovelock's Gaia hypothesis. Social structures are both the pre-condition and the unintended outcome of people's agency. People draw upon them in order to engage in their daily social practices, and in so doing they cannot help but reproduce the very same structures. For example, when we speak we necessarily draw upon the rules of our language, and as we use language we continually reproduce and transform the very same semantic structures. Thus social structures both enable us to interact and are also reproduced by our interactions. Giddens calls this the "duality of structure" and he acknowledges the similarity to the circular nature of self-regulating networks in biology.

The conceptual links to Gaia theory are even more evident when we turn to Giddens' view of human agency. He insists that agency does not consist of discrete acts but is a continuous flow of conduct. Similarly, a living metabolic network embodies an ongoing process of life. And as the components of the living network continually transform or replace other components, so the actions in the flow of human conduit have a "transformative capacity" (*Op. Cit*). Thus we have a social system which is linked to the living Earth.

Culture as a Living System

The New Webster's Dictionary (1992) defines culture as "the social and religious structures and intellectual and artistic manifestations etc. that characterise society." This definition can be further elucidated by saying that culture results from an integrated system of socially acquired values, beliefs, and rules of conduct that limit the range of accepted behaviours in a society. In other words, culture arises from a complex, highly non-linear dynamic. It is created by a social network involving multiple feedback loops through which values, beliefs, and rules of conduct are continually communicated, modified and sustained. It emerges from a network of communications among individuals, and as it emerges it produces constraints on their actions. In other words, the social structures, or rules of behaviour that constrain the actions of the individuals are produced and continually reinforced by their own network of communications.

Cultural behaviour, therefore, is not a form essentially different from other learned behaviours. It is peculiar in that it arises as a consequence of social living over many generations while its members are continuously replaced.

The social network also produces a shared body of knowledge – including information, ideas and skills – that shapes the culture's distinctive way of life in addition to its values and beliefs.

Moreover, the culture's values and beliefs affect its body of knowledge. They are part of the lens through which we see the world. They help us to interpret our experiences and to decide what kind of knowledge is meaningful. This meaningful knowledge, continually modified by the network of communications, is passed on from generation to generation together with the culture's values, beliefs and rules of conduct.

The system of shared values and beliefs creates an identity among the members of the social network, based on a sense of belonging. The socialisation of the young child thus becomes of paramount importance. The agency which is primarily responsible for this process is the family.

The Family doing Gaia's Work

Bloom (1981) says that, in studies undertaken by him and from international studies involving some twenty-two nations, it has become clear that family life is a most powerful factor in determining the amount of learning that a child achieves. He also maintains that the home environment is a far stronger influence than any curriculum which has been drawn up for educational purposes. The interaction and support of parents for their children has thus been found to be vital.

Interaction and support within the family as in the larger society of which it is a part, is made up of a network of organisation with many feedback loops. This is what Stern (1977) is referring to as the "dance of life". The important thing to remember is that both the parents and the children will have 'mis-steps' from time to time but that each of the players because of the feedback loops will adjust (if they are sensitive) and this adjustment is one of the more exciting aspects of this 'dance of life'.

The network between the family and the broader society can be to a greater or lesser extent 'open' or 'closed'. This obviously has implications for interactions and learning. Minuchin's (1974) "enmeshed" and "disengaged" family styles are useful classifications for thinking about the ways in which some families encourage their children to befriend adults and children. "Enmeshed" families prefer to enlist only close relatives, while "disengaged" families are more open to non-relatives. Shorter (1975) draws attention to the "post-modern family" where a number of problems exist. Shorter says that recent family life in

Western Society has been characterised by three main criteria:

(1) instability in the life of the adult couples.
(2) A 'systematic destruction of the nest'.
(3) Indifference to or rejection on the part of adolescent children of the values and family orientation of older generations.

None of these things are the fault of the young child but they all impact upon the node, which is the child, in the interactive network, which is the society into which the child is born.

Gaia, The Family and Pre-School Provision

Bronfenbrenner's (1977,1979) concentric circle model of ecology of human development is a useful device for analysing the influences being brought to bear on the life of the very young child. The innermost circle represents the micro-system, the individual's most immediate setting. Enclosing this is the meso-system, other settings and relationships which impinge on the child's experiences, for example, provision attended, the ways in which communication between the adults involved and the parents operates, and whether the child experiences continuity of experience or discontinuities, due to either changes in provider or differences in philosophy and culture between parent or teacher or minder. Many studies (for example, Cleave *et al.*, 1982; Powell, 1980) indicate that most children experience discontinuity and fragmentation at the interface between family and provision. Bronfenbrenner's next layer, the exo-system, is made up of those structures which impinge less directly upon the children's lives but influence them through their parents, for example, parental employment, or the availability of a local childcare committee committed to the provision of pre-school facilities. The outer circle represents the macro-system, the overarching ideology and organisation existing in the culture or sub-culture in which the child is growing up. This would include beliefs about the position of women and children in society, attitudes to single-parenthood, maternal employment and so on.

Bronfenbrenner's model is represented here in diagrammatic form.

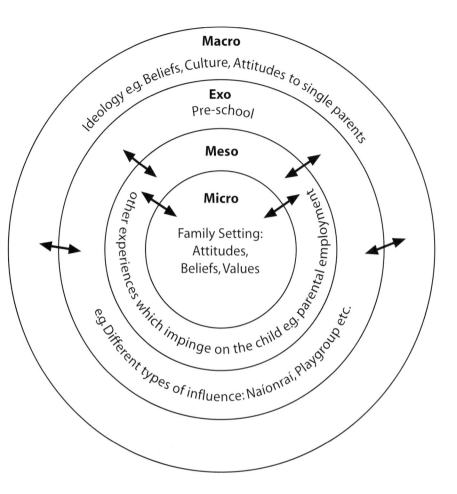

The Ecology of Pre-School Provision (From Bronfenbrenner 1977;1979)

The above is a dynamic model with constant interaction through 'feedback loops' between the different layers and as such the power of a situation, and the interpretation of that situation, can both have a bearing on its implementation.

Gaia's World of Social Scientists

All human beings, including young children, observe and collect data, detect correlation and co-variation, infer cause and effect and nowhere is this more apparent than in the pre-school. Like all social scientists young children make mistakes, they have problems of selective recall, they find that some things stand out in their mind more than others (Nisbett and Ross, 1980; Taylor and Thompson, 1982; Borgida and Nisbett, 1977) and they are influenced by their theories of what their data should look like. We all have stereotypes of different people and situations and many of these become self-fulfilling (Heider,1958; Kelley, 1967). If we infer that something about the person is primarily responsible for their behaviour then our inference is called an internal or dispositional attribution. If, on the other hand, we conclude that some external cause is primarily responsible for the behaviour it is called an external or situational attribution.

According to Heider (1958) in Western Society we give too much weight to the person and too little to the situation. This is known as "the fundamental attribution error" (Ross, 1977). Bem (1972) in a similar way suggests that adults and children may mistakenly rely on external cues in order to make judgements about their inner states. For example, we are not beautiful unless someone else tells us so.

Invariably, when we are forming our attitudes we place a great emphasis on the importance of consistency. As human beings we like to think that we are consistent and we are motivated to change our beliefs until we think we are. Nevertheless, much of our behaviour and many of our beliefs and attitudes emanate from our subconscious and are determined as much by emotion as rational thought. There is in fact a constant interchange between our conscious and subconscious in the form of feedback loops.

Attitudes tend to predict behaviour best when they are a) strong and consistent; b) based on a person's direct experience and c) specifically related to the behaviour being predicted. If children obey a very mild request not to play with an attractive toy, they come to believe that the toy is not as attractive as they first thought – a belief that is consistent with their observation that they are not playing with it. But if the children refrain from playing with the toy under a strong threat of punishment they do not change their liking for the toy (Aronson and Carlsmith, 1963; Freedman, 1965).

Interpersonal attraction can also be an important component of social interaction. Physically attractive boys and girls (five and six years of age) are more popular with their peers than are less attractive children (Dion and

Berscheid, 1972). Even adults are affected by a child's physical attractiveness (Dion, 1972).

Gaia – The Integrated World

In this paper we have traced Lovelock's Gaia theory of the living Earth. We have hypothesised that the distinction between living and non-living systems is a false one. In doing this we have hypothesised that there is a strong connection between plants, micro-organisms, animals and humans on the one hand and rocks, oceans and the atmosphere on the other. The environment of life is really part of life. Using 'feedback loops' we have shown how mental images, form, matter, process and meaning integrates social structures with the world we live in. Society's culture can indeed be seen as a 'living' system. At the centre of this culture we can see the influence of the family where a system of shared values and beliefs creates an identity which is based on a sense of belonging. The socialisation of the young child thus becomes of paramount importance. Although the major influence on this socialisation process comes from the family an important component nevertheless can result from pre-school provision.

Finally, in their desire to make sense of their environment young children, like all human beings, become social scientists. Our attitudes are formed and broken as a direct result of the interplay between our actions and the ripples which they cause reaching out to the rocks and oceans of our World. Likewise, through complex 'feedback loops' we are influenced by multitudinous dynamic variables emanating from the World around us.

In educating young children we are thus conscious of the World in which we live. We are part of this World and if we are to be happy we have to be at one with it. The secret lies in our culture which as Giddens has shown is a living system connected to everything else. Many people look to the past for this "ideal" culture. They see a society which they perceive as embracing things which they are now missing. They may see strong local communities and extended families, living spiritual traditions shared by the whole culture, the spontaneity and urgency of daily life and the symbolic richness of daily eating, living and dying, the care and awe devoted to the design of everyday implements like eating utensils and boats, the simple, repetitive pattern of everyday life, seasonal crops and festivals. But we all know that these things, if they ever existed in their totality, are no longer features of our present culture.

Nevertheless, we all yearn for a spiritual existence filled with over-arching meaning. We want our daily life, and that of our children, to be embedded in a cultural spiritual richness.

The essential difference between these "old" cultures and our present Western World is that their values are underpinned by habits and traditions. Such cultures thrive on recognition and repetition of familiar patterns. They are cultures which echo Jung's archetypes of the unconscious or Freud's "primary process".

If we view people as having a rational outer layer (ego), an emotional middle layer (associative) and a spiritual (uniative) centre we see that these "old" cultures belong to the middle layer.

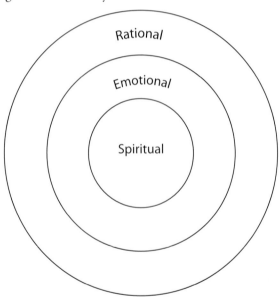

A well balanced person needs something from each layer. Children brought up in these "old" cultures have the advantage that the traditions of the community encapsulate deeper spiritual insights and values, so that the child relates to the spiritual centre through his or her culture and its traditions. Children don't have to relate directly to the centre on their own as individuals. Nevertheless, the child who surmounts this far greater challenge will have answered the question "Why?" for themselves and will be capable of relating their rational being to their emotional being, to their spiritual being and vica-versa.

The weakness is that without the shared community with its shared values children and adults will be deeply undernourished in the middle emotional layer of their being. Modern Western children have few collective traditions that point beyond the prosaic everyday level of life. Our children have few "gods" and "goddesses" as collective heroes whose lives exemplify some deeper layer of human possibility or aspiration and touch our own lives with a sense of grace. One very obvious recent exception to the above was the global mourning that followed the death of Diana, Princess of Wales. Hers was a life that exemplified a spontaneity, a warmth, a quality of love, a vulnerability that we long to contact through some collective symbol or icon.

In the absence of such "heroes" we are left to find or create our own meanings or just to feel their loss. In a world where creativity is not emphasised children thus end up in despair. There is a tremendous pressure in Western society to over emphasise the importance of the individual (the ego) thus leading to a lack of balance. Thus individual needs, aspirations and ourselves become of paramount importance. This often leads to distorted or peripheral activities like materialism, promiscuous sex, pointless rebellion, violence, drug abuse or 'New Age' occultism. In other words the 'feedback loops' between the spiritual centre, the emotional middle and the rational outer layer cease to function. This is contrary to the theory of Gaia.

Turning Gaia theory in its extended form above into practice for the pre-school child requires the child to have a sense of 'something beyond'. This 'something more' requires the following:

1) A Deeper Social Reality.

The Social Development of the young child is of the utmost importance for as MacMurray (1961) says, " Any philosophy which finds itself required by its own logic to ask the question "How do we know that there are other persons? Has refuted itself ..."

In a practical sense there are many concerns for the Early Years Educator. Young children can exhibit difficulty in separating from their parent/caregiver even leading, in extreme cases, to refusal to attend pre-school. They can be solitary and lonely, lack confidence with other children and adults and be over dependent or over confident. They can be self contained and self sufficient or crave for recognition by a particular group. They can be self-centred or aggressive. All these traits, and many more, can inhibit the child in achieving their full potential as a human being

Babies begin their social development at birth (or even before) making significant contact with their mother or care-person. They always find people more interesting than toys. During the period from six to twelve months of age they actively take part in social games where they interact with their adult carer.

The development of the child's social world can be greatly enhanced through socio-dramatic play which involves the following components: imitative role play; make-believe in regard to objects; make-believe in regard to actions and situations; interaction with play-partners; verbal communication related to the play episode and; persistence in the play episode. These attributes can be encouraged by the Educator through the provision of a suitable play environment and possibly, intervention at appropriate times. The latter is a highly skilled undertaking which is often neglected by parents/caregivers and pre-school educators. It is interesting to note that socio-dramatic play is linked closely to creativity and one's sense of awe and wonder which is the essence of spirituality

2) An Awareness of the Mythological, Archetypal or Religious dimensions of our situation. Much of this arises from one's Culture.
Cultural Development is concerned with knowledge of the World's people, their customs and language. An important aspect of this is anti-bias education which is closely linked to spiritual, moral and emotional development. It is based on the age old commandment "Love thy neighbour as Thyself". It includes all discrimination and feelings of superiority and articulates social morality – the good of the World Community. The child is viewed as at one with the planet as argued in this paper and expresses Froebel's concept of 'unity' and Montessori's 'Greater Cosmos'.

It is a fundamental truth that knowledge rather than prejudice leads to greater understanding, is an expression of 'unity', is part of the Gaia experience, and is part of the child's holistic development. Thus the attitude of the child and adult, is of significant importance.

Prejudice starts young – some would say that it is imbibed with the mother's milk – and hence parent education is vital. Parents and children have to learn to celebrate and have tolerance of difference. Uniformity is not the aim. In this celebration, the virtues of joy, love, peace, patience, goodness, kindness, trustfulness, gentleness and self-control should all be emphasised.

To achieve these aims a structured, developmentally appropriate programme has to be instituted. The Educator, having made careful observations of a particular child, can influence them by both activity and discussion.

Activity must respond to the child's specific interests and concerns. Discussion must be designed to find out whether the individual understands, requires knowledge or wishes to comment. The focus will, nevertheless, be targeted at different languages, customs and processes of socialisation.

The objective is to increase the children's knowledge of the way in which different groups live (within Ireland and without) and to bring about a more tolerant attitude. Finally, the educator should ask the question, "How are children's attitudes to learning, self-esteem, expectations of other children and their own aspirations and performance affected by society's stereotyping and labelling?"

In the words of Louise Derman-Sparks (1989), "Everybody has the capacity to change but some people die before they do!"

3) Some More Profound Level Of Truth Or Beauty. This is related to human Creativity.
Creativity is the quality which leads to the production of something new and desirable. The product may be new to society, or merely new to the individual who creates it. Novelty, however, is not enough for if it were, we could end up with a whole collection of oddities! Not only is novelty a requirement but so too is appropriateness, transformation and endurance.

The adult who wrote down 'playpen' when asked to think of uses for a rubber band and a four year old talking to himself in the bath and describing the water as 'devil deep', were both using novel expressions but the latter was more appropriate. Obviously, appropriateness on its own is insufficient. For example, to say that a tin of boot polish can be used for cleaning shoes is appropriate but not novel and so not creative.

Transformation allows people to see something in a new way. In its most radical form, transformation allows us to make a shift in approach towards a subject (or the handling of material), the kind of shift occasioned by Einstein's "Theory of Relativity" or Barnes Wallace's "Bouncing Bomb".

Transformation involves the creation of new forms. But to be really creative they also have to have an enduring quality that warrants close and repeated examination. This is what gives them their spiritual quality. They do not divulge their total meaning at their first viewing or listening. They offer something new each time we experience them. They have an intensity and concentration of meaning that requires constant contemplation.

Torrance (1979) analysed the letters of 150 parents in the U.S.A. who described their children as being creative. The following were the most frequently observed behaviours: Overactive physically and mentally; Annoying curiosity; Forgetful and absent minded; Good sense of humour; Read while friends played; Liked to work alone; Sensitive; Daydreaming; Imaginative (enjoyed pretending); And friends thought that he or she was slightly strange. Torrance is not suggesting that that these things should be encouraged, but merely that they are indicative of the creative mind. Perhaps the most striking aspect of the above is the important part that personality plays (rather than just intellectual ability). The complexity of the creative personality is such that no one characteristic can be viewed in isolation. In some cases a child that daydreams will be a source of annoyance, in other cases it may well be the facet that makes an individual creative. Upon the judgement of the adult the decision must lie. Research carried out in University College, Cork [Horgan, M (1987); Dunlea (1990); Douglas (1993); Horgan, S (1996) and Dwane (1998)] found that in most cases no sustained effort was observed in various different types of pre-school provision whereby adults fostered creativity in the scientific and artistic domains. Much more could be attempted in order to realise children's full potential for the future.

4) An Attunement to a deeper, Cosmic sense of Wholeness, a sense that our actions are part of some greater universal process

This, in essence, is what we have been striving to achieve in this paper with our Gaia hypothesis. Everything is related to everything else. Indeed, our life on this earth consists of four essential elements. Firstly, we live together with others. Secondly, we do so on this earth. Thirdly, we ourselves are part of this earth. And Fourthly, we as human beings are endowed with a certain freedom and spiritual quality. These are also the main elements from which our happiness is composed.

We do not live in isolation. Our life is lived in common and nowhere is this inescapable fact illustrated more strongly than with the relationship between children and adults. They cannot exist without each other. We could not speak or think of love. We could not even survive at birth. The child's mother and father are not simply there to look after the baby. In the long run, child care could perhaps be mechanised but the results would be disastrous. We are human beings not machines.

The baby needs his or her father and mother as human beings. Society is a tissue of personal relationships expressed through mutual confidence and love. Within this love all people are included and without it society degenerates. Life in common is one of the great answers to the quest for meaning and happiness. Love and solidarity mean fulfilment. Life is uncertain and every child and adult needs somewhere to turn which is non-judgemental and secure.

The baby relates to others but also to the world. From the very first cry, if not before, the baby is reaching out, making contact, touching, grasping, feeding, playing. The child works at things, builds, admires and ponders. This is a joyful task. The child, like the adult, works to change his or her environment to make the world a better place. In so doing the child not only impacts on their physical world but also develops themselves. Children grow and become adults through their work.

The third element in our existence is that we ourselves form part of the material world. We seem to be made of the same material as the earth and plants and animals around us. The very fibres of our being are so much part of the universe that we cannot make a decision without chemical and electrical processes taking place within our brain. This is not a humiliation it is a miracle of creation.

The fourth main element is that men and women and children are more than their bodies. The reactions of animals are largely determined by their senses and to that extent they are not free. Human beings, on the other hand, are faced with many choices. Human beings like the animals live by sense impressions but we also have a certain clearness of mind that can consciously survey and consider everything, even our own thought. This is the irreducible mystery of our personal consciousness and of course here lies our responsibility because we are not merely at the mercy of stimuli and reflexes like the animals. We also have a certain freedom. This is also part of the fulfilment of existence, that we are a thinking, conscious, responsive part of the world, that in growing freedom we can choose the good.

This 'something more' confers added meaning and value on where we are now. This spiritual 'something more' may be a deeper social reality or social web of meaning. It may be an awareness of, or attunement to, the mythological, archetypal or religious dimensions of our situation. It may be a sense of some more profound level of truth or beauty. And/or it may be an attunement to some deeper, cosmic sense of wholeness, a sense that our actions are part of some greater universal process. Whatever it is children and adults all experience a despair and an impoverishment when it is not there. We need to be aware that it is the love of the pre-school practitioner who through their care, empathy and consideration will lead the young child towards a greater meaning in life. And we need to be aware that it is even more so the love of a parent or caregiver who will fill the child with a sense of awe and wonder. Such is the magic of life.

Bibliography

Aronson, E. and Carlsmith, J.M. (1963). The effect of the severity of threat on the devaluation of forbidden behaviour. *Journal of Abnormal and Social Psychology*, 66, 584-588.

Baert, P. (1998) *Social Theory in the Twentieth Century* New York University Press.

Bem, D.J. (1972) Self Perception Theory. In L. Berkowitz (Ed) *Advances in Experimental Social Psychology* (Vol. 6) New York: Academic Press.

Bloom, B.S. (1981) *All our children Learning*. McGraw Hill.

Borgida, E. and Nisbett, R.E. (1977). The differential impact of abstract vs. concrete information on decisions. *Journal of Applied Social Psychology*, 42, 444-445.

Bronfenbrenner,U. (1977) Towards an experimental ecology of human development. *American Psychologist*, 32, 513-31.

Bronfenbrenner, U. (1979) *The ecology of human development*. Cambridge, M.A. Harvard University Press.

Cleave, S. Jowett, S. and Bate, M. (1982) *And so to School.* Windsor, NFER-Nelson.

Derman-Sparks, L. (1989). *The ABC Taskforce Anti-bias Curriculum.* Washington D.C. : National Association for the Education of Young Children.

Dion, K.K. and Berscheid, D.E. (1972) *Physical attractiveness and social perception of peers in pre-school children.* Unpublished manuscript, University of Minnesota, Minneapolis.

Dion, K.K. (1972) Physical attractiveness and evaluations of children's transgressions. *Journal of Personality and Social Psychology,* 24, 207-213.

Douglas, F.G. (1993) A Study of Pre-School Education in the Republic of Ireland with Particular Reference to those Pre-Schools which are listed by the Irish Pre-School Playgroups Association in Cork City and County. Ph.D. Dissertation, University of Hull.

Dunlea, C.P. (1990). The Relevance of Montessori Education: A Study of Montessori Schools in the Cork Area. M.Ed. Dissertation. University College, Cork.

Dwane,C.A. (1998). A Study of the Linguistic and Cognitive Development of Children in Naionrai in Cork City and County. M.Ed. Dissertation. University College, Cork.

Freedman, J.J. (1965). Long-term behavioural effects of cognitive dissonance. *Journal of Experimental Social Psychology,* 1, 145-155.

Heider, F. (1958) The psychology of interpersonal relations. New York: Wiley.

Horgan, M.A. (1987). A Study of the Importance of Play in the Education of Junior Infant Class Children in Cork City and County. M.Ed. Dissertation, University College, Cork.

Horgan, S.(1995). A Study of the Linguistic and Cognitive Development of Junior Infant Class Children in Gaelscoileanna in Cork City and County. M. Ed. Dissertation, University College, Cork.

Kelley, H.H. (1967). Attribution theory in social psychology. In D. Levine (Ed) *Nebraska symposium on motivation* (Vol. 15) Lincoln: University of Nebraska Press.

Kenny, A. (1998) *A Brief History of Western Philosophy,* Blackwell Pub. Ltd. Oxford.

Lovelock, J. (1979) *Gaia,* Oxford University Press.

MacMurray, J. (1961) *Persons in Relation.* London: Faber and Faber.

Margulis, L. (1989) Gaia: The Living Earth, *The Elmwood Newsletter,* Berkeley,

Cal, Vol 5, No. 2.

Minuchin, S. (1974). *Families and Family Therapy.* London. Tavistock.

New Webster's Dictionary (1992) Lexicon Publications, Inc.

Nisbett, R.E. and Ross, L. (1980) *Human inference: Strategies and shortcomings of social judgment.* Englewood Cliffs, NJ: Prentice Hall.

Powell, D.R. (1980) Towards a socio-ecological perspective of relations between parents and care programs in S. Kilmer (ed), *Advances in early education and day care*, Vol. 1. Greenwich, CT, JAI Press.

Ross, L. (1977). The intuitive psychologist and his shortcomings: Distortions in the attribution process. In L Berkowitz, (Ed). *Advances in experimental social psychology* (Vol. 10) New York: Academic Press.

Shorter, E. (1975) *The making of the modern family.* New York. Basic Books.

Stern, D. (1977) *The first relationship: infant and mother.* London, Fontana/Open Books.

Taylor, S.E. and Thompson, S.C. (1982) Stalking the elusive "vividness" effect. *Psychological Review*, 89. 155-181.

Torrance, E.P. (1979). *Creative Learning and Teaching.* New York: Dodd-Mead.

New Books

Developing the Whole Child – The Importance of the Emotional, Social, Moral and Spiritual in Early Years Education and Care

by Mary Catherine Daly

Published by The Edwin Mellen Press

"This work is a powerful reminder to parents, policy makers and practitioners that attention to young children's emotional, social, moral and spiritual development is absolutely essential. Mary Daly provides a moving account of her own reasons for seeing these elements of a holistic view of human development as fundamental. In a world where economics and speed seem to take precedence over all other aspects of life, many people are recognising that this simply is not a basis for bringing up and educating our children ... Mary's analysis includes evidence about meditation, which is not only a key spiritual process, helping children find oases of peace in a troubled, noisy world, but also has benefits for physical as well as mental health ... This is a book to be read and re-read, and pondered over. Above all, it is a book to inform staff training, to evaluate existing practice and to stimulate action for the development of truly appropriate provision in early childhood education and care settings." – (from the Commendatory Preface) Tricia David BSc, MA, PhD, FRSA, Professor Emeritus, Canterbury Christ Church University College, England.

ISBN 0-7734-6166-3   356pp.   Published 2004

Further Details From: The Edwin Mellen Press, Mellen House, Unit 17 Llambed Business Park, Lampeter, Ceredigion, SA48 8LT, Wales, U.K. Tel: 01570 423356 Fax: 01570 423775 email: emp@mellon.demon.co.uk www.mellenpress.com